How to Read the Constitution

Originalism, Constitutional Interpretation, and Judicial Power

Christopher Wolfe

ROWMAN & LITTLEFIELD PUBLISHERS, INC.
Lanham · Boulder · New York · London

ROWMAN & LITTLEFIELD PUBLISHERS, INC.

Published in the United States of America
by Rowman & Littlefield Publishers, Inc.
4720 Boston Way, Lanham, Maryland 20706

3 Henrietta Street, London WC2E 8LU, England

British Cataloging in Publication Information Available

Library of Congress Cataloging-in-Publication Data

Wolfe, Christopher.
How to read the constitution : orginalism, constitutional
interpretation, and judicial power / by Christopher Wolfe.
p.   cm.
Includes bibliographical references and index.
1. United States—Constitutional law—Interpretation and construction.
2. Judicial power—United States.   3. Judicial review—United States.
I. Title.
KF4552.W63   1996   342.73'02—dc20   [347.3022]   96-12526 CIP

ISBN 0–8476–8234–X (cloth : alk. paper)
ISBN 0–8476–8235–8 (pbk.: alk. paper)

Printed in the United States of America

The paper used in this publication meets the minimum requirements of
American National Standard for Information Sciences—Permanence of
Paper for Printed Library Materials, ANSI Z39.48–1984.

To my beloved Anne

Contents

Acknowledgments

Permission to include previously published articles as chapters in this book is gratefully acknowledged:

Chapter 1 originally appeared in *Constitutionalism in Perspective*, Volume III: *The United States Constitution in Twentieth Century Politics*, ed. S. Thurow (Lanham, Md.: University Press of America, 1988).

Chapter 2 was published in *The Bill of Rights: Original Meaning and Current Understanding*, ed. E. Hickok, Jr. (Charlottesville, Va.: University Press of Virginia).

Chapter 4 was published in the *Harvard Journal of Law and Public Policy* 10, no. 3 (Summer 1987). Copyright 1987 by the Harvard Society for Law and Public Policy, Inc.

Chapters 5 and 6 were published originally in 70 *Texas Law Review* 1325 (1992). Copyright 1992 by the Texas Law Review Association. Reprinted by permission.

Chapter 7 was published in *Law and Social Inquiry* 15, no. 4 (Fall 1990). Copyright 1991 American Bar Foundation.

Chapter 8 was originally part of the Program in American Constitutionalism Lecture Series at Southwest Texas State University (March 1994).

Grateful acknowledgment also is owed to the Bradley Institute for Democracy and Public Values at Marquette University for the summer fellowship that made chapter 3 possible.

Introduction

This book is an effort to extend and apply the "originalist" position on constitutional interpretation and judicial review that I set out in *The Rise of Modern Judicial Review* (Basic Books, 1986) and *Judicial Activism* (Brooks/Cole, 1990). In the former, I presented an outline of a history of constitutional interpretation and judicial review in America. The heart of that book was an effort to compare and contrast the "traditional" approach of early American constitutional thinkers with the "modern" approach that has been dominant on the Supreme Court since 1937. In the latter book, I tried to present a dialectical argument on the pros and cons of modern judicial power, concluding that it provides "too precarious" a security for our rights and that we would do well to return to the political principles—including a more limited judicial power—of the founders of American government.

The debate over "interpretivism" and "noninterpretivism" that began in the 1970s was the most significant challenge to the prevailing orthodoxy since its establishment earlier in the century. Legal intellectual elites reacted strongly to the attack, producing a plethora of constitutional theories that were variations on the same theme: the deficiencies of the ordinary democratic political process and the superiority of judges (especially the Supreme Court) in articulating—and enforcing—our fundamental political principles. The challenge to modern judicial power may be receding for the moment, with the failure of recent Republican presidents to change the character of the Court fundamentally and with the 1992 election of a Democrat committed to modern judicial power. But I do not think that this is because originalism "lost" the debate. I am today as convinced as ever that originalism properly understood is the correct approach to constitutional interpretation and judicial review, despite the many recent efforts to discredit it. In this book, I want to carry on the debate, clarifying originalism, distinguishing its best form from weaker forms, analyzing modern judicial power and its implications, and responding to some recent legal scholarship.

While this book consists of essays written on different occasions, they fit together easily and coherently because they are all part of a larger effort to develop and extend the approach described in my earlier books. The first series of essays (Part I) deals with the approach to constitutional interpretation and judicial review that was dominant in the founding and in the traditional era (roughly 1789 to 1890). Chapter 1 provides a statement of this era's basic approach to constitutional interpretation. It describes what is today typically called originalism, but argues that it could be better characterized as a "real meaning" position. Chapter 2 then applies that approach to a particularly important area—the due process clause, which has been the basis for most constitutional law for much of our history—showing that the due process clause is not a deliberately vague statement of a very general principle, a situation that would make it a functional equivalent of a blank check for judges. Finally, Part I concludes with an extensive discussion of an often-cited article that claims to refute originalism on its own grounds, H. Jefferson Powell's "The Original Understanding of Original Intention" (chapter 3). Ironically, we will discover that, while it defeats the well-known form of originalism represented by Raoul Berger, Powell's essay actually ends up making a case for originalism properly understood.

Part II takes up twentieth-century issues of interpretation and judicial power. The first chapter in this part is an overview of how constitutional law became decisively detached from the Constitution itself, except at so general a level as to be without significance (chapter 4). The next three chapters deal with contemporary legal scholarship—the efforts in the academy to give legitimacy to the transformation of judicial power discussed earlier. Chapter 5 summarizes and criticizes *On Reading the Constitution* by the noted liberal constitutional commentator Laurence Tribe, together with Michael Dorf. Chapter 6 does the same to *Interpreting the Constitution* by former Yale Law School Dean Harry Wellington. These two books are a kind of "counterattack" to the originalist assault on modern Supreme Court power during the late 1970s and 1980s, but neither provides a persuasive case for the broad modern form of judicial review. In fact, they provide much evidence to reinforce the case against it. Chapter 7 is a review of *Red, White, and Blue* by Mark

Tushnet, a "critical legal studies" (radical) legal commentator who teaches at Georgetown Law Center. It contains my response to the more sophisticated modern critiques of the possibility of "objective" interpretation, as well as a critique of contemporary left-wing "republican" thought in constitutional law.

The final chapter deals with the topic of "Originalism and Precedent." It takes up the question of what a "traditional" or "originalist" justice should do when confronted with a large body of constitutional law that is not rooted deeply (or, often, not at all rooted) in the Constitution. It rejects two extreme positions (reject all precedent, accept all precedent) and tries to give a principled ground for distinguishing between authoritative and nonauthoritative precedents.

We do not know where the future will take us. If mainstream modern judicial power has survived a significant challenge, we do not know whether that challenge has exhausted its resources or is biding its time after a temporary setback, preparing for a renewed effort. But whatever the future holds, it is always worthwhile for us to renew our acquaintance with the moderate liberal democratic principles that inspired the founders of American government.

As I conclude this project on judicial review in American life and prepare to move on to more substantive discussions of American public philosophy, I hope that my efforts will at least have encouraged my readers—whatever their stance on judicial power—to take the political philosophy of the American founding more seriously, resisting the tendencies either to accommodate its thought to our own or to dismiss it as antiquated. Whatever the limits of that political philosophy *sub specie aeternitatis*—and there are grounds on which I would criticize it—it provided for a long time the foundations for a government of a generally free and decent people. Given a fair reading of history, that was an extraordinary accomplishment.

If current theorists of liberal democracy have their way (often through the aggressive use of a broad judicial power), extending the democratic principles of equality and liberty into a principle of the autonomous human self, losing sight of a transcendent and natural order of right that serves as an essential guide and limit to human choices, then we may have unfortunate occasion for appreciating more fully the virtues of the political principles on which the nation was founded.

Part I

The Founding and
Constitutional Interpretation

1

How to Read and Interpret
the Constitution

My particular focus in this initial chapter will be on the question, "How should we read or interpret the Constitution?" After examining how the founders would have answered that question, I will offer a brief description, by way of contrast, of how more modern Courts and commentators might answer it and offer some brief comments on the relation of the different answers to the power of judicial review and the role of the Supreme Court in American politics.

Traditional Interpretation

The founders acted on an understanding of interpretation that was dominant during the first, or what I call the traditional, era of U.S. constitutional history, which ran from the founding until the end of the nineteenth century. During this era, there was substantial agreement about general rules of interpretation, although, as students of U.S. history know, there was also substantial disagreement about the particular interpretations of the Constitution that resulted from the application of those common rules.[1]

One of the most striking facts about rules of interpretation in the founding was the relative rarity of discussions about them. This may have reflected, one might argue, a certain kind of thoughtlessness, but I believe that it was more a matter of widespread agreement on them, which limited the need for such discussion. Constitutional interpretation was viewed as a special case of legal interpretation, drawing es-

3

pecially on the background of rules for legal interpretation developed
in English law. Blackstone, for example, has a section on rules of interpretation at the beginning of his influential *Commentaries on the Laws
of England*, published shortly before the American Revolution. I will
use this as an example of what the framers assumed as part of the background for their efforts to establish and implement—which required interpreting—the Constitution.[2]

Blackstone on Interpretation

Blackstone says that the best way to interpret the law is to explore the
intention of the lawgiver at the time the law was made "by signs the
most natural and probable." There are five basic signs: "the words, the
context, the subject-matter, the effects and consequences, or the spirit
and reason of the law." The words are to be understood "in their most
usual and most known signification . . . their general and popular use."
This is especially true for the American Constitution, since the document was written for the people, who are the ultimate authority in the
United States government, and one should assume that a writer is using words as they are understood by those with whom he wishes to communicate.

The one apparent exception to relying on the normal "popular" usage of words is that there may be some technical terms, for example,
legal terms such as "writ of habeas corpus" or "ex post facto law." But
then, one might argue that, in a certain sense, the technical definition
is the "popular" usage in those cases. What other usage is there for such
a term in ordinary discourse, especially when the use of Latin suggests
rather directly that it is a technical term? Of course, there might be more
doubt with respect to some other terms, for example, in how technical
a sense the word "contract" should be taken, in Article I, section 10.

If the meaning of the words is dubious (e.g., ambiguous, equivocal,
or intricate), Blackstone says, then the meaning can be established from
the context. This refers not only to the immediate verbal context, but
to broader senses of context. Two examples he gives are: first, the preamble of the law whose meaning is in question and second, the use of
the word or words in similar laws passed by the same legislature and
relating to the same subject or point.

Words are also to be understood in relation to the subject-matter with
which the legislator is dealing. If a word has several legitimate meanings, it may be that one of them is particularly apt when the speaker is

dealing with one kind of subject, and therefore attention to that context will help to indicate which meaning the legislator intended.

The next "sign" Blackstone mentions must be interpreted carefully: deriving aid from the "effects and consequences" of different meanings. This does not mean that the legislator is free to reject a meaning if he does not like the consequences, in the sense that he favors a different policy view. Rather, the rule is applicable to more extreme cases, namely, "where the words bear either none, or a very absurd signification, if literally understood." The classic example was the law of the city of Bologna that prohibited "drawing blood," which could have been applied not only to criminals, but also to doctors, for whom "drawing blood" was a standard medical procedure. The absurdity of prohibiting the latter justified a narrower interpretation.

But "the most universal and effectual way of discovering the true meaning of the law, when the words are dubious, is by considering the reason and spirit of it; or the cause which moved the legislator to enact it." Thus, for example, a law ought not to be extended to cases where the reason for the law is inapplicable, if the words do not require it.

On what foundation, one might ask, do these rules lie? Where did Blackstone (and those before him, on whom he relied) get them? Hamilton suggests the answer in a remark in the *Federalist*, where he says that the "rules of legal interpretation are rules of common sense, adopted by the courts in the construction of the laws."[3] Rules of legal interpretation are not the result of some kind of abstruse or hidden technical analysis, but simply a set of commonsense rules for ascertaining the meaning of a speech or document, put into a more or less systematic order on the basis of generations of experience applying them in cases.

The Founders and Interpretation

The English rules of legal interpretation were so well established that there was very little discussion of rules of interpretation in the founding period. The rules were simply adapted to the interpretation of a constitution, taking into account the breadth of the subject-matter and the nature of such a document. There was a great deal of discussion about *particular interpretations*, but little about the general principles or rules about how to interpret a constitution. One might conclude from the disagreements that quickly arose on important issues of interpretation that the appearance of general agreement on rules of interpretation was misleading. Without being able to demonstrate it here, I will say that an examination of early constitutional controversies shows that this is not the case.[4] The differences of interpretation arise not from the application of different rules but from different conclusions drawn from application of the same rules.

For those who wish to pursue this study, I recommend the following sources: 1) constitutional exposition contemporaneous with the proposing and ratifying of the Constitution, both in the state debates and in public writing on the subject, especially in the *Federalist*; 2) early constitutional controversies in the ordinary political process, such as the disputes over the executive removal power, the congressional power to establish a national bank, the relation of the House of Representatives to the treaty power, the breadth of the general welfare clause, and the Alien and Sedition Acts; 3) early Supreme Court cases involving constitutional questions, such as *Hayburn's Case* (where justices refused to accept duties as commissioners that Congress assigned them), *Ware v. Hylton* (the treaty power and state legislation), *Hylton v. U.S.* (the power of Congress to lay an unapportioned tax on carriages), and *Calder v. Bull* (the power of a state to provide a new trial, relative to a challenge under the prohibition of *ex post facto* laws); 4) the great constitutional cases of the Marshall Court, such as *Marbury v. Madison*, *Fletcher v. Peck*, *Martin v. Hunter's Lessee*, *McCulloch v. Maryland*, *Dartmouth College v. Woodward*, *Cohens v. Virginia*, *Ogden v. Saunders*, *Gibbons v. Ogden*, and *Barron v. Baltimore*; and 5) early constitutional commentators, especially Justice Joseph Story in his *Commentaries on the Constitution of the United States*.[5]

Marshall states the rules briefly in *Ogden v. Saunders*:

> To say that the intention of the instrument must prevail; that this intention must be collected from its words; that its words are to be understood in that sense in which they are generally used by those for whom the instrument was intended; that its provisions are neither to be restricted into insignificance, nor extended to objects not comprehended in them, nor contemplated by its framers; is to repeat what has been already said more at large, and is all that can be necessary.[6]

The method of ascertaining the "objects," which are especially important to note in cases where the words bear more than one meaning, is to examine "the subject, the context, and the intention of the person using [the words]."[7]

We can get a fair idea of the meaning of the subject and context by looking at Blackstone's discussion, but it is also worth noting some special factors that arise when it is a question of constitutional interpretation. Two parts of the subject and context are what might be called the "normal requirements of government" and "the nature of a written constitution." With respect to the normal requirements of government, if a particular power belongs to governments universally, that would suggest strongly that a fair reading that allowed for it is superior to a reading that does not. At this point, a consideration of "mischievous consequences" could enter: where the results of a particular interpretation would seriously harm the ability of government to perform its functions, the case for that interpretation must be quite strong to justify it (assuming that there is another plausible reading that would not lead to such harm).[8]

The "nature of a written constitution" might enter as a factor if one interpretation seems to require something contrary to it. For example, something like the "necessary and proper" clause seems to be implicit in the nature of a constitution, because otherwise the list of government powers would have to be much longer than any constitution could tolerate and even then would not be able to provide for the future very well.[9]

In ascertaining the meaning of the Constitution by adverting to the "intention," it is very important to distinguish between finding the intention in the document and seeking it by examining extrinsic sources. The founders emphasized the former approach. For example, in *McCulloch v. Maryland* Marshall dealt with intention largely by noting the *terms* of the clause at issue (the necessary and proper clause) and its *placement* in the document, arguing to what he says "must have been the intention" of those who wrote the Constitution, "as manifested in the whole clause."[10]

Extrinsic sources of intent, such as the historical circumstances of its writing, the debates in the Constitutional Convention or in Congress, the ratification debates, contemporary exposition of the document (in newspapers, books, public debates, etc.), and writers cited by its authors, are subordinate but admissible evidence as long as they are employed with some caution. They are not to be used against the text but to explain it; they carry weight proportionate to the evidence that they represented the general understanding of the provision, rather than that of a person or group only; and their authority touches only the *meaning* of the provision, not putative *applications* of it.

It is worth stressing how subordinate the latter kind of evidence was. The framers emphasized that it was the fair reading of the document that took precedence, and they tended to downplay extrinsic sources of intention. For example, in the debate over the national bank, Hamilton argued (with respect to a proposition discussed at the Constitutional

Convention) that "whatever may have been the nature of the proposition, or the reasons for rejecting it, it concludes nothing with respect to the real merits of the question . . . whatever the intentions of the framers of the Constitution or of a law, that intention is to be sought for in the instrument itself, according to the usual and established rules of construction."[11]

Hamilton's views on this issue were echoed in early constitutional debates by others, including Madison.[12] This subordination of extrinsic historical sources explains why the framers were in no hurry to publish the *Journal* of the convention and why most of what we know about it comes from a personal, private source, Madison's notes, rather than from an official document.

The central reason for this is that the only absolutely clear basis for authority that we have is the ratification vote that was taken on the words of the document itself. We cannot know with the same certainty that anyone's opinion about the meaning of the document was meant to be given authority. To rely on extrinsic sources of the meaning of the document as the primary source would be to undercut the clarity and certainty that are such essential elements of the rule of law. Moreover, the language of the document will inevitably be our only guide in many cases, since the framers (and ratifiers) will not have thought of an increasing number of problems arising over time.

Even in regard to the language of the document, however, certain "historical" considerations are essential. The words are to be understood as they were understood by those for whom they were written, and therefore we must know what those understandings were. This implies the necessity of recourse to some study of the founding era (and of those eras that produced amendments), especially the explanations of constitutional provisions by those who proposed them. Such study is a kind of cross-check to ensure that the words as we understand them today have the same meaning as when they were adopted.[13]

Nonetheless, as long as we have made all the appropriate qualifications, extrinsic sources may be a legitimate factor to take into consideration, an auxiliary aid, in our efforts to ascertain the intention of the document. If law is to govern, it must first be understood, and why would we object to any aids in discerning the meaning of the law as long as they are trustworthy?

To the extent that the framers were good draftsmen, extrinsic sources of evidence would never clearly show that a provision was intended to mean something contrary to or different from a fair reading of the document. Of course, the quality of the drafting is an empirical question, and assertions that the framers had failed that way would have to be addressed case by case. (I doubt that such a case exists.) More likely, however, might be a case where a plausible but disputable case built on extrinsic sources differs from a plausible but disputable case built on a fair reading of the document itself. I believe, for the reasons given above, that the framers would tend to give preference in such cases to the fair reading of the document itself. (A separate case, on which I will reserve comment until later in this chapter, is what the framers would say about the exercise of judicial review in plausible but doubtful cases—whether such judicial review is appropriate, based either on reading the document or on studying extrinsic historical sources.)

To summarize briefly, then, the approach to constitutional interpretation employed in the early years of American government: an interpreter is to begin with the words of the document in their ordinary popular usage and understand them in light of their context. That context includes the words of the provision of which it is a part, but also extends to the much broader context of the document as a whole, especially its structure and the subject-matter with which it deals. The intent of provisions is commonly ascertainable from the terms and structure of the document, that is, it can be grasped by an analysis of the document itself, taken as a whole.

An important assumption behind these rules is that the document is not a mere grab bag of disparate provisions but a coherent whole, with objects or purposes that can be inferred from it and in light of which it ought to be read. Constitutional interpretation can, indeed, be likened to a dialectic that moves back and forth from specific words and phrases of the Constitution and its broader objects.[14]

Which of the various "signs" that Blackstone gives will be the most important in a given case of interpretation, which will be the surest guide to the intended meaning of the provision, cannot be specified abstractly. Indeed, the method of reasoning here, as in many other instances, is one that leads to certitude by a path other than logical demonstration. This kind of reasoning is described in John Henry Newman's *A Grammar of Assent*. It is a form of "concrete" reasoning in which the mind reaches the conclusion that "it can be no other way"

> by the strength, variety, or multiplicity of premises, which are only probable, not by invincible syllogisms,—by objections overcome, by adverse theories neutralized, by difficulties gradually clearing up, by exceptions proving the rule, by unlooked-for correlations found with received truths, by suspense and delay in the process issuing in triumphant reactions,—by all these ways and many others . . .[15]

In many matters, it is the "cumulation of concurring probabilities" that leads the human mind to certitude (the certitude "appropriate to the subject-matter," of course, as Aristotle would indicate[16]). So it is, in constitutional interpretation.

The deeper assumption underlying these early rules of interpretation was a fairly traditional realist epistemology: that the Constitution has a fixed, determinate meaning intelligible to those who give it a fair reading. Communication through human language is possible, the founders thought, unlike some modern philosophical schools (e.g., deconstructionism) that stress the inevitable and radical subjectivity of all language, which stands as a bar to genuine communication. Under modern assumptions, a constitution is unavoidably made up or created by interpreters (an individual, group, or the society at large), to a greater or lesser extent, as they go along. The framers of the Constitution, on the contrary, looked to the Constitution as an intelligible fixed standard that made possible a republican rule of law, rather than of men.

Perhaps it would be worthwhile to give one brief example of a particular application of the approach to interpretation I have been describing. The case of *Barron v. Baltimore*[17] confronts the question, "Does the original Bill of Rights apply to states as well as to the national government?" The First Amendment refers specifically to Congress, but that does not settle the issue for the other amendments (two through eight), which do not refer to any specific level of government. This led to an early court case in which the owner of a wharf in Baltimore damaged by the city's action to change the path of a river sued in court for just compensation under the terms of the Fifth Amendment. Chief Justice John Marshall employed a variety of arguments to show that the claim was insupportable.

Marshall rightly notes that the words themselves are not determinate here, since the Fifth Amendment (unlike the First) does not specify that the limitation applies to Congress. Marshall therefore appeals to the broad nature of the Constitution, viz., the "federal" character of the government (which, of course, has solid grounding in the text): the Constitution establishes the national government (the states' existence being assumed), so that the limits in the document that are not specifically applicable to a particular level of government should be understood as applying to the national government (the states already being limited by their own state constitutions).

Marshall then considers a counterargument: the Constitution, in fact, limits not only the national government but also state governments, as can be seen especially in Article I, section 10. He is able to appeal to the context of these limits, however, to draw out a rule of interpretation that supports his own reading: The limits on state government in Article I, section 10 are specifically addressed to states, while some of the limits of Article I, section 9 are indefinite—these obviously apply to the national government, though they do not explicitly say that.

Marshall then moves back to broader considerations, asking whether there is any strong reason to depart from his initial findings. He finds, rather, further reasons to support it: if the fears that prompted the Bill of Rights had been directed against state governments, it would have been easier to deal with these fears by state constitutional amendment or, if limitations had been included in the Bill of Rights, Congress would have made such a purpose clear. But in fact—Marshall continues to appeal to the broad character of the document as a whole, which is not part of the "text," but which provides a sure or objective context for understanding it—"it is universally understood" and "it is part of the history of the day" that the fears that gave rise to the Bill of Rights were directed at the new national government, not the states. It was these causes that led state ratifying conventions to recommend amendments, and Congress eventually acted in response to them by passing the Bill of Rights.

Is Marshall's argument conclusive? In my opinion, absolutely. Is it free of any considerations that cannot be derived directly from the text? No. But its objectivity is not endangered if the dialectical process includes clear and noncontroversial—"objective"[18]—points from outside the text, and continually "tests" them against the text (and alternative interpretations), to make sure that they reveal the inner meaning of the text (its reason and spirit) rather than being impositions upon it.

Marshall's typically cogent argument looks both to general characteristics of the Constitution and to its more particular phraseology, combining the two to make a very convincing case—a pattern typical of most Marshallian constitutional opinions.

A truly adequate examination of the founders' approach to interpretation would involve the study and explication of many such opinions. My experience is that the only way to really get a feeling for how traditional interpreters went about interpretation is to immerse oneself in their opinions. In evaluating their approach there is, moreover, no alternative but to examine what they did: the only way to find out whether that approach worked is to get down to specifics and evaluate the arguments.

One danger—possible source of distortion—that a person faces when doing this is that he is likely to be very impressed by both sides of the argument in many of these early controversies—so much so as to be tempted to adopt the sophist's position, that there are no right or wrong answers but only more or less plausible (but not compelling) argumentation. But the fact that good arguments can be made on both (or many) sides does not prove that there is no answer. It may mean that the answer is difficult to arrive at, or it may even mean that the answer in some cases is that a given provision could fairly be read in more than one way. But those are both fair answers.

It is worthwhile emphasizing that these rules of interpretation emerge from a study of the whole range of constitutional interpretation in the first years of American government and not merely judicial instances of it. Much of the outstanding debate over the meaning of the Constitution came, in these early days, within the Cabinet and within Congress and in public debates (e.g., the debate over the constitutionality of the national bank, the removal power debate, and the controversy surrounding the Alien and Sedition Acts). No one assumed then, as some people do today, that constitutional interpretation is the special (virtually exclusive) prerogative of the judiciary. While there was certainly a great deal of disagreement about very important questions of constitutional interpretation in early American history, especially federalism and slavery, the more striking fact (the forest that should not be lost sight of for the trees) is the general agreement that existed on the question of *how* to go about interpreting the Constitution, what the rules of interpretation were. That did not eliminate controversy, but it did limit it and provide generally accepted criteria for resolving such questions. The most fundamental assumption shared by all was that the Constitution did have an ascertainable meaning—one given it by its authors—and that that "original intention" was the end or object of constitutional interpretation—it was authoritative.

This does not mean that the meaning of all provisions of the Constitution was completely clear. Early constitutional interpreters would not have suggested this possibility. The "meaning" of the Constitution in unclear cases was more a question of limiting the possible readings than of finding the one sole legitimate reading. "Interpretation" resulted in the conclusion that several readings were plausible, and it ended at that point; that is, to go beyond noting the legitimate possible readings by choosing one of them (making it authoritative) was to take a step beyond simply "interpreting" the document.

Characteristics of Traditional Interpretation

I would like to make six disparate observations about this general approach to interpretation, elaborating on some issues and pointing out some of the more important implications. First, careful study of early rules of interpretation suggests the inadequacy of the frequently used dichotomy between "strict" or "narrow construction" and "broad" or "loose construction." At the very least, one should distinguish between a "narrow construction" on one extreme, a "loose construction" on the other, and a "broad but strict construction" in the middle. Narrow construction would be the tendency to read the words more narrowly than a fair reading of the text requires. Loose construction would be the tendency to read them more broadly (in ways I shall describe briefly below). Broad but strict construction is the recognition, flowing from a faithful (or "strict") interpretation of the text, of the appropriate breadth of government powers and limitations, without permitting them to be expanded improperly. (To put some more flesh on those characterizations, although I do not have the space to defend my assertions here, a good example of narrow construction is the approach of Thomas Jefferson, who read the Constitution more narrowly than a fair reading would require; John Marshall is a good example of broad but strict construction; and the typical modern form of constitutional interpretation, which involves balancing of broad and vague constitutional principles against competing governmental interests, is loose construction.[19])

The simple dichotomy of strict and broad (or loose) construction is made to the detriment of clarity; it usually submerges strict construction in narrow construction and/or broad construction in loose construction, both of which are improper; as Marshall showed, strict construction ought not to be narrow, and broad construction ought not to be loose.

Second, the approach to interpretation in the founding was not, I think, merely "an" approach to interpretation. That is what is implicit in its characterization today by some as "interpretivism."[20] It is, rather, interpretation in the primary or strict sense of that word. That is not to say that there are not secondary or, as is sometimes said, "improper" senses of the word "interpretation." An example of the secondary meaning may be taken from the world of drama, in which an actor may be said to "interpret" a role quite apart from any understanding of that role on the part of the playwright. By this I mean not merely that the actor sees in the role aspects that the playwright himself may not have thought of specifically—a fair possibility even with the stricter sense of interpretation, as long as those potentialities flow "fairly" from what the playwright has written. Rather, the actor imposes his own (different though not *necessarily* hostile) theoretical framework on the materials with which he is dealing to produce a "new" character, one that is not fairly traceable to the playwright. (The *most* that could be said is that the new character is not demonstrably *contrary* to any particular and definite aspect of what the playwright intended, although it cannot be shown to flow from the original design of the playwright. More often than not, however, such new "interpretations" lead to some changes that do not do full justice to at least some aspect of the original design.[21])

It would, however, be equivocal to use the word "interpretation" in this extended, or "improper," sense with regard to constitutional interpretation. To do so would be to use language in a way that undermines the very purpose of a written constitution as it was understood by the framers and as it is still understood by most people today. The whole point of the written constitution was to provide a fixed reference point by which to preserve—even against the legislature—a government of laws rather than of men. To adopt a notion of interpretation as a vehicle for change rather than a means of defending fixed principles runs contrary to this understanding of a constitution. One sign of this is that even those who embrace an "evolving constitution" philosophy are often very upset when the Constitution "is evolved" by others, rather than themselves.[22]

Third, the Constitution understood according to a traditional approach to interpretation is "adaptable" in a particular sense. Identifying that sense is crucial, since the most obvious criticism of maintaining the original meaning of the document is that it will become outdated and inadequate for new and modern circumstances. In what does the adaptability of the Constitution lie? Not, it should be said in the first place, in the ability of an interpreter to read new meaning into the document in order to bring it up to date. Rather, the adaptability lies in three factors: 1) the broad language used by the framers—it provides for regulating, not horses and buggies or steamships, but "commerce," and permits Congress to supply the nation, not with muskets and cannon, but with "armies"; 2) the substantial discretion left to the ordinary political process in choosing which means are best used according to the particular circumstances of a given time in order to implement the broad powers of the Constitution, especially in the necessary and proper clause; and 3) the power of amendment, by which the nation could add new powers to or impose new limits on government, as long as there was broad national consensus on doing so.

There could be a lengthy discussion of whether this degree of adaptability is adequate. Moreover, even if one concluded that it was inadequate, there could be an equally long discussion as to which institution of government could make up for its inadequacy. After all, even if the Constitution does not provide enough power or limits on power, it is not by any means clear that the judiciary ought to be the branch to "adapt" the Constitution by adding new powers or imposing new limits. But that is a separate question I have dealt with elsewhere.[23] For now, let me simply say that assertions of the outdated character of the Constitution, understood as it was understood by those who wrote and ratified it, are often found persuasive by those who wrongly accept the dictates of historicism (the necessary "timeboundedness" of all human thought) and assume the outdatedness rather than proving it. And, moreover, all too often allegations of outdatedness are more subtly based on altogether controversial contentions that amount to little more than the personal preferences of some particular individual or group, which do not have—as they ought not to have—special authority in a republican government. "Outdatedness" may not simply be in the eye of the beholder, but it is controversial enough to require decision by some prescribed authoritative process, such as constitutional amendment.

Fourth, the approach to interpretation of early American political life cannot be fairly characterized as "mechanical jurisprudence," as it sometimes has been. This approach is not based on the contention that an answer to every problem may be deduced from the Constitution. Rather, it is adequate primarily because it provides a form of government that is empowered to deal with various problems.

This does not mean that it is not based on any fixed principles or that those principles are only procedural. There are some fixed substantive principles, for example, the protection of rights to life, liberty, and property. But the founders prudently realized that there was substantial variability in the specific ways to accomplish those fixed goals, and so they did not try to hamstring future governments with too-narrow conceptions of either the powers of government or the limits thereon.

Nor was interpretation reduced to merely verbal analysis, as if it were simply parsing out the words, phrases, sentences, and paragraphs of the document. The rules of interpretation requiring attention to context, subject matter, and the reason and spirit of the law guaranteed that statesmanlike interpretation could be done only with a fair measure of political prudence.

Fifth, the traditional approach to interpretation did not pretend to remove all possible sources of controversy. No one ever claimed that any approach to interpretation could do that. As Hamilton pointed out, some constitutional questions were quite clear, and others were less so.[24] In some parts of the Constitution, inevitably, either because of the limits of the framers' language or thought or because they could not know future questions that would arise under various constitutional provisions, they wrote provisions that were ambiguous, either in general or as applied to specific cases. In these cases, "interpretation" could only narrow down the fair readings of the document, leaving the determination of which of these meanings was preferable to *choice*. Who would make that choice was an important question, but a question separate from the question of interpretation. Given that judicial review was rooted in the special judicial task of *interpreting* the Constitution, putting interpretation aside meant putting judicial review aside as well. According to the political philosophy of the Constitution and the founding, little commended the position that the judges ought to be the ones to choose among various more or less equally plausible meanings of constitutional provisions, in the context of judicial review. By this sort of extension, "originalism," which starts out as a theory of interpretation, becomes a theory of adjudication as well.

Reasonable people, then, could certainly have different reasonable interpretations of some constitutional provisions. But 1) some provisions would be relatively clear, 2) there would be widely agreed-upon norms of interpretation to serve as a common standard or reference point in the debate over less clear provisions, and 3) where there was no clear conflict between Constitution and act, essential conditions for the exercise of judicial review were absent. Thus, the debate over controversial constitutional questions would at least be substantially narrowed.

Finally, sixth, I should make clear in what sense I would refer to the position I have been elaborating as an "original intent" position. In some ways, that characterization can be misleading, if it is understood as referring to the motives or purposes or intentions of the particular individuals who wrote and ratified the Constitution. The true original intention position, according to the "original intention" of the founders, was that the document did have a meaning and that meaning was binding. The original intention was the intention embodied in the document, and it was understood primarily—indeed overwhelmingly— by a careful reading of that document. The various intentions or purposes of those who contributed to its writing and ratification could be useful evidence as to the original intent, if they met certain standards (e.g., if one could show that they reflected the views of the majority of those who ratified the document, which is the way it obtained its political authority in our form of government), but even they were subordinate to the very best evidence of intent, namely, what the framers wrote and the ratifiers adopted.

For the record, it must be pointed out (with Madison) that the document should be understood not simply in light of the intention of the framers but in light of those for whom it was framed.[25] Coming from the convention that produced it, by itself, the Constitution had no authority. Its authority was derived from its ratification by the people of the United States, in the various state ratifying conventions. Ultimately, Madison traced the question of the authority of the Constitution back to the Declaration of Independence: the people have the right to establish, and to alter, government in order to achieve the goal of protecting the fundamental rights of man, among them, life, liberty, and the pursuit of happiness.[26]

Because these principles were so widely accepted in American political life, the framers should be assumed to have stated their meaning in plain language, and normally there should be no conflict between the Constitution as understood by its framers and the Constitution as understood by its ratifiers. Of course, it is an empirical question open to argument whether this assumption is true. Should there be a conflict, the Constitution is authoritative in the sense in which it was understood by those for whom it was written and from whom it received its authority. But the burden of proof rests upon those who would contend that the Constitution was understood by its ratifiers differently from the way it was written by its authors.

Moreover, this original intention concerns the principles embodied in the document, which can be distinguished from the expectations of the framers as to how the principles would be applied in concrete cases. What the Constitution embodied was not the expectations, but the principles.

At the same time, the burden is strongly on those who would contend that expectations widely shared by the authors and ratifiers of the Constitution are not necessary implications of the document. After all, constitutional principles are frequently formulated by generalizing from specific problems or abuses, and those problems or abuses are often a significant source of light on the meaning of the general principles, at least where there is virtually universal agreement on the particular problems that gave rise to a provision. The presumption, then, should be that contemporaneous understandings of the application of a provision generally shared by those proposing it are proper applications of it.

Nonetheless, one can imagine a situation in which expectations—perhaps even widely shared expectations—do not correspond with the intrinsic requirements of the principles of the document. For example, it cannot be properly contended—as it was by at least one Congressman voting for the Fourteenth Amendment—that its protections against racial discrimination apply to Negroes but not to Chinese.[27] Nor could it properly be contended that the First Amendment's guarantee of free exercise of religion applies to Protestants (or Christians) but not to Catholics (or Jews or Muslims), as some in the founding generation argued.[28]

The "original intention" or meaning of the Constitution, then, is to be found in the principles embodied in the document, as its language was understood by those for whom it was framed.

Understood this way, it is fair to call the position I have elaborated the "original intent" position, though one could justify as easily its characterization as the "original meaning" or, even more provocatively, the "real meaning" of the Constitution.

Modern Constitutional Interpretation

It may help to clarify my position on how the framers thought the Constitution ought to be interpreted if I describe briefly what I see as the major alternative to that view, one that has come to dominate legal scholarship in the twentieth century.

Let me begin with the critique of the traditional approach.[29] The approach to constitutional interpretation in the early years of American government has been subjected to criticism on two major grounds. First, it is argued, it is unrealizable since interpretation of a document with some of the Constitution's vague general phrases inevitably involves the personal views and preferences of the interpreter. The ideal of an interpreter who serves merely as a "mouthpiece of the law" is a dream, not a reality. One has only to look at the constitutional interpretation of the greatest figure of this period, John Marshall, to see that constitutional interpretation is not above politics; Marshall's great decisions consist largely of reading his own Federalist party predilections into the Constitution. Whether it would really be ideal to have such self-abnegating judges as the traditional approach espouses, the simple fact is that it is not possible, and it is better to be honest about it, whether you want to restrain judges or increase their power.

Nor is Marshall's failure an accident, it is argued. It flows directly from the traditional rules of interpretation themselves, which necessarily involve an interpreter's own personal conceptions rather than merely those of some disembodied law. For example, the rules requiring the interpreter to consider the subject-matter and context, including such indeterminate factors as "the normal requirements of government" and "the nature of a written constitution," inevitably lead to the importation of personal preferences into the process. (Jefferson's differences with Marshall often flowed from precisely these considerations, where the Constitution itself provides no answers.)

Second, even were it possible to restrict the interpreter of the Constitution to being a "mouthpiece of the law," it would not be desirable.

Especially when one is dealing with a constitution, the notion of a static, unchanging law is not an ideal but a nightmare. The broad principles of a constitution must be constantly applied and adapted to the different circumstances of new eras, and without that adaptation the constitution would soon be outdated. An especially important aspect of this role of adapting a constitution would be expanding the sphere of liberty against the various attempts of the dominant forces of society to impose their will on minorities from generation to generation. Protection of minority rights in the name of human freedom and dignity is a function essential for any government, for democracies no less than for others. This requires an institution that can 1) confront and defeat newly devised ways of undermining rights, of which the framers of a document written long ago could not have known, and 2) devise new ways of expanding rights to which the framers would likely have been hostile, given the limits of their world-view.

In light of this critique of traditional notions of interpretation, what is a more adequate conception according to modern commentators?[30] Modern constitutional interpretation generally is based on a reading of particular constitutional phrases as very broad, general *presumptions* or guiding principles, as opposed to absolutes to be construed literally and applied mechanically. The difference between traditional and modern interpretation, then, begins with differences over the meaning of certain key phrases, such as "due process" and "equal protection."[31] Were these phrases intended to have, or do they in fact have—the argument can be made either by invoking or dismissing original intent— some relatively determinate content that interpreters are to focus on, or were they intended to be, or are they in fact, "open-ended" provisions whose content must be established and reestablished by courts over time?

The most important phrases have been the due process clauses of the Fifth and Fourteenth Amendments, the Fourteenth Amendment's equal protection clause, and the guarantees of freedom of speech and religion in the First Amendment. Modern interpreters (following those of the "transitional" era from 1890 to 1937, when the Court often mandated laissez-faire policy in its review of economic legislation) have attributed a very broad meaning to the due process clause: it is a guarantee of fundamental rights against arbitrary deprivation. Which rights are fundamental and what constitutes arbitrary deprivation are not specified—that is the job of the "interpreter." Likewise, the equal protection clause is a guarantee against unreasonably unequal or different treatment; the standard formulation is that people situated similarly must be treated equally. The specification of what kinds of different treat-

ment would be unreasonable would be the job of the interpreter. The
First Amendment guarantee of free speech establishes the principle that
free speech is very important, and it lays down a requirement that state
interests must be very important ones to justify restrictions on free
speech. The guarantee of free exercise of religion means that religious
belief cannot be mandated or prohibited and that religiously based action can be restricted only for very important state interests.[32]

The modern Court (and many of its supporters) tends to argue that
these phrases were intended by their authors to be open-ended. In this
sense, they can be viewed as delegations of power to future interpreters to determine certain questions. Others would prescind from the issue of original intent and simply say that the provisions obviously and
inevitably are open-ended, since any attempt to establish provisions with
specific content would have been both impossible and undesirable. The
main job of interpretation in the modern era, then, is not so much ob-
taining the meaning of the words of the Constitution—the vague general principles are relatively easy to establish as such—but applying
those general meanings to particular cases in order to give them specific content in regard to the issues involved.

This is often characterized as a "balancing" process. In each case,
judges must evaluate, first, the importance of the asserted right (especially in the form in which it is presented in the case), second, the importance of the state interests that are said to justify impinging on the
right, and third, whether the state interests justify such impingement
upon the right as the case involves. As a general rule, modern judges
engage in this process with something of a presumption in favor of the
right (i.e., the burden of proof is on the government, at least after a
prima facie showing that a constitutional right has been restricted in
some way, which typically is not difficult), although the extent of that
presumption varies.

The content of the balancing process reveals clearly the similarity
between the judges' duty and what goes on in the normal legislative
process (or, some would argue, what would go on in the ordinary legislative process if it chose to be more concerned about rights than it
tends to be). It is not a question of simply applying a clear principle
to facts that fall within the operation of the principle. Rather, it is a
question of defining or giving content to a vague principle in cases
involving its application to various factual circumstances. This is what
Justice Oliver Wendell Holmes Jr. and others referred to as legislating
in the "gaps of the law."[33] The major considerations shaping a judge's
decisions are notions of what is good public policy, in the broad sense
of "sorting out the enduring values of society."[34] The judge's task could

perhaps be viewed as discerning what the Constitution *ought to be understood* to say more than as what it was *meant* to say (though some will see the two as identical).

The Response

The advocate of the traditional approach to interpretation would respond to the modern critique in several ways. Without defending every decision made by early Supreme Courts—in fact, any given constitutional commentator will find a good many cases to have been wrongly argued and decided—he would maintain that there was general acceptance of the rules, even when they were used poorly (as in *Dred Scott*, for example[35]). To the argument that Marshall read his own Federalist opinions into the document, the response would be that he did not have to—they were already there, since the Constitution was, after all, fundamentally a Federalist document.

Modern "realist" critics often stumble into a contradiction when they go back in history and try to prove that judges are invariably moved by policy considerations rather than by legal reasoning by proving that some decisions were obviously decided wrongly, contrary to fair legal reasoning. For example, Marshall is often condemned for extending the contract clause beyond a fair reading. That very argument, of course, assumes the possibility of reading the Constitution fairly—it avows that a right interpretation can be known, by its assertion that Marshall was wrong. (That is why more cautious realists must restrict their critical analysis of decisions to the position that "other interpretations were equally plausible.")

No one that I know of has ever argued that Marshall or other traditional interpreters were infallible. *Of course* the traditional notion of interpretation is an ideal, and *of course* the ideal is only approximated. The crucial question (in response to the argument that such interpretation is impossible) is whether it can be operative enough to be "substantially" true, in the only way that all non-Utopian ideals are true. I think that the founders in general showed that it was, although they were men who differed sharply on many political and specific constitutional issues.

To the more radical and serious criticism that the rules of interpretation necessarily involve the interpreter's personal predilections (e.g., in regard to the "normal requirements of government" and "the nature of a written constitution"), the response is more complex.[36] First, that people may differ about the normal requirements of government or the nature of a written constitution is no proof in itself that interpreters must necessarily import dubious notions of them into the interpretive process. Some things are obviously much more necessary for government than others, and a good interpreter will distinguish between what is clearly so and what is more debatable. The fact is that there are *some* requirements of government that are obviously necessary (e.g., something like a necessary and proper clause—though its breadth is certainly subject to debate), and they can legitimately be considered in *ascertaining* the meaning of a constitution.

Second, in the work of the best representatives of the traditional approach to interpretation these factors are used primarily to confirm the natural import, or at least a strongly plausible usage, of words in the Constitution. They ought not to be used *against* the natural import of words, Marshall said, except in extreme cases, where "all mankind would, without hesitation, unite in rejecting the application."[37]

Third, Marshall and other traditional interpreters would argue that the proper use of broad considerations should find direct or indirect support in the Constitution. One example of this is Marshall's assertion in *Cohens v. Virginia* (and elsewhere) that the Constitution ought to be understood as intended "to endure for ages to come."[38] One might ask (Jefferson certainly would have) whether this was simply Marshall's own belief, unsupported by the Constitution itself. Careful examination suggests that Marshall is right in finding it implicit there. Some of the evidence includes: 1) the purpose of establishing a "more perfect Union" than the Articles, which were made "in perpetuity"; 2) the Preamble's expectations that the Constitution will bring liberty not only to ourselves but to "our posterity"; 3) the absence of any specified number of states or seats in the House of Representatives, which suggests the contemplation of an expanding future; 4) the lack of an explicit reference to slavery in the Constitution, reflecting—as Lincoln argued—the framers' long-term expectation (and desire) that slavery would be eliminated and their desire not to saddle the long-living document with the term after the peculiar and unjust institution had disappeared; 5) the general language of the Constitution ("commerce," not "stagecoaches" and other particular forms of conveyance in 1787, and "war," not "muskets" and other weapons of 1787), which makes it readily applicable to future, unforeseen circumstances; 6) its provision for emergencies that might arise in the course of time, for example, suspension of the writ of habeas corpus in times of threat to public safety, such as rebellion or invasion; 7) the absence of any provision for termination of the Constitution; and 8) provision for amendment, to make possible such changes as future circumstances might seem to require, but with a requirement of an extraordinary majority, thereby suggesting that frequent recourse to this power was not anticipated.[39]

The rules requiring an interpreter to consider the subject and context of constitutional provisions, including broad considerations such as the normal requirements of government and the nature of a written constitution, could, of course, be abused. Then, however, one ought to criticize the abuse rather than the rules, unless one can show that the abuse flowed inevitably from the rules. Again, the constitutional interpretation of figures such as Hamilton, Madison, and Marshall demonstrates that there was no such inevitability.

In examining the alternative, modern conception of interpretation, a defender of more traditional principles would simply deny that the phrases most commonly employed by the modern Court are the vague generalities they are alleged to be. The due process clause, he would argue, for example, is much narrower than it is typically considered, being limited to procedural questions and even there a relatively narrow guarantee to defendants of the prevailing law.[40] Moreover, to treat provisions such as the First Amendment as mere "presumptions" is simply to give up the attempt to interpret them in any serious way, since no possible reading of the language could sustain *that* view.

Beyond Interpretation

Another traditionalist ground of objection to the modern position is based on the following line of reasoning. To say that the Constitution is fundamentally ambiguous, as the modern form of interpretation does, is to say that there are multiple possible fair readings of the document. Even after careful efforts to ascertain the meaning, one is left with more than one very plausible (not just possible, but very defensible or "not clearly refutable") interpretation. The *choice* between or among these different readings, then, is not properly interpretation. It is an assertion not of judgment but of will.

At this point, the topic of interpretation yields to a different topic. The modern critique of traditional interpretation given above contained a second point, not yet dealt with. That is the argument that even were the traditional approach to interpretation possible, it would not be desirable, since it would shackle us with a static law incapable of reflecting (and contributing to) the progress of our society. That argument is not so much for a particular kind of "interpretation" as it is against "merely interpreting" the document. It leads us to a judiciary that is regarded as *the* authoritative source of the meaning of the Constitution, a source that can choose, as well as find, that meaning. This form of judicial review, based on (allegedly) ambiguous provisions of the Constitution, is fundamentally different from the traditional approach to judicial review, which had to find a clear violation of the Constitution.

The most profound difference is that in the traditional approach, the judge is able to assert the traditional "democratic credentials" of judicial review, namely, that he is enforcing the will of the people, contained in the document, rather than some other will, such as his own. In the case where a judge *chooses* which of several fair readings of a constitutional provision to make authoritative, one could only say that the judge's choice *might* reflect the popular will.

This is true whether or not the ambiguity was deliberate. One could imagine not only accidental ambiguity—cases where the framers intended something but did not state it well enough to make their will clear—but also deliberate ambiguity; that is, the framers either could only agree on something by leaving it ambiguous or intended to leave room for various future interpretations. Even in the case of deliberate ambiguity, a judge could only say that his chosen interpretation of the provision was compatible with the constitutional provision, not that it was what the people had intended (even in a very general way). For the record, however, I think it is highly doubtful whether any of the framers (whether of the original Constitution or of the Fourteenth Amendment) intended the Constitution to be deliberately ambiguous with a view to *judicial* specification of its generalities.[41]

What should be clear by now is that the nature of judicial review is determined particularly by the conception of "interpretation" that one adopts as the foundation for judicial review or, to state my case more exactly, it is determined by the choice of *whether* to adopt interpretation in the stricter sense of that term. The founders would argue that what they called "interpretation" was not merely one variant but the real thing. The alternative to the conception of judicial review dominant in the founding, based on interpretation, is a form of judicial review based on something other than intepretation, not merely on a different form of interpretation; probably "judicial legislation" is the best term for it.[42]

I make no pretense of having proven here that the founders' conceptions were better. Even if everyone agreed with what I have been saying here—that judicial review has, indeed, been transformed into a new kind of power—the issue would remain unsettled. One could either lament the departure from the original intention of the Constitution (the departure from "interpretation") that I have described, or one could praise the "adaptability of our living, evolving Constitution" and applaud the decision to transcend "mere" interpretation.

But what I have said does make clear, I hope, that there is a genuine alternative to today's contending theories of modern judicial power, one based on genuine interpretation of the Constitution. A careful examination of the founders' thought provides a different approach that cannot be glibly dismissed on shallow historicist grounds. Whatever the differences between now and then, the founders' thought has not become simply or automatically "outdated." They themslves did not confine their thought and action to narrow and very time-bound questions but dealt carefully with the fundamental and perennial questions of republican government. We owe it to ourselves not to study them merely as objects of antiquarian interest. We owe them at least the courtesy of a continuing participation in our debates about the institutions they established and the principles they erected as the foundation of our government. And, in fact, I believe that we will find the most adequate conceptions of interpretation and of judicial review by recurring to the original intent, the original understanding, of "interpretation."

2

The Original Meaning of the Due Process Clause

Of all the phrases in the Constitution that have been invoked to justify judicial voiding of legislative and executive acts, none can match the historical record of the due process clause. Indeed, until the explosion of equal protection law under the Warren Court and its successors, no clause could even come close to dominating constitutional law as did due process cases. Most modern scholars regard it as the greatest of the Constitution's "majestic generalities."

My argument in this chapter is simple. It is that virtually all of the constitutional law built on the due process clause is built upon sand, because the original meaning of the due process clause was rather narrow.

The effort to ascertain the original meaning of the due process clause of the Fifth Amendment will turn out to be a relatively typical case of constitutional interpretation: a cursory reading of the document will reveal several possible meanings, of which one is strongly suggested by a more careful reading in context; historical sources will provide some basis for several positions, but generally support the fairest reading of the text.

The Original Meaning of Fifth Amendment Due Process: The Words

Fifth Amendment due process was quite limited in scope. The key phrase is "due process of law." What does the wording suggest? "Pro-

27

cess," especially process of law, would normally be taken to mean some legal proceedings or legal procedure. That is, some kind of legal process must be followed before depriving someone of life, liberty, or property.[1]

For this procedural content of due process, several different major interpretations flow from different answers to the question, "What is *due* process of law?" What criterion or reference point determines what is "due" or owed a person?

The narrower interpretation would be that a person has a right to that process due to a person under the law. What is due a person is the legal process specified by the law—that is, by the Constitution, statutes, and common law. The broader interpretation would be that a person has a right to just or proper legal procedure—that is, what is necessary to guarantee fairness as a matter of natural rights or natural law. The latter interpretation of the clause, unlike the narrower interpretation, would significantly limit the legislature as well as the executive and judiciary.[2] Another interpretation would lie between the first two. The law that would be the norm for due process would be the 1789 common law.[3] This would make the norm a limit on the legislature because the source of this law would be something other than the legislature itself, but it would also give it a more clear-cut or specified source, since the common law is a definite received body of doctrine whose content can be established with less controversy (than the natural law).

The common law could be considered guaranteed in two senses: the specific, determinate law of 1789, or at least the general principles underlying that law (leaving open the possibility of new forms of procedure being acceptable as long as they continue to guarantee the general principles).[4]

The wording by itself, then, suggests several possibilities.

Turning from the words of the particular provision to its context, it is important to note that the Bill of Rights has at least some rough order—it is not a mere grab bag of rights. The organization of the Bill of Rights appears to be something like the following:

I. Substantive Rights
    A. I: a) Freedom of Religion (establishment prohibited
                 and free exercise guaranteed)
              b) Freedom of Speech, Press
              c) Freedom to Assemble and Petition for Redress of
                 Grievances
    B. II: The Right to Bear Arms

C. III: Limitations on Quartering of Soldiers in Citizens'
Homes [which leads into the Fourth Amendment . . .]
II. Procedural Rights
A. IV: Freedom from Unreasonable Searches and Seizures
(including requirements for warrants)
B. V: Rules Governing Proceedings Against Life, Liberty, and
Property (applicable especially to pretrial matters and
general trial procedure)
1. Grand jury requirement;
2. Double jeopardy prohibition;
3. Self-incrimination prohibition, due process requirement;
4. Just compensation requirement.
C. VI: Procedural Rights of Individual Once Charged with a
Crime
1. Speedy and public trial, by impartial local jury, notice
of accusation;
2. Confrontation of witnesses;
3. Compulsory process for defendant's witnesses, and
permission of assistance of counsel for defense.
D. VII: Trial by Jury in Civil Cases
E. VIII: a) No Excessive Bail
b) No Excessive Fines
c) No Cruel and Unusual Punishments
III. Rules of Construction
A. Regarding the Enumeration of Rights
IX: Enumeration of Some Rights Not to Deny or Disparage
Others
B. Relation of Federal Powers to States and People
X: Powers Not Delegated to the U.S. or Prohibited to States
Are Reserved to the Individual States or the People.[5]

Some roughness in the organization (as is common with committee
work) should not obscure the existence of a basic structure. Due process is in a section generally concerned with procedural matters. Within that section, it is in the third of five amendments; and within that
amendment, it is in the second half of the third (of four) sections (each
separated by semi-colons). This placement—"buried" in the midst of
several specific rights—suggests rather strongly that due process is a
fairly limited right rather than a broad general one. On its face, the
placement makes quite unlikely the very broad form of "procedural due
process," according to which it is a general guarantee of fair or just
legal process. Such a broad guarantee would have been singled out as
a separate amendment (like trial by jury in civil cases) or at least placed
at the beginning or, more likely, the end of the procedural guarantees.

The placement also casts doubt on the interpretation of the due process clause that says that it is a perpetual guarantee of the whole 1789 common-law legal process and, as such, is a limit on all three branches of government. Such an interpretation appears to be a variant of the very broad interpretation (the "natural law"—at least regarding legal procedure—approach) with this difference: the "natural law" guarantees would be assumed to have been comprehensively and permanently embodied in the common law, as it stood in 1789.

The interpretation most supported by the placement is the narrower one: a person is guaranteed that process specified by law. The common law would be the source of this law, for the most part, but would not be the standard in such a way as to proscribe legislative modifications thereof.[6]

Another important aspect of the context of the due process clause suggests that it has a (relatively) narrow meaning. The other provisions of the Bill of Rights include many specific procedural guarantees, for example, grand jury, double jeopardy, self-incrimination, trial by jury, notice and hearing, confrontation of witnesses, assistance of counsel. If due process were a general guarantee that included all of these, then those provisions would be redundant or superfluous and would not have been included. That they were included suggests that due process was not understood to cover them (i.e., was very narrow) or covered them only in the sense that they were part of the standing law at the time of the framing of the Bill of Rights (a standing law subject to modification through the ordinary lawmaking process.)[7] Redundancy is thus avoided, and the clause is given an intelligible content, if it is interpreted as a reference to the standing laws regarding legal procedure (i.e., the common law of the courts, as modified by the legislature).

The most questionable part of the organization is the placement of the takings clause as the last of the four clauses in the Fifth Amendment. In one way, that supports my argument by emphasizing the focus on the executive (since my interpretation of the due process clause makes it primarily a limit on the executive and judicial branches). The requirement of just compensation would seem to be directed especially at the executive agents of government, who preside over the paradigm case of "takings": eminent domain.

However, the requirement of just compensation for a taking is quite different from the deprivation of life, liberty, or property as a punishment in ordinary criminal justice. The just compensation clause somewhat undercuts the more narrowly "procedural" character of the Fifth Amendment, as I have described it above. And since the takings clause focuses especially on property rights, that fact might buttress the broader, more "substantive" interpretation of due process, which came to be historically associated with property rights in the late nineteenth century. Alternatively, perhaps it was merely a precaution to prevent due process from being read as a barrier to the power of eminent domain by pointing out that private property *could* be taken under some circumstances.

The most important response to the argument rests on a semi-colon— the one that follows the due process clause, leaving due process more closely connected with the (procedural) guarantee against self-incrimination that precedes it, rather than the (more substantive) takings clause that follows it.

The interpretation I argue for here—confining due process to a guarantee of the standing law, whatever that might be—is sometimes criticized for guaranteeing the "obvious": why bother to *say* that "whatever the law regarding procedure is, people have a right to it"—isn't that obvious without a due process clause? What is essential to remember is that many "obvious" rights have been violated throughout history. English history provided the framers with numerous examples of tyrannical acts of Parliament or the King (and their agents) depriving particular individuals or groups of life, liberty, and property without legal procedure according to the standing law. Moreover, the purpose of the Bill of Rights was primarily to quiet the fears of opponents to the national government by cautionary *explanations*. Many Federalists, such as Madison, argued that the Bill of Rights was not strictly necessary, but that it was a prudent measure to calm Anti-Federalists' fears.

The Original Intention of Due Process: History

One of the most important facets of the historical evidence on the meaning of the due process clause of the Fifth Amendment is what was *not* said. First, there was hardly any debate or controversy about the due process clause in the Congressional discussion of the Bill of Rights, or (from what little we know of them) in the state ratification debates on the Bill of Rights. Second, the Fifth Amendment due process clause was seldom used for the first century of its existence. The first major Supreme Court case defining it did not come until 1856.[8] Both of these facts strongly suggest that due process did not have a broad meaning.

What was its historical meaning at the time of the adoption of the Fifth Amendment? Its origin was taken to have been the Magna Carta provision that no freeman would be imprisoned, dispossessed, banished, or destroyed "except by the lawful judgment of his peers or by the law

of the land." A later reissue of the charter (in 1354 by Edward III) used
"due process of law" in place of "by the law of the land." Coke seemed
to identify the phrases with each other, defining due process as requiring "indictment and presentment of good and lawful men, and trial and
conviction in consequence." Keith Jurow, in a fascinating article, "Un-
timely Thoughts: A Reconsideration of the Origins of Due Process of
Law," shows that this assumed equivalence is doubtful.[9] In fact, due
process was a very narrow right associated with use of the proper writ
to bring an accused person before a court.

    More evidence of the narrow meaning of due process in English law
at the time of the founding can be found in Sir William Blackstone's
Commentaries on the Laws of England. In Book IV, he discusses public wrongs and the method of punishing them. His outline of this part
of the book is as follows:

VI. The method of punishment, wherein of
    1. The Several Courts of Criminal Jurisdiction
    2. The Proceedings There
        1. Summary
        2. Regular; by
            1. Arrest
            2. Commitment and Bail
            3. Prosecution; by
                1. Presentment
                2. Indictment
                3. Information
                4. Appeal
            4. Process
            5. Arraignment and its Incidents
            6. Plea, and Issue
            7. Trial, and Conviction
        Etc.

Note that process is situated between the initial prosecution (presentment or indictment) and arraignment. In this chapter (IV, 24) Blackstone identifies such "process" with "due process of law":

> . . . for the indictment cannot be tried unless he personally appears,
> according to the rules of equity in all cases, and the express provision
> of statute Edw. III, 3 in capital ones, that no man shall be put to death
> without being brought to answer by due process of law.

The two-page discussion that follows indicates 1) that "due process" consisted in using the proper writ to bring before the court a person who was indicted without being present, and 2) that this was the usual time to transfer certain cases from inferior courts to the Court of King's Bench. It is clear, then, that for Blackstone, "due process of law" was an extremely narrow matter.

Blackstone's authority is not determinative, however. His *Commentaries* were published in England from 1765–69 and had just become available in America at the time of the Revolution. Older commentators such as Coke were probably still the more frequently cited authorities, even by the time of the First Congress, which passed the Bill of Rights.

Early American legal commentators give a broader reading to due process, following Coke in identifying it with the Magna Carta provision that the king will not take or imprison or dispossess or outlaw or exile any freeman "except by the lawful judgment of his peers or by the law of the land." Hamilton cites Coke in defining New York State's law of the land clause in 1786: it means "due process of law, that is . . . *by indictment or presentment of good and lawful men*, and trial and conviction in consequence."[10] Kent also cites Coke,[11] as does Story, who summarizes the clause more broadly when he concludes: "So that this clause in effect affirms the right of trial according to the process of proceedings of the common law."[12]

What remains ambiguous in Story's statement is the relation of the "proceedings of the common law" to the legislature. It is clear from Hamilton that the legislature is limited by the clause—it cannot authorize wholesale arbitrary punishment of a class of people (Tories, in that particular case) without a legal determination of guilt beforehand: the legislature "cannot, without tyranny, disfranchise or punish whole classes of citizens by general descriptions, without trial and conviction of offenses known by laws previously established, declaring the offense and prescribing the penalty."[13] But this seems to be a reference to legislative attempts to impose penalties directly, without permitting a regular course of judicial proceedings. What of more properly "legislative" acts: that is, a modification of common-law procedure by general rules or laws? Nothing suggests that the forms of the common law of 1790 were engraved in the Constitution, beyond such legislative modification, by the Fifth Amendment due process clause. (If that was what the framers had intended, it would not have been difficult to say that—but they did not.) "Common law," therefore, could have been (likely was) understood as "the prevailing law," that is, the law of the courts, as codified or modified by statute. Whatever the legal procedures guaranteed by the standing law, they had to be accorded people before punishing them, by deprivation of life (capital punishment), liberty (jail), or property (fine). It is as if the framers of the Fifth Amendment were saying: "In addition to these specific rights we have mentioned, which are constitutionally guaranteed beyond legislative modification, the other rules of legal proceedings in effect at a given time—whatever they may be— are also to be accorded persons before punishing them."

The first major due process case defining the due process clause was *Murray's Lessee v. Hoboken Land & Improvement Co.* (1856). Justice Curtis's opinion for a unanimous Court argued that this clause is a limit on the legislature: Congress cannot make any process "due process of law" merely by its will. What, then, are the criteria for *due* process? They are 1) the Constitution's provisions and 2)

> Those settled usages and modes of proceeding existing in the common and statute law of England, before the emigration of our ancestors, and which are shown not to have been unsuited to their civil and political condition by having been acted on by them after the settlement of this country.[14]

Since the kind of "distress warrant" at issue in this case was clearly provided for in the common law, Curtis's discussion needed to go no further. He did not need to address himself to the possible issue of the validity of some legislative modification of common-law legal procedure.[15]

When pointing to the common law, did Curtis mean that its usages and proceedings as of 1789 were "locked into" the Constitution by the Fifth Amendment due process clause? It is not possible to answer this question with certitude, but given the very nature of the common law, it seems unlikely. First, the common law throughout its history showed itself to be very adaptable to new circumstances, and accordingly, it was continually developed and modified rather than fixed in all its facets. This flexible development of the common law would not be possible were it absolutely fixed in its form in a given year.[16] Second, the common law—Coke's efforts to the contrary notwithstanding—was subject to statutory modification by Parliament. This traditional legislative discretion would be eliminated if the common-law procedural guarantees as of 1789 were made permanent, subject to alteration only by constitutional amendment.

If Curtis did not mean to say that the 1789 common-law legal procedures became fixed by means of Fifth Amendment due process, what did he mean? Perhaps, as Crosskey suggested, he would say that legislative modifications of the common law were legitimate, but subject to the power of the courts "to pass on the 'reasonableness' and essential 'fairness' of any legislative innovations on Common Law,"[17] with (I would add) the customary deference the courts owe legislative judgments. Or perhaps, as the Court itself was to suggest in *Hurtado v. California* (1884),[18] the common-law legal procedure's *principles* were constitutionally protected, while the "forms" were subject to legislative modification (as long as the principles or *purposes* of the older forms were adequately preserved by the new forms). The common-law protections might be guaranteed through different forms, but they could not be abolished altogether.

The placement of the due process clause indicates that Curtis's reading of the clause expands it vis-a-vis its original intent. Even this broader reading of the due process clause, however, should be understood in light of an important characteristic of early judicial review: it was limited by the traditional understanding that, in the absence of *clear* constitutional standards, "reasonable" legislative opinions as to the constitutionality of legislation precluded judicial review. Had Curtis's interpretation prevailed until the present, due process law would be a much smaller section of contemporary casebooks.

The Other Side

If the evidence, both interpretive and historical, suggests so strongly a narrow meaning for the due process clause (relative to its amorphous boundaries today), how can one account for the change? That puzzled Justice Samuel Miller, too, who in *Davidson v. New Orleans* (1878) noted:

> It is not a little remarkable, that this provision has been in the Constitution of the United States, as a restraint upon the authority of the Federal Government, for nearly a century, and while, during all that time, the manner in which the powers of that Government have been exercised has been watched with jealousy, and subjected to the most rigid criticism in all its branches, this special limitation upon its powers has rarely been invoked in the judicial forum or the more enlarged theater of public discussion. But while it has been a part of the Constitution as a restraint upon the power of the States, only a very few years, the docket of this Court is crowded with [such] cases . . . There is here abundant evidence that there exists some strange misconception of the scope of this provision as found in the Fourteenth Amendment.[19]

The question, then, must be asked again: Why, despite such strong evidence of the relatively narrow character of this clause, was it able to be transformed as it has been into what sometimes seems like a blank check for judicial notions of justice, in the area of procedural due process and even beyond, in the area of substantive due process, as exemplified by modern "privacy" cases such as *Griswold v. Connecticut* and *Roe v. Wade*? The answer is complicated, but there is at least a partial explanation.

There did exist in early American courts, especially at the state level, a string of cases that gave a broader reading to "due process of law," by emphasizing the last word especially: *law*. If the law under which one is being deprived of life, liberty, or property turns out not to be a law really—if it lacks some essential element of "law"—then it might be argued that such a "law" violated the due process clause, and that punishments under it (deprivations of life, liberty, and property) were invalid and prohibited.

What is "law"? Whatever the exact definition, there was widespread agreement that it had to be *general*—not, for example, a decree as to particular persons. (This suggests the reasoning behind the prohibition of bills of attainder.) This characteristic of law—its generality—was lacking in an action such as arbitrarily taking property from A and giving it to B. In this way, some early state court decisions were able to invoke the due process clause of the state constitutions (or "the law of the land" clause, which was generally considered to be its equivalent) to protect property rights against "arbitrary legislative deprivation."

For example, in *University of North Carolina v. Foy*[20] the North Carolina courts held unconstitutional a legislative repeal of an earlier grant of land to the university, invoking the "law of the land" clause. The property rights could be taken away from the trustees only after the judiciary "in the usual and common form" pronounced them guilty of some acts that would justify forfeiture of their rights.

Likewise, in *Dartmouth College v. Woodward*, Daniel Webster cited New Hampshire's law of the land provision (again, widely regarded as equivalent to due process) in this way: "By the law of the land is most clearly intended the general law; a law which hears before it condemns; which proceeds upon inquiry, and renders judgment only after trial." This sounds "procedural," but it was used to attack the New Hampshire legislature's unilateral altering of Dartmouth College's charter, on the grounds that these acts were "particular acts of the legislature, which have no relation to the community in general, and which are rather sentences than laws."[21]

In New York, both the "law of the land" and the "due process" clauses were held to be violated in *Taylor v. Porter* by a law that permitted individuals to condemn the property of others in order to build private highways.[22] Eminent domain was legitimate only when used for public purposes. In the absence of a public purpose, property could be taken only when the normal judicial channels had ascertained guilt of a kind that justified the deprivation.[23]

On the federal level, some pieces of evidence could be invoked to support this reading. First, in the wording and placement of words in the Constitution itself there is something suggestive. While most of the amendments of the Bill of Rights are broadly procedural (IV–VIII), and the due process clause is found in the middle of these amendments, and while the Fifth Amendment itself is largely a collection of procedural guarantees (such as grand jury indictment, double jeopardy, and self-incrimination), still there is something rather less procedural about the last clause of the Fifth Amendment, which immediately follows the due process clause: namely, the just compensation clause. This provided that private property could not be taken for public purposes, unless just compensation were given for it. This might be read to deal not with procedure but with the substance of law as it affects property rights, since it would preclude a legislative act authorizing the taking of private property for public purposes without just compensation (and also, presumably, a law authorizing the taking of private property for private purposes). Thus interpreted, this clause might provide a less rigorously procedural context for the foregoing due process clause and support a less procedural application of it.

Again, for reasons given above, I do not find this reasoning particularly persuasive. Most importantly for establishing the context, the due process clause is connected with the self-incrimination clause—only a comma separates them—rather than with the just compensation clause—a semi-colon stands between them. And recurring to our earlier analysis of the broad context, why include a broad substantive guarantee against arbitrary government action here?

Second, another factor at the federal level that supports a broader reading of due process is the flirtation with "natural justice judicial review" in John Marshall's opinion in *Fletcher v. Peck*,[24] which contains reasoning relative to the nature of the law. The argument is essentially that depriving certain people of their land is a judicial act rather than a legislative one:

> It may well be doubted whether the nature of society and of government does not prescribe some limits to the legislative power . . . To the

legislative all legislature power is granted; but the question, whether the act of transferring the property of an individual to the public, to be in the nature of the legislative power, is well worthy of serious reflection. It is the peculiar province of the legislature to prescribe general rules for the government of society; the application of those rules to individuals in society would seem to be the duty of other departments.[25]

Marshall suggests that the legislature is limited by such intrinsic requirements of law. While these remarks did not concern due process, a similar line of reasoning contributed to the origin of substantive due process.

Such "natural justice judicial review" (i.e., judicial review apart from the language of the document itself) did exist in the founding, but I believe that it was an anomaly (which helps to explain why it died out). In Marshall's case, I would point out that he used rather tentative language in *Fletcher*, which suggests some ambivalence, and that he abandoned this approach—though it would seem to be just as applicable, and indeed, Webster used it in his argument to the Court—in *Dartmouth College v. Woodward*, preferring the more clear-cut contract clause argument.

Third, a *dictum* in an early Supreme Court case supports the broader view of due process. Justice Johnson wrote the opinion for the Court in *Bank of Columbia v. Okely* and gave a brief but broad reading of Maryland's "law of the land" clause, widely regarded as equivalent to the due process clause (following Coke). These words, he said, "were intended to secure the individual from the arbitrary exercise of the powers of government, unrestrained by the established principles of private rights and distributive justice."[26]

Justice Johnson's ideas on private rights and the Constitution were, however, generally idiosyncratic. This can be seen best by examining the long note to his opinion in *Satterlee v. Matthewson*, arguing that the most important protection for private rights in the Constitution was the *ex post facto* law prohibition of Article I, sections 9 and 10. Over his objections, the Supreme Court had consistently maintained its earlier interpretation of those clauses, confining them to criminal law.[27]

Substantive due process, then, does have some (relatively tenuous) roots on the federal level in the early (or traditional) era of constitutional interpretation and judicial review. On the state-court level these principles developed earlier, and in 1856 the New York State Court of Appeals used them to strike down a law that forbade the sale of liquor (except for medicinal purposes) in *Wynehamer v. New York*.

The judges explicitly disavowed a straightforward "natural justice" basis for their opinion and argued that certain legislative actions could not be done "even by the forms which belong to due process of law."[28]

Only a year later, in the *Dred Scott* case, we see the only significant pre-Civil War use of substantive due process on the federal level—though it is a weak precedent. The reliance on substantive due process occurs in Taney's plurality (three of the seven justices) rather than a Court opinion. Even Taney's opinion refers to it only once and not in any developed way:

> An act of Congress which deprives a citizen of the United States of his liberty or property merely because he came himself or brought his property into a particular territory of the United States and who had committed no offense against the law could hardly be dignified with the name due process of law.[29]

Of course, a precedent such as *Dred Scott* did not lend much weight to a doctrine in the wake of the Civil War.

Still, this account suggests that some historical evidence could be used to support a broader reading of the due process clause.[30]

Besides reasons noted above, which limit the weight of some of these arguments, I would emphasize three facts. First, this historical evidence comes well after the founding, for the most part, which limits the weight one should attach to it. Relying on such evidence is only legitimate to the extent that it can be shown that it was simply a continuation of ideas already prevalent earlier, when the Constitution was being written. But the evidence—perhaps especially the *absence* of similar cases earlier in constitutional history—suggests the contrary.

Second, I would reemphasize the placement of the due process clause. Were the due process clause intended to be what some have argued it is—a general prohibition of arbitrary legislation—then its position in the Bill of Rights is very difficult to explain.

Third, again, is the absence of debate or discussion about the due process clause in the Congress that passed the Fifth Amendment and (insofar as we know) the state legislatures that ratified it. If the clause had been intended to be the broad guarantee against arbitrary government that it is alleged to be, it seems very extremely unlikely that such debate would be absent. For example, the due process clause would have been cited as an important bulwark against a too-powerful central government by those who were defending the Constitution against charges of "consolidation," or pressed for by those who were making such charges.

A Final Consideration and a Qualification

One last point involves a return to more general considerations of constitutional interpretation and judicial review. Defenders of an expansive
due process clause typically try to muster *some* evidence that due process is a broad guarantee against arbitrary government action and conclude that—given their evidence and the contrary evidence that suggests
a narrower meaning—the clause is a "majestic generality" and must be
left to the courts to "interpret."

The sifting of the evidence above, however, suggests that the most
minimal conclusion one could draw is that the due process clause is
not *clearly* either a general guarantee against arbitrary action or even
a general guarantee of procedural fairness. (Again, a less crabbed evaluation of the evidence seems to me to suggest overwhelmingly that it
is no more than a guarantee of the judicial proceedings appropriate under the standing law.) Under the traditional rationale for judicial review,
judges were not to employ one particular interpretation of a provision
to override a legislative enactment that was based on another interpretation of the provision that was also a "fair" reading of the document
(plausible not merely on a first glance, but after careful interpretation).

This defense was rooted in an essential part of the theoretical foundation for judicial review in a democratic republic: it was not judges
applying their own will but judges applying only the will of the people in the Constitution (see also *Federalist* No. 78). Unless the judges
had a clear constitutional basis for judicial review they had no authority to strike down an act.[31]

The main argument against this position is that it would make judicial review very infrequent and thus an ineffective bulwark protecting
constitutional rights. My response to this is, first, that judicial review
was not necessarily expected to be frequent, second, that even infre-
quently used judicial review can serve a useful function (since its benefits include not only the acts that are overturned but also those that
are forestalled), and third, that the founders looked not only to the judiciary but also and perhaps especially to the political process to vin-
dicate constitutional rights (see especially *Federalist* No. 10). Whether
this approach to judicial review is an adequate one may, of course, be
debated. Whatever its merits, though, I think it can be shown to be the
prevailing view among the founders of American government. All debates over the "original intention" of particular provisions of the Constitution must be carried on in light of this more fundamental aspect
of original intention.

In light of this understanding of judicial review, it is fair to assume that the due process clause would *not* be a legitimate ground for many exercises of judicial review. The only acts that would *clearly* violate it would be acts that deprive people of life, personal liberty, or property without according them the procedures guaranteed by the standing (common and statutory) law. Confining constitutional law to this original understanding of the due process clause would, of course, dramatically curtail judicial power as we know it today. Whether such an original intention ought to be the norm of present Supreme Court decisions—especially in light of the disruption of precedent it would cause—is a question that must be confronted even by those who generally favor "original intent" as the norm of constitutional interpretation. But it is at least desirable for us to confront the issue, rather than remaining ignorant of its existence.

Finally, I should end by adding a very important qualification. What I have been arguing here applies to the original intention of the due process clause of the Fifth Amendment. As I have indicated above, however, by the time of the *Murray v. Hoboken* case of 1856, a broader view of the clause had been adopted, so that it was viewed as a limit not only on the executive and judiciary but on the legislature as well. And it is the understanding of *Murray v. Hoboken* that was the touchstone for the understanding of due process by the framers of the Fourteenth Amendment.[32]

While this modifies my argument somewhat, as it applies to use of the Fourteenth Amendment due process clause (which is, after all, most due process cases), my argument against the broad modern reading of the due process clause remains intact in two essential respects. First, the Court's description of due process in *Murray* still confines it to *procedural* due process, not extending it to substantive due process. Second, even with respect to procedural due process, there is little evidence in *Murray* of a general power of the Court to define and require "just legal procedure" on the basis of the due process clause. The actual use of the due process clause in *Murray* was to uphold a particular form of procedure, on the ground that it was part of the common law. That holding, as *Hurtado v. California* argues persuasively, does not preclude all legislative modifications of common law procedures, but only those that would undercut the fundamental *principles* of common law procedures. The example in *Hurtado* itself was that indictment by information fulfilled the same purpose as indictment by grand jury, though normally in a murder case, common law indictment by grand jury would have been required. And this interpretation of the Court finds compelling support, in my opinion, in the fact that various states that ratified the Fourteenth Amendment provided for indictment

by information, without any sense of inconsistency between those provisions and the new amendment.[33] I would add, finally, that judicial
evaluation of legislative enactments under the due process clause, on
the issue of whether they squared with the principles of common law,
would have been done, on early standards of judicial review, with the
normal deference to the legislature in all cases where the challenged law
did not clearly violate the Constitution.

I would conclude, therefore, that the Fourteenth Amendment due process clause ought to be read more broadly than the original meaning
of the Fifth Amendment due process clause, since the settled interpretation of the latter was the reference point for defining the former at
the time of its drafting. Nonetheless, for reasons I have noted, the original ("real") meaning of the Fourteenth Amendment due process clause
is still dramatically narrower than what has come to be its twentieth-
century reading.

3

Between Scylla and Charybdis: Powell and Berger on the Framers and Original Intention

In the debate of recent years, both scholarly and public, about the role of original intent in constitutional interpretation, much of the criticism of original intent is directed at its alleged undesirability. That is, according to the argument, even assuming that we can know and apply original intent, we would be wrong to use that as the touchstone for interpreting the Constitution. The mistake would rest on two ideas: that the Constitution is and always has been fundamentally defective (generally or in particular but important respects) or because what was once an appropriate document for its era is now outdated.

But original intent has been attacked on other grounds as well. Not only is this approach undesirable; it is also neither feasible nor coherent. It is not feasible because we cannot know and apply original intent in such a way as to derive from it the guidance its adherents claim to derive, and it is not coherent because it fails its own test: reliance on original intent was not the original intent of the Constitution's framers. This chapter will focus on the latter criticism.

One of the most cited articles on this topic is H. Jefferson Powell's "The Original Understanding of Original Intent," published in the *Harvard Law Review* in 1985.[1] This article has become the outstanding example of nonoriginalism's refutation of originalism on originalism's own grounds.[2] Powell argues that "[i]t is commonly assumed that the 'interpretive intention' of the Constitution's framers was that the Constitution would be construed in accordance with what future interpreters could gather of the framers' own purposes, expectations, and intentions. Inquiry shows that assumption to be incorrect" (948).

43

Powell's article elicited a major response from the chief standard-bearer of original intent in contemporary legal circles, Raoul Berger. His "'Original Intention' in Historical Perspective" carefully analyzes Powell's arguments and evidence and comes to the conclusion that "alas, it represents merely another case of special pleading for judicial paramountcy" (296).[3]

These articles draw the battle lines neatly, but neither is victorious because both positions are fundamentally defective. Powell's article separates too sharply the letter and the spirit of the founders' approach to interpretation, using the letter to undermine the spirit. Moreover, on close analysis, he makes major concessions that substantially undermine his basic thesis regarding the impropriety of relying on extratextual sources of the Constitution's intention. But Berger, who is more closely in accord with the founders' ultimate "interpretive intention," the "spirit" of their position, overstates the case for extratextual sources of intention and actually describes the founders' approach to interpretation less accurately than does Powell. This chapter is a defense of original intent against Powell's critique that at the same time tries to preserve original intent from the harm that Berger's argument does to it.[4]

I will proceed by using Powell's outline as a framework, summarizing his arguments one section at a time, describing Berger's response to each one, and then suggesting the problems with both their positions in light of the founders' understanding of constitutional interpretation.[5]

Hermeneutical Traditions in 1787

The Cultural Rejection of Interpretation

Powell's article begins by describing the tension between the two main sources of principles of interpretation used by the authors and ratifiers of the Constitution. The first of these was a flat rejection of interpretation. British Protestants had inherited from the Reformation a deep suspicion of interpretation, as opposed to "the plain meaning," of the Bible. This suspicion was translated into political terms in the views of what has come to be called the "country ideology" in eighteenth-century British politics. And at the same time, Enlightenment *philosophes* contributed to the distrust of interpretation, viewing it as a corruption of meaning. All three of these traditions—British Protestantism, the country ideology, and Enlightenment thought—were major influences on the thought of late-eighteenth-century Americans, and predisposed them to be suspicious of *any* interpretation of legal (as well as religious) texts.

Berger points out that Powell's observations apply not so much to construction per se as to "twisted" construction. In the country ideology, that concern led to a fear that judicial construction would undermine the prerogatives of the legislature.

The import of this tendency to be suspicious of interpretation is ambiguous, it should be noted, because it can cut in several directions. One could derive from it a very strong orientation toward a "plain meaning" position (which, of course, is one form of "interpretation"), with heavy emphasis on the letter of the text. Equally plausibly, it could lead, as shown by Powell's citation of Jefferson to exemplify the fear of construction, to a deemphasis on the text and a shift to a kind of "plain meaning" version of historical intent.[6]

Interpretation and the Common Law

Powell

The first area of major substantive dispute between Powell and Berger involves the common law and its principles of interpretation. However suspicious some English circles were of interpretation, "the necessity of judicial construction had already engendered a second—and conflicting—source of influence: the rich common-law tradition of legal interpretation" (894). Powell argues that "the concept central to the common law's hermeneutic, and to later American discussion of constitutional interpretation, was the notion of the 'intention' or 'intent' underlying a text" (894). The problem with this apparently simple statement is the ambiguity of "intent." It could mean "the meaning that the drafters wished to communicate" or "the meaning the reader was warranted in deriving from the text" (895). It is the latter meaning that was dominant in the common-law tradition, says Powell:

> At common law, then, the "intent" of the maker of a legal document and the "intent" of the document itself were one and the same; "intent" did not depend upon the subjective purposes of the author. The late eighteenth century common lawyer conceived an instrument's "intent"— and therefore its meaning—not as what the drafters meant by their words but rather as what judges, employing the "artificial reason and judgment of law," understood "the reasonable and legal meaning" of those words to be. (895–96, footnotes omitted)

Apparently different interpretive methodologies were applied to different instruments: statutes, wills, deeds, and contracts. For example, Blackstone is typical in seeming to place particular emphasis on the "subjective intentions" of those who drafted statutes and wills. But this apparent "concern for the drafters' purposes was largely illusory" (896). While the construction should be "as near the minds and apparent intents of the parties, as the rules of law will admit," the court was not "free to disregard the rule of law governing the 'apparent intent' of the testator's words: 'the construction must also be reasonable, and agreeable to common understanding.'" Thus, Powell says, "Blackstone was cautioning against hypercritical readings of the words of unlearned laypersons, not endorsing an extratextual search for the purposes underlying those words" (896–97).

Statutory interpretation was similar. "The modern practice of interpreting law by reference to its legislative history was almost wholly nonexistent." The "intent of the act" and "the intent of the legislature" were interchangeable, and for both of them the evidence consisted of the words of the text and the common-law background of the statute. Judges were free to correct a text obviously defective on its face, to substitute coherence for gibberish. But the more serious interpretive problem was ambiguity in the wording. "It was generally agreed," Powell asserts, "that such *ambiguitas patens* could not be resolved by extrinsic evidence as to Parliament's purpose" and, instead, courts read acts against the background of the common law, for example, the mischief unprovided for and the parliamentary remedy (898). They could advert to the preamble as a key to legislative purposes and also to "the practical exposition of the statute supplied by usage under it" (899). But the most important source of meaning beyond the actual text was judicial precedent—"not the 'private interpretation[ ]' of an individual, but rather the authoritative 'resolution[ ] of judges in Courts of Justice" (899, citing Coke). In a revealing formulation, Powell says that this "followed almost by definition from the basic notion of 'intent' as a product of the interpretive process rather than something locked into the text by its author" (899). Powell concludes this section by noting that "[m]ost of the Americans influential in the framing, ratification, and early interpretation of the federal Constitution were intimately familiar with the common law, and gleaned from it . . . a general approach to constitutional interpretation—one centering on a search for the Constitution's 'intention,'" as that term was understood in common law. (Powell left unresolved, however, other important questions about constitutional interpretation, which are the subject of the next section.)

Berger

Berger begins by citing the sixteenth-century work, *A Discourse Upon Statutes*:

those that were the penners and devisors of statutes [have] bene the grettest lighte for exposicion of statutes. If they have not gyven anie declaracion of theire myndes, then is to be sene howe the statute hathe bene put in use, & theire authoritye muste persuade us that were mooste neerest the statute, and that we do see muche receyved & leaned unto in bookes. (299)

The respect for the judgment of those nearest the statute is maintained under the rubric of "contemporaneous construction," based on the fact that contemporaries of the Constitution "had the best opportunities of informing themselves of the understanding of the framers . . . and of the sense put upon it by the people when it was adopted by them" (299– 300, citing Justice William Johnson). Berger deduces from this (and that it is a "deduction" worthy of notice) that "it is difficult to conclude that judges who deferred to the 'understanding of the framers' when it was received at second hand would have rejected the drafters' own record- ed explanation of their intentions" (300). Much of Berger's discussion of the common law consists of citations of authorities who emphasize intent, with critical evaluation of some of Powell's citations. For ex- ample, Powell cites Coke as saying, in *Edrich's Case*, that there should be no construction against the express letter of the statute, because "nothing can so express the meaning of the makers of the Act, as their own direct words, for *index animi sermo* ['the word is the sign or the indicator of the soul']." But Berger quotes Coke's following sentence as well: "And it would be dangerous to give scope to make a construc- tion in any case against the express words, *when the meaning of the makers doth not appear to the contrary*" (300, Berger's emphasis). For Coke, Berger says, "intent prevails over 'words'" (300). Judicial pre- cedent certainly deserves more weight than interpretation of a private individual, but "that is a far cry from Coke's reservation in *Edrich's Case* for" cases "when the meaning of the makers doth not appear to the contrary" (300, note 31).

One of Berger's many citations is from Plowden's *Commentaries*: "[E]verything which is within the intent of the makers of the Act, al- though it be not within the letter, is as strongly within the Act as that which is within the letter and intent also" (301). Some of Powell's ci- tations, he points out, are rejections of intent on the basis of unsatis- factory evidence: cases ought not to be "controlled by averment of the parties to be *proved by the uncertain testimony of slippery memory*" (301, Berger's emphasis). Obviously, intent must be proved: "whenso- ever there is departure from the words to the *intent*, that *must be well proved* that there is such meaning" (302, quoting Lord Chancellor Hatton, Berger's emphasis). Since resort to intention depends upon adequate proof, "it is difficult to conceive" that unmistakable evidence of the author's intention would be excluded. He adds that "leading legal historian" Samuel Thorne concluded that "[a]ctual intent . . . is controlling from Hengham's day to that of Lord Nottingham (1678)" (302–303).

Berger takes up Powell's argument on the ambiguity of intent. He first contends that, if there is such ambiguity, then the prior judicial statements he has cited to show that the meaning of the makers prevails over the words ought to tip the scales in favor of that approach to intent. More fundamentally, he denies that the common law operated on such a "bifurcated-intention theory," reviewing Powell's citations and revising their import (304). For example, Powell cites Selden to the effect that the court determines the intention of the king solely on the basis of the words of the law. Berger points out that in the context of that statement there is no occasion to examine opposition between word and intent.

Powell misreads Blackstone, Berger argues, citing other passages to show that his emphasis on subjective intentions is not illusory; for example, "where the *intention is clear*, too minute a stress be not laid on the strict and precise signification of *words*" (305, emphasis partly Blackstone's, partly Berger's). Likewise, Coke's reference to the "artificial reason and judgment of law" is said to have been wrenched out of a context that was unrelated to "intent."

Powell contends that the preamble of a law is *the* key to the purposes of its makers, Berger points out, by citing a jurist's statement that it is *a* key. Statutes were to be interpreted, Powell says, to suppress the mischief and advance the remedy. But besides resorting to the preamble, one could know the mischief by learning from the "lyvinge voice" of the Parliament (citing *A Discourse Upon Statutes*) and "following in the footsteps of those who were contemporaries of the statute" (306–307). The overarching principle was that "where the intent is evident it must prevail" (307). Again, Berger reasons that

> It offends common sense to conclude that, if other unmistakable evidence of the "makers'" intention to cure a certain mischief was available, it would be rejected because, for example, it was not a "contemporaneous construction" that itself carried weight only because it was deemed a reflection of that intention. (307)

To Powell's "triumphantly" asserting that "the modern practice of interpreting a law by reference to its legislative history was almost wholly nonexistent," Berger makes the simple response that "there was no legislative history" to cite (307). (Parliamentary debates, the Journal and Madison's notes of the Convention of 1787, and the state ratifying convention debates all appeared only in the nineteenth century.) Resort to legislative history is simply an instance of permitting an old concept to embrace new applications: as "commerce" includes "planes" no less than ox carts, so does "intent" include "recorded intent," that is, legislative history.

Berger concludes:

> Manifestly, Powell has failed to demonstrate that "[a]t common law . . . 'intent' did not depend upon the subjective purpose of the author." In truth, the common law looked to the intention of the draftsmen.

Analysis

There are key problems with the way both Powell and Berger employ the evidence regarding the common law.

Powell is correct in making his crucial distinction between "the meaning that the drafters wished to communicate" and "the meaning the reader was warranted in deriving from the text," though one would have to be careful with the word "warranted"—it means not that the reader is authorized to draw any meaning from the text but that he must submit himself to the text. The meaning or "intention" of the law is the intention expressed in the text of the law itself rather than the unstated, subjective purposes of the lawmakers.

But if Powell is correct in this, it is disturbing and revealing that he never seems to ask where the "meaning of the text" came from. *Why* is it that the meaning of the text is the meaning of the law? It makes no sense to take one's orientation from the "extreme" case (the "failure") in which there is a disjunction between the meaning of the law and the intentions of its makers. The "normal" case is that the meaning of the text *is* the meaning the drafters wished to communicate. The words of the law, Blackstone tells us, are the best "sign" of the intention. Law, in the common-law period and well into the twentieth century, was based on a faith—now under challenge—that language could in fact express human purposes with tolerable accuracy. The law expressed in language could be—and normally was—an accurate reflection of the purposes of the lawgiver. This is only the starting point of the discussion, because one must also consider that language is but an imperfect means of expressing human purposes. Yet that starting point is important, and it emphasizes the tie between the text of the law and the subjective purposes of the lawgivers rather than the potential conflict.

Powell says that "the 'intent' of the maker of a legal document and the 'intent' of the document were one and the same; intent did not depend upon the subjective purposes of the author" (895). In one very important sense that is true. Legal intent is normally found by a fair reading of the text of the law, not by recourse to extratextual sources. The rule of law required that the law be public, known, and fixed. It would not be possible if the "real" law were in the mind[s] of some lawgiver[s] and might be definitively revealed only *after* the performance of actions that could be judged under such a law. It was never open to the lawgiver to say, "That is not the law, because that is not what I meant," for such a power would threaten essential features of good law: intelligibility and impartiality. In another sense, however, it is too extreme to say that legal intent does not "depend" on the subjective purposes of the author. It may not depend on it (retrospectively) in the sense that those subjective purposes are to be investigated to discover the meaning of the law, but it does depend on it in the sense that those subjective purposes are precisely the origin and source of legal intent. If the intent of the law owes its existence to the subjective purposes of its author[s]—if they "put" the meaning there—then one can hardly deny that there is a certain kind of dependence.

Powell does not deny this, but he downplays it to the point of ignoring it in his discussion. This is important for two reasons. First, when the "normal" case of interpretation does not exist—especially where the law is ambiguous after the "usual" means of ascertaining its meaning have been employed—then one must approach these "hard cases" with the overarching character of the law in mind. If the intention of the law has its origin in the intentions of its authors, then even if the normal rule is to employ rules of interpretation that focus exclusively on the text, it might be possible in exceptional cases (those where the normal rules are not adequate) to advert to this origin. As we shall see below, I believe that Powell himself concedes this at certain points, though his general statement of his thesis would seem to deny it.

The second reason why Powell's downplaying of the connection between legal intent and subjective purposes is important is that, taken together with several of Powell's statements, it raises the question of whether Powell's underlying purpose is to prevent the Constitution from being "fixed" or unchanging. For example, Powell says: "This followed almost by definition from the basic notion of 'intent' as a product of the interpretive process rather than something locked into the text by its author" (899). This formulation is, I think, a distinctively modern one that common lawyers would have strongly objected to. The contention that intent is a "product" of the interpretive process suggests that the interpreter produces or *creates* the meaning of the law rather than discovering it in the instrument itself (where it "preexists," in a sense)—a notion that does not appear in the work of leading legal figures before the nineteenth century. There also seems to be an implied criticism of a meaning being "locked into the text by its author." "Locked into" is a pejorative formulation of "fixed." But common-law jurists would not have had the aversion to a "fixed" meaning of written law that is more characteristic of modern, post-Darwinian thinkers. Even if the chief *evidence* to discover intent was the application of rules of interpretation to the text, the overarching purpose of interpretation was to discover and apply the authors' ("fixed") intent.

In his discussion of statutory construction, and especially the harder case where the words are ambiguous, Powell says that the common-law interpreter would look to the common law background of an act, and particularly how it was a remedy for a mischief not provided for in the common law. The preamble is one possible source for this. Another is previous judicial opinions, which, Powell argues, were authoritative, not merely the interpretations of private individuals. But where did previous judicial opinions discover the mischief and the remedy? Reliance on previous judicial opinions is a case of a present interpreter relying on a previous interpreter. But from what source did those previous interpreters—especially the first, often contemporaneous, ones—derive their knowledge of the mischief and remedy? No "official" legislative history was available. But wasn't there a kind of "unwritten" legislative history, according to which "educated public opinion," indeed "everybody," knew (in general) what the law was meant to do and that provided judges with the necessary knowledge of mischief and remedy?[7] Powell's emphasis on the importance of previous judicial opinions is, in fact, a way of smuggling "extratextual sources of intent" into the interpretive process. Much the same thing can be said of relying on "the practical exposition of the statute supplied by usage under it," which Powell also accepts as legitimate evidence of intent.[8]

But if this "unwritten" legislative history was sometimes legitimately employed by the earliest interpreters of a law, why not use written legislative history, once it became available? Berger deduces from the willingness to resort to contemporaneous construction to discover evidence of intention—on the grounds that contemporaneous interpreters were closer to the original understanding—the propriety of accepting more direct evidence (if sufficient) of the lawmakers' intent. That seems a logical deduction.

And yet Berger's critique of Powell is generally problematic as well. The most significant difficulty is that most of Berger's citations proving the importance—indeed, the preeminence—of intent do so in a way that is perfectly compatible with Powell's distinction between legal intent and subjective author's intent. None of Berger's evidence shows that the intent of the lawgiver is to be determined by evidence other than the words of the law. For example, Berger does not give us common-law cases in which a judge has actually gone to extratextual sources for intent. (As I will indicate below, I think that this could probably be done, but that we will find that it was a relatively rare resort, used only in exceptional cases.)

Nor is Berger's argument automatically borne out when a judge makes a distinction between the "intent" and the "letter" of the law. At first glance, this seems to suggest that the judge is moving from the text to some extratextual source of intent. But it is obviously possible to have one interpretation based on the strict letter and another interpretation based on a broader reading of the text that still does not appeal to any extratextual sources.

Blackstone, for example, says that interpretation ought to be done by "signs the most natural and probable" of the intent of the lawgiver at the time the law was made.[9] The first, most obvious sign is the words, but there also are others: context (including the preamble and other laws by the same legislator relating to the same subject), subject matter, effects and consequences (in cases where literal interpretation leads to the words having no meaning or an absurd one), and the reason and spirit of the law. But these other signs—while perhaps leading to an interpretation other than that suggested by the letter of the law—do not necessarily require going beyond the text to some historical evidence of subjective intent. For instance, the example of the "reason and spirit" of the law given by Blackstone is the case of a law relating to property on a ship in a storm: those who deserted the ship forfeited their property on it, and those who stayed took possession of the ship's property. But the reason and spirit of the law led to denial of a claim to a ship's property by a man who was the only one to stay on board in a tempest—but only because he was too sick to be able to leave. Since the law was ("obviously"—we do not need to research legislative debates) made to encourage efforts to save ships, it could not be invoked by someone whose motives and actions had nothing to do with that purpose.

Berger's shaft, then, goes wide of the mark when he tries to refute Powell with Matthew Bacon's statements that, "Every Thing which is within the Intention of the Makers of a Statute is, although it be not within the Letter thereof, as much within the Statute as that which is within the Letter" and "[T]hat which is within the Letter of a Statute is not within such Statute, if it be not within the Intention of the Makers thereof" (305). His argument is simply circular when he employs these quotations, because he is assuming the very meaning of "intention" that is the object of dispute between Powell and himself.

Berger rejects Powell's reading of Blackstone (to the effect that concern regarding the subjective intentions of a testator is "largely illusory"), citing Blackstone's dictum

> That the construction be *favorable*, and as near the minds and apparent intents of the parties, as the rules of law will admit. For the maxims of the law are, that *"verba intentioni [et non contra] debent inservire"* [words ought to wait upon the intention, not the reverse]. (305, Blackstone's emphasis)

He also cites Blackstone's observation that "where the *intention is clear*, too minute a stress be not laid on the strict and precise signification of *words*" (305, emphasis partly Blackstone's, partly Berger's).

At this point, one might reasonably ask, with Berger: If there are two interpretations of a will, both of which are "reasonable and agreeable to common understanding," and one of them is supported by clear extratextual evidence of the testator's mind and intent, should not such evidence be considered? (The immediate question, remember, is not whether this is abstractly reasonable, but whether Blackstone and other common lawyers provided for it.)

The first argument against this line of reasoning is an argument from silence, which does carry significant weight. If Blackstone would employ extratextual evidence of a testator's intent, why does he not say so? In a three-page discussion of "general rules and maxims . . . for construction and exposition," there is no clear reference to extratextual sources of intent. The references to intent consist of the two Berger citations just quoted and another maxim (the seventh) that says to pursue the will of the devisor even if for want of advice or learning he may have omitted the legal or proper phrases. The question is, then, how is one to know "the minds and apparent intents of the parties," "the intention," "the will of the devisor?" All of these can be interpreted, as Powell does, as being the intention *as expressed in the whole instrument*.

An early commentator on Blackstone, Christian, discussing a case in connection with this section, says that he

entirely concurs with that learned judge that it is the first and great
rule in the exposition of wills, and to which all other rules must bend,
that the intention of the testator, expressed in his will, shall prevail,
provided it be *consistent with the rules of law*—that is, provided it can
be effectuated consistently with the limits and bounds which the law
prescribes.[10]

In this statement, Christian appears to *assume as a matter of course*
that the will of the devisor to which Blackstone refers is "expressed in
his will," not derived from some other source.

Again, the argument from silence is quite strong. One of Blackstone's other rules of construction is that, if there are two clauses in
an instrument that are totally repugnant to each other and cannot stand
together, then in a deed the first (i.e., earlier) shall be received and in
a will the latter (i.e., most recent) shall stand. But in extreme cases like
this, would it not be especially useful to recur to extratextual sources
of intent? Yet Blackstone makes no mention of them.

If there is a problem with citing extratextual sources, the chief one
seems to be the high degree of variability in the trustworthiness of such
sources. Berger's logical response is simply that extratextual sources
ought to receive the credence they deserve: if they show evidence of high
reliability, employ them, and if they don't, don't. But would not a commentator such as Blackstone, *if* he really did accept the propriety of
employing extratextual sources of intent, devote part of a section that
sums up maxims of construction to the task of indicating which extratextual sources were more or less reliable, or at least providing some
general criteria of reliability? The silence *is* deafening.

Virtually all of Berger's citations to the effect that "intent prevails
over words" are subject to this objection of circularity. What is needed
to make his case is a) citations that unambiguously refer to extratextual sources of intent and b) examples of cases in which extratextual
sources of intent are actually used. My suspicion is that such evidence
will be obtainable but so exceptional as to prove Powell's rule.

One of Berger's most important observations is that one cannot find
examples of appeal to *legislative history* because it did not exist before the nineteenth century. But that argument cuts both ways. It does
enable Berger to explain the absence of such appeals, but it also damages Berger's case substantially by raising the further question: *Why*
was there no legislative history? If Berger is right that intent in his
sense was the key norm of interpretation back into the fifteenth or six-
teenth century, then why was legislative history not recorded until the
nineteenth century? Its absence for so long a period suggests strongly

that earlier common lawyers did not consider that kind of evidence of intent necessary or appropriate.

Berger's case is really more a deduction from or extension of common law principles: Why not, he asks, use satisfactory evidence of intent (outside of the law itself), if discovering the intention of the lawmaker is the aim (as all must agree that it was)? But putting aside for the moment the abstract propriety of that deduction or extension, the question remains: Did practitioners during the pre-Constitution common-law period make that deduction or extension? The answer appears to be no, at least as a very general rule. Why not? Perhaps they generalized (or, Berger might argue, overgeneralized) from the evidentiary difficulties that often beset extratextual sources of intent and concluded that the utility of such sources was offset by the difficulties or potential distortions of trying to use them. Perhaps the reason may be found in their having a different conception of law (especially a more positive attitude toward unwritten customary law, and a correspondingly lesser emphasis on formal written law). But whatever the reason, the fact that legislative history did not exist before the nineteenth century obviously indicates that it was not considered important.

In regard to the common law, then, we find that Berger has not succeeded in refuting Powell's case, but we also find that Powell's (and the common law's) reliance on previous judicial opinions and upon practice under a law, in difficult cases, may be a way of smuggling at least some extratextual sources of intent into the interpretive process. As we turn to early American history, we may find that the extent of that smuggling increases.

Early American Views on Interpreting the Constitution

The Framers and the Battle for Ratification

Powell

Powell maintains that the "framers' primary expectation regarding constitutional interpretation was that the Constitution, like any other legal document, would be interpreted in accord with its express language" (903). This was indicated especially by their efforts to refine the document's wording in order to eliminate vagueness and to allay fears that overprecise language would be taken literally, thereby defeating the aim of a provision. "There is no indication that they expected or intended future interpreters to refer to any extratextual intentions revealed in the convention's secretly conducted debates" (903). They "shared the traditional common law view . . . that the import of the document they were framing would be determined by reference to the intrinsic meaning of the words or through the usual judicial process of case-by-case interpretation" (903–904). When there was doubt about the meaning of "*ex post facto* laws," for example, they looked not to "their own intention" but to other sources, such as Blackstone, to discover its meaning.

The framers were not strict literalists—"they accepted the inevitability and propriety of construction" (904). For example, James Wilson recognized that a power to create monopolies was implicit in the commerce clause. Madison was concerned about the judicial power to decide cases arising under the Constitution, worrying that this might be interpreted as a right to expound the Constitution even in cases that were not "of a judiciary nature." He was reassured, however, when it was agreed without dissent that "the jurisdiction given was constructively limited to cases of a judiciary nature" (904). So the framers accepted construction, according to the then-prevalent rules of statutory construction.

Powell argues that in the struggle over ratification both Federalists and Anti-Federalists agreed that the Constitution ought to be interpreted according to the common rules of statutory interpretation. Anti-Federalists used this to argue that judges and legislators would read into the Constitution doctrines present only constructively, not textually— an open invitation to corruption and usurpation. Federalists responded that the people's unquestionably republican intent, evinced in the plain, obvious meaning of the text, would control future interpretation.

Powell describes the attack on the Constitution by "Brutus" and the response to that attack by Hamilton in the last part of the *Federalist*. Brutus argued that federal courts could interpret the Constitution according its reasoning spirit without being confined by its words or letter, thus enabling them to mold the government into the shape they pleased. The ordinary rules of construction, with their emphasis on the purposes of the law, as described in the Preamble, would easily justify consolidation of the states into one government. The framers had erred in writing a document requiring interpretation, rather than a plain compact between a people and their rulers that would not require artificial techniques of interpretation.

Madison had argued in *Federalist* No. 37 that all human writing and laws were subject to some ambiguity:

laws, though penned with the greatest technical skill, and passed on the fullest and most mature deliberation, are considered as more or less obscure and equivocal, until their meaning be liquidated and ascertained by a series of particular discussions and adjudications.[11]

Powell characterizes this (revealingly) as a

> restatement in somewhat abstract terms of the old common law assumption, shared by the Philadelphia framers, that the "intent" of any legal document is the product of the interpretive process and not some fixed meaning that the author locks into the document's text at the outset. (910)

Hamilton, says Powell, responds to the Anti-Federalist attack based on the Constitution's ambiguity by arguing that rules of legal interpretation are rules of common sense, which do not make judges superior to the will of the people, but enable them to enforce it. The Federalists rejected the Anti-Federalist reliance on the anti-interpretive tradition of Protestant and Enlightenment thought, embracing common-law hermeneutics as a developed tradition that enabled the people to predict with confidence the results of future constitutional construction.

Berger

Berger argues that Americans were raised on the single common-law tradition of Coke (according to which express words govern "when the meaning of the makers doth not appear to the contrary"), not "Powell's bifurcated view." As evidence he cites Marshall's view in *U.S. v. Fisher* that "where the mind labors to discover the design of the legislature, *it seizes every thing* from which aid can be derived" (309, emphasis added). Powell mentions these remarks of Marshall, but dismisses them because neither the lawyers nor Marshall suggests an investigation of congressional debates. How could they, asks Berger, since the Annals of Congress had not yet been published?

Berger notes that George Washington took steps in his final will to make sure that his own subjective intentions controlled, unfettered by law or legal determination. But if Washington was so concerned about the wiles of judicial construction in his own will, why would he give them a freer hand with respect to the founders' intentions? In this, Washington represented Americans' profound fear of judicial independence and discretion. Thus, equivocal statements should not be read as a bar to resort to "original intention," since that intention serves as a restraint on judicial free-wheeling.

The founders never contemplated that judges would take over poli-cy-making. Judges were not to be legislators, they agreed. And the founders were also attached to a fixed constitution, not to be altered by the wiles of judicial construction. That is why Hamilton could say that the judiciary was beyond comparison the weakest of the three branches. Fear of the Supreme Court, Berger says, has turned out to be only too well founded.

With this as background, Berger turns to Powell's discussion of the founders. Berger agrees that the founders thought that future interpret-ers would adhere to then-prevalent methods of statutory construction, but argues that Powell tries to burden the founders with his own view of the common law, that is, that the import of the document would be determined by the intrinsic meaning of its words. For example, Powell argues in a footnote that convention debates show that the meaning of "ex post facto law" was not controlled by the intentions of the dele-gates to the convention. But his citations refer only to Dickinson's de-scription of Blackstone's definition of the term and Mason's concern that the meaning of the provision (in particular, its limitation to crimi-nal cases) is not clear enough. At most, Berger points out, these cita-tions reveal differences over the meaning of a common-law term. If anything, they suggest that later interpreters did not rely on the bare words.

Powell also cites the framers' attempts to eliminate vagueness as an indication that they expected the Constitution to be interpreted in ac-cord with its express language. But Berger argues that the search for precision demonstrates a fear of judicial discretion in the construction of vague terms, not an intention to facilitate wide-roving construction.

Powell argues that there is no indication that the framers expected or intended future interpreters to refer to any extratextual intentions re-vealed in the convention's secretly conducted debates. Berger says that this is simply not so. For example, secrecy was intended to make it easier to voice and change opinions as the draft was hammered out and to avoid enkindling partisan debate that might hinder compromise. Lat-er, after discussion, the framers decided not to destroy the journal and records of the convention. James Wilson argued for preserving them so that it would be possible to contradict false suggestions about the con-vention, thus implying that it mattered that the framers' intentions be known. Prominent framers did in fact resort to original intention: Wash-ington (in the Jay Treaty debate), Rufus King (in the Massachusetts ratifying convention), and Roger Sherman and Abraham Baldwin (in the First Congress). Moreover, silence on the point would have meant con-tinuation of the common-law emphasis on intent.

Berger and Powell agree that Madison's proposal to limit federal court jurisdiction to "cases of a judiciary nature" demonstrates an acceptance of then-prevalent methods of statutory construction. The question is whether those methods included resort to original intention. But Berger asserts that, if the Court had later claimed jurisdiction of a case not of a "judiciary nature," Madison could hardly have felt foreclosed from complaining of a breach of the reassurance given him on this point in the debates.

One North Carolina ratifying convention delegate stated that the "constitution is only a mere proposal . . . If the people approve of it, it becomes their act." Powell wrongly tries to draw from this the inference that the plain, obvious meaning of the text would control future interpretations. But, says Berger, advocates of the Constitution were repeatedly constrained to explain that the words of the Constitution did not contain the sweeping meanings they were alleged to have. The Constitution was defeated in the first North Carolina convention, but if it had not been, it would be absurd to bar resort to the reassuring explanations on the basis of which the delegates voted.

Analysis

Powell and Berger generally agree that the Constitution was to be interpreted on the basis of common-law rules of statutory construction, but they differ on what these were. Were interpreters to rely only on the express language or could they legitimately resort to extratextual sources of intent as well?

Powell's argument that the framers were careful about the language they chose proves nothing. Even someone willing to accept resort to extratextual sources of intention would not thereby cease to care about precision in the drafting of the Constitution. Similarly, the debate about the meaning of "ex post facto laws" does show that the framers were trying to be careful in their choice of language so as not to be misunderstood, but that is not necessarily evidence against later reliance on extratextual sources.

On the other hand, Wilson's argument for preservation of the convention records and journal does not prove what Berger claims it does. When Wilson says that they should be preserved in order to contradict false suggestions about the convention, he might be referring to broadly political arguments rather than more narrowly legal or interpretive ones. For example, if an opponent in the ratifying debates argued that the convention was a deliberate attempt to abolish the states and establish a monarchy, the convention records would be useful evidence to the contrary. But the utility of records in that regard does not mean that

Wilson would necessarily have considered them admissible evidence for judicial construction of a constitutional provision. That is probably why, in the same debate about preserving the records, Wilson could say that "he had at one time liked the first [proposal—the expedient of destroying the journals] best . . ."[12] If Wilson regarded the journals as useful evidence of intent—and if the then-prevalent methods of statutory construction included extratextual sources—then why did Wilson have to change his mind on the subject? We are back at this point to the most significant weakness in Berger's case: the implications of the widespread *nonpractice* of maintaining and using accurate reports of legislative debates.[13]

Washington's will cuts both ways, since it suggests a fear of construction (evidence for a narrow view of judicial interpretation) that is, from another perspective, an expectation of it (evidence for a broader view). Berger asks whether Washington, who was so careful to prevent departure from his actual intention in the case of his will, would be likely to grant judges a freer hand in regard to the Constitution. The least one can say is that the answer to that question is unclear, since there are obvious differences between a will and a constitution. For example, a will has one single author and is therefore less likely to have the ambiguities that can arise from multiple authorship, ambiguities that could arguably call for a freer judicial hand. Moreover, a will does not require the long-term application to many varied circumstances that a constitution would.[14]

Some of Berger's arguments are assertion without much to support them, for example, that it is "hardly conceivable" that Madison would have felt foreclosed to complain of a breach of the assurance that judges were limited to cases of a judiciary nature. It is simply not clear that Madison would have felt able to say, in a public debate in Congress, for example, "but they told me it did not mean that." (More about Madison below.)

In discussing a statement made in the first North Carolina ratifying convention (which rejected the Constitution), Berger argues against relying simply on the plain, obvious meaning of the text. If ratifying conventions voted for the document on the basis of reassuring explanations by its framers, it would be absurd to bar resort to those explanations, he says. That may be plausible reasoning, but he fails to note one interpretation of that whole event, which cuts the other way: perhaps the North Carolina convention rejected the Constitution because it did not believe that those reassuring explanations carried sufficient weight in the ordinary process of legal interpretation to be credible.

Berger emphasizes that the framers were opposed to judicial

policy-making, which would undermine the notion of a fixed Constitution. That is true, of course, but it does not prove the need for resort to extratextual sources of intention. For example, if a judge adopted Powell's reliance on the express language, interpreted according to ordinary rules of statutory construction (assuming, *arguendo*, that these do not include reliance on extratextual sources), there is no necessary reason why such a judge would have to be a policymaker acting contrary to a fixed constitution. That *might* happen, but it would depend completely on the way in which the power of interpretation (and especially judicial review) was exercised. If the judge adhered to the principle of legislative deference—that is, if he did not exercise the power of judicial review unless the language of the document, fairly interpreted, was clearly incompatible with a challenged law—then he would not be a policymaker.

Powell is not clear about how judicial power should be used, but there is at least some reason to be concerned about his commitment to a fixed constitution. For example, he refers at one point to "the old common-law assumption, shared by the Philadelphia framers, that the 'intent' of any legal document is the product of the interpretive process and not some fixed meaning that the author locks into the document's text at the outset" (910). I think that the intent of a legal document is precisely the fixed meaning—the principle—the author locks into the document's text at the outset. That meaning is not the *product* of the interpretive process: it is discovered, not made, in the process of interpretation, properly understood. Powell may, however, only be making the unobjectionable observation that a provision with a fixed meaning or principle may have different *applications* in different situations. If so, though, his language here is imprecise and subject to easy misinterpretation.

Berger is able to point to some framers who resorted to extratextual intentions in later political debates (e.g., Washington, King, Sherman, and Baldwin), and this constitutes an important argument against Powell's seemingly absolute statements excluding extratextual sources.

On the other hand, it is difficult to find in Berger's own description of statutory construction the reasons why resort to extratextual sources is rather rare. As one reads early constitutional debates, one *is* struck by the infrequency of resort to the framers' intentions.[15] From this perspective, Powell gives a more accurate sense of the "normal" method of constitutional interpretation in early American history. It is fair to say that resort to extratextual sources is very much the exception rather than the rule. Unfortunately, that is not what Powell says. But then, it is not what Berger says either.[16]

The Beginnings of Constitutional Interpretation

Powell

Most of Powell's examination of early constitutional interpretation focuses on two major disputes. In particular, Powell describes Hamilton's and Jefferson's views on the constitutionality of the national bank and then examines the Congressional debate over the Jay Treaty.

Hamilton explicitly argued in the bank debate that the intention of the Constitution is to be sought for in the document itself, according to the usual and established rules of construction. He said that "[n]othing is more common than for laws to express and effect, more or less than was intended," rejecting the idea that arguments "drawn from extrinsic sources, regarding the intention of the convention" could overcome a fair textual implication. This was not to reject the intention of the convention, which Hamilton had cited in the same document, but simply to make the text the authoritative source of knowledge about that intention. Jefferson's argument also started from traditional common-law statutory interpretation, but in Powell's view Jefferson ultimately smuggles in presumptions against change of common-law rules that are not justified.

In the Jay Treaty debate, several Congressmen cited discussions of the Constitution's meaning from the framing and ratification period. Powell says that "[t]his use of history was related but not identical to that of modern intentionalism." These "contemporaneous expositions" included not only the Philadelphia convention and state ratifying conventions, but also defenses of the Constitution published by its proponents and even some critical interpretations of its opponents. Powell notes that "those who cited evidence from the ratification period invariably linked it with other expressions of constitutional opinion" (e.g., the practice of Congress, a "well-understood" Supreme Court opinion, state legislative resolutions on earlier treaties, and views on federal powers under the Articles of Confederation) (918).

Powell argues that those who advanced historical materials did so with caution, giving them only modest weight. Even this cautious use of history was vigorously attacked. Powell says that "[r]esort to materials from the ratification era as one species of evidence as to the Constitution's context was in fact only mildly innovative" (919). But this falls short of modern intentionalism, which is, however, represented by one Congressman's direct appeal to those who had been at the convention to clear up doubts about some difficulties.

This suggestion drew a sharp response from Albert Gallatin, and only one voice was raised in (at least partial) support of it: George Washington, in his message rejecting the House's call for papers related to the treaty. Washington's citation of the convention journal, in regard to a specific motion rejected in the Convention, again brought an explicit protest, this time from James Madison: he "did not believe a single instance could be cited in which the sense of the Convention had been required or admitted as material [to] any Constitutional question" (921).

Berger

Berger takes up Hamilton's argument in favor of Congressional power to establish a national bank in some detail. He argues that the "Convention records plainly show that the framers rejected a proposal empowering Congress to grant charters of incorporation" (315), even a proposal as limited as one to establish corporations for canals. Hamilton "pretended" to find the facts confused and locked out "*unimpeachable* evidence" by restricting the search for the intention to the document itself (316), attempting finally to "secure by 'interpretation' of the Necessary and Proper Clause what the Convention unmistakably had rejected" (316). With regard to the Jay Treaty, Berger interprets attacks on resort to historical materials as reflections of "the bias of heated factionalism" (318). Perhaps only one voice was raised on behalf of modern intentionalism, but it was the voice of George Washington! If Madison criticized Washington now, we will see soon that, by Powell's own admission, he came to embrace intentionalism in the Virginia Resolutions.

Analysis

Berger's observation about heated factionalism in the Jay Treaty debate is worth keeping in mind. It may be that in given instances early debaters were affected by whose ox was being gored. Moreover, some of the objections to the use of history may have related more to the adequacy of the particular historical analysis being put forward and less to the principle of using history itself.

What I find very striking in this section, however, is that Berger does not pounce more vigorously on Powell's concessions. Historical materials were put forward with "caution," given only "modest weight," and overall this was only a "mild innovation." But they were used, Powell concedes! This seems a far cry from his seemingly blanket rejection of "historical inquiry into the expectations of individuals involved in framing and ratifying the Constitution" earlier (888).

Powell seems to minimize this concession by distinguishing this use of historical materials from modern intentionalism. What he is describing here is the use of historical materials "as one species of evidence as to the Constitution's context" (919). Modern intentionalism is different, apparently because it appeals directly to the subjective intentions of those who wrote and framed the Constitution, as the authoritative determinant of the meaning of the document.

But doesn't the line between these two notions get pretty fuzzy? Doesn't the "context" of the Constitution include the purposes, specifically the public purposes, of those individuals and groups involved in its writing and ratification? Those purposes, after all—what the founding generation often referred to as the reason and spirit of the law—"in-form" the meaning of the document, the whole and its parts. It is difficult to see any sharp distinction between what Powell regards as only a mild innovation and what he rejects completely.

Powell is absolutely right that the founders were extremely cautious with historical materials, that these were typically used to confirm other arguments (primarily textual ones), and only resorted to when there was doubt about the text. But having laid down those conditions, one can go on to say that they accepted the careful and limited use of historical materials to help establish the intention or meaning of constitutional provisions.[17]

But if Powell almost concedes the case here, Berger pushes well beyond the founders' own understanding of what was acceptable in constitutional interpretation, in his discussion of the national bank debate. He does so by giving a primacy to historical materials that is unwarranted and by seeing in them a clarity that is not there. Berger rejects Hamilton's argument in defense of the power to establish a national bank, an argument that Powell rightly sees as "a clear picture of what the Constitution was and how it should be construed" (917).

Berger points out that the framers rejected a proposal empowering Congress to grant charters of incorporation, which he regards as "unimpeachable evidence of a preclusive intent" (316). In fact, the rejection of that proposal is not a clear statement about anything. The discussion came at the very end of the Convention, when many delegates were no longer in a mood to sit around arguing details. Berger ignores the important fact that those who voted against the proposal could have done so equally well on either of two diametrically opposed grounds: first, because they did not want Congress to have a general power to incorporate or, second, because they thought that Congress already had the power to incorporate insofar as it was necessary to have it (especially through the necessary and proper clause), but did not want to wave it like a red flag in the faces of those opposed to the Constitution. (And not spelling out every implication is not the same as a deliberate intent to deceive, either.)

Berger's error lies in seeming to imagine that there was some kind of obligation recognized by all the delegates to give their reasons for voting one way, if they disagreed with the reasons for voting that way proposed by someone else. Thus, if some opposed the bank because they wished Congress not to have the power, those who opposed the motion for opposite reasons had to speak up or be discounted later. There was no such obligation. (Nor was there any indication that the debates would have any authority later, as I explained earlier in regard to Wilson's preference for preserving the records.)

I agree with Berger in rejecting the arguments of modern opponents of original intention, who often seem to suggest that there is hardly ever clarity about original intention. But Berger weakens the case for original intention jurisprudence when he claims a spurious clarity from historical materials, especially on issues such as the bank, where his clear answer is not only not clear, but wrong. In fact, I believe that the Constitution is fairly clear on the power of Congress to establish a national bank—not explicitly, but by the implications of text and context that Hamilton so powerfully demonstrates. (Part of the strength of that case is the severe difficulties of maintaining Jefferson's and Madison's case, without inventing a distinction between "merely technical means" and "broad independent powers as means" that has no constitutional grounding).

The Constitution and the New Supreme Court

Powell

Powell rightly sees in *Chisholm v. Georgia* a case study of interpretation based on rules of construction even in the face of very strong historical evidence for a different construction. During the ratification debates, Federalists had frequently denied that the Constitution would work any change in the sovereign immunity of the states from suits by their own citizens. Yet in *Chisholm* the Court upheld the right of a Georgia citizen to sue his own state.

Berger

Berger emphasizes the response to *Chisholm*: it was quickly overruled by the Eleventh Amendment. This quick response does not support Powell, but signifies the people's determination to have their intention obeyed even in the face of a Court determined to thwart that intention.

At this point, Berger engages in something of a discursus on Justice Joseph Story, whom Powell mentions in passing. It seems to make sense for Berger to do so, since Story gives a telling critique of excessive reliance on historical evidence of intention in his *Commentaries on the Constitution of the United States.* While Berger does not say so, his attack on Story is also implicitly an attack on Chief Justice John Marshall, who may be regarded as indistinguishable from Story on rules of constitutional interpretation.

Berger is critical of Story for regarding Blackstone's listing of factors in interpretation (words, context, subject matter, effects and consequences, and spirit and reason of the law) as preclusive rather than illustrative, since Blackstone respects the expression of a clear intention. What, Berger (not Blackstone) adds, could be clearer than the draftsman's contemporary explanation? Blackstone's omission of legislative intention is understandable in the absence of published parliamentary debates.

Berger is almost puzzled by Story's criticism of reliance on historical evidence of intention, given his emphasis on "the intention of the parties" and "the objects for which [power] was given" and his acceptance of secondary evidence (e.g., contemporaneous construction and the mischief to be cured) (321).

Story's objections to use of historical materials go, in fact, to the weight of the evidence, not its admissibility. For example, we have records from five state ratifying conventions and cannot just assume that they represent the views of the others. Berger responds in two ways: first, *ad hominem*, that "[u]nderstandably, a judge who would enjoy the freedom the 'text' permits may prefer *no* evidence to some evidence of intention that confutes his personal views" (321), and second, it is not unreasonable to assume that the general agreement of five states on major issues reflects the sentiments in six adjoining states.

Story also objects that there may be a disparity of views in any one convention. But Berger argues that at least on some issues (including two he had studied) there was "remarkable unanimity" in the five conventions, and so this evidence should be accepted when it is available.

Story asks whether the *Federalist* or other authors are to be followed. Berger replies by pointing out Story's own continuous citation of the *Federalist*, the esteem for it of both Marshall and Jefferson, and the fact that (according to Jefferson and Corwin) it tried to set forth the views of the Convention.

Story stresses that "[n]othing but the text itself was adopted by the people." But, says Berger, it was the text as explained by the advocates of adoption (explanations that Story sometimes relies on himself). Moreover, the text makes no mention of judicial review, so on Story's reasoning it has no footing in the Constitution (particularly since he rejects evidence that the founders meant to and had provided for it).

Berger then relies on Powell to discover that Story was writing his *Commentaries* as an opponent of democracy bent on frustrating the results of the political process by a body of antimajoritarian constitutional law. Thus, the *Commentaries*, according to Powell (and Berger, following Powell), were a massive self-vindication as well as a bitter indictment of Story's personal enemy, Jefferson. Story wrote to thwart Jefferson's revolution of 1800, carried forward by Andrew Jackson. Berger's conclusion is that "Story's thin, make-weight arguments" result from the fact that his scholarship is "animated by personal bias" (324).

Analysis

Chisholm is a difficult question for me because it is one of the relatively few cases in which a strong argument can be made for history over plain text. The text is not absolutely decisive, but if we had no other source, then the Court's decision would certainly have been a plausible one. But the historical materials are very clear, and so they might reasonably have been called on in this case, where the text was not dispositive.

But note that Berger's case is not unproblematic. The person who would seem to have had the greatest incentive to make the same argument that Berger does—Justice Iredell, who dissented in the case—does not. (And a footnote by Powell suggests that he would not as a matter of principle [922n.202].) Moreover, the historical case against *Chisholm* is not iron-clad for several reasons. First, some remarks in ratifying conventions presaged the decision in *Chisholm* (notably by Randolph and Nicholas in Virginia and by Wilson in Pennsylvania), though they were a minority.[18] Second, some conventions passed resolutions suggesting an amendment to protect states from suit—what is unclear is whether these were intended to modify the Constitution or explain it. (At the very least they suggest a fearful expectation of something like *Chisholm*, in the absence of an amendment.) Third, the violence of the reaction against *Chisholm* came, in great measure, from Anti-Federalists who had used as an argument against ratification of the Constitution the argument that under it states would be amenable to suits! Nonetheless, this instance is one of Berger's stronger cases for

heavy consideration of historical materials, especially since the text is
not dispositive.

Berger's discursus on Story is strange and frustrating. I believe that
Story is not nearly as far from Berger as Berger thinks, and Berger's
occasionally harsh critique of someone who in general should be one
of his foremost allies seems woefully misplaced. Berger, for example,
points out that Story's arguments go to the weight, not the admissibility of historical evidence. That is true—so why does Berger attack him
so strongly? Story is criticizing the *abuse* of historical materials by Jef-
fersonians (a legitimate concern), not denying that they can ever be resorted to. At the end of his critique of Jefferson's excessive reliance
on extrinsic sources of intent—that is, Jefferson's own sense of public
opinion at the time of the framing—Story says: "The people adopted
the Constitution according to the words of the text in their reasonable
interpretation, and not according to the private interpretation of any
particular men. *The opinions of the latter may sometimes aid us in arriving at just results*; but they can never be conclusive."[19] Story is not
less concerned than Berger about attaining interpretation in accord with
original intent—he is (ironically, I think) just much more confident than
Berger that a fair reading of the text will attain original intention and
more sensitive to the limitations of extrinsic sources of intent.

Berger attacks Story's assumption that Blackstone's list of aids in
construction is complete or preclusive rather than illustrative, but there
is absolutely nothing in Blackstone's argument that suggests these aids
are only *some* of the factors in interpretation. Berger argues that, after
all, Blackstone respects the intention of the lawgiver, but that is a return to Berger's circular argument about the common-law meaning of
intention. "What could be clearer than the draftsman's intention?" Berger asks. But then we can ask: "Why does Blackstone omit from his list
what Berger regards as the *clearest* indication of intention?" It is understandable that Blackstone does not include legislative intention, since
records of these debates were not yet published. But, as usual, Berger
does not stop to ask why there were no published debates, if legislative intention (as he understands it) was so dispositive.

Berger takes an unjustifiable shot at Story with the remark that
"[u]nderstandably, a judge who would enjoy the freedom the 'text' permits may prefer *no* evidence to some evidence of intention that confutes his personal views" (321). Nothing in Story supports this implicit
attribution to him of the view that the text gives the judge the freedom
to pursue his personal views. Everything Story says about rules of interpretation indicates that the text is the vehicle for recognizing the in-

tention of the lawgiver. Again, Berger reveals a lack of faith in textual interpretation, perhaps because he has seen so much manipulation of it. Story would undoubtedly counsel Berger not to give up on textual interpretation per se but to emphasize sharply the distinction between good and bad textual interpretation.

As to the problems with the weight of the evidence, Berger tries to refute Story with simple assertions. Story points out that we have debates from only five of the state ratifying conventions. Berger retorts that "it is not unreasonable to assume that the general agreement of the five states on major issues reflects the sentiments of the six adjoining states" (321). That is true as a generalization, but it is also "not unreasonable" to believe that *sometimes* it would not do so. This does not mean that such evidence is without weight, but only that, as Story says, it "can never be conclusive."

Berger places great weight on the *Federalist*, as he should and (as he points out) as Story does. But again, what the *Federalist* says is not "conclusive." For example, *Federalist* No. 77 argues that officials appointed by the president with the advice and consent of the Senate can only be removed with the advice and consent of the Senate—a proposition thoroughly rejected by the First Congress and almost everybody else since.

When Story says that "[n]othing but the text itself was adopted by the people," Berger responds that on this reasoning judicial review "has no footing in the Constitution," since the text makes no mention of it, especially since Story "rejects the evidence that the founders contemplated and thought that they had provided for judicial review" (322). But Story, first, does not completely reject that evidence (contemporaneous construction, he says, "may sometimes aid us in arriving at just results") and, second, would never limit the text to what is explicit in it, since implications fairly derived from the text are a part of the "text" too.

Finally—the strangest thing of all—upon whom does Berger rely to establish that Story's *Commentaries* were "a massive self-vindication . . . animated by personal bias" (324) and should therefore be discounted? Powell! There is certainly no question that Story had no love lost for Jefferson (or Andrew Jackson), but that does not lead necessarily—as Berger seems to contend—to the conclusion that Story's scholarship can be reduced to bias. An alternative view is that the *Commentaries* are a *successful* vindication of the principles of the Constitution, as they were (correctly) understood by Story. And in general, I believe that those principles are not far from Berger's own understanding.[20]

Sovereign States and Later
Theories of Constitutional Intent

The Doctrines of '98

I will not spend much time on Powell's discussion of the Virginia and
Kentucky Resolutions, since he and Berger basically agree that these
are "intentionalist." But I will note briefly why I believe that these
Resolutions do not represent the birth of intentionalism in American
political history.

Powell argues that the Resolutions proposed "an interpretive strategy centered on a search for the Constitution's underlying and original
'intent'" (927). Their view represented a coherent reading of the Constitution based on contractual imagery and eighteenth-century notions
of sovereignty, not an appeal to the subjective purposes of the framers.
"The intentionalism of the Resolutions was therefore a form of structural interpretation carried out largely by inference from the nature both
of compacts and of sovereignty" (931). This reliance on "state" intentions was for the most part traditional, but it broke new ground in
suggesting "the possibility that some extratextual historical evidence
might be relevant to constitutional interpretation," especially "the proposed amendments and declarations of reserved rights that accompanied
several of the states' ratification resolutions" (932).

As Powell notes, insofar as this form of interpretation was *structural* interpretation, it was traditional. What is new, he says, was acceptance of some extratextual historical evidence. But earlier, in his
discussion of the Jay Treaty congressional debate (a debate that pre-
dated the Resolutions), Powell told us that "[r]esort to materials from
the ratification era as one species of evidence as to the Constitution's
context was in fact only mildly innovative" (919).

The fact is that it was not new in 1798, nor was it "innovative" at
all, even mildly, in 1796. One can go back to Madison's Congressional speech against the constitutionality of a national bank in February
of 1791 and find him appealing to the "expositions of friends of the
Constitution whilst depending before the public; . . . the apparent intention of the parties which ratified the Constitution [especially "the
explanatory declarations and amendments accompanying the ratifications
of the several States"]; . . . the explanatory amendments proposed by
Congress themselves to the Constitution."[21] Of course, for Madison, as
for Story, those forms of evidence were combined with—and primarily
confirmative of—a more authoritative source of intent: an analysis of

the text itself. Extrinsic sources of intent were *subordinate* to textual interpretation, but they *were* legitimate "aids."

James Madison's Theory of Constitutional Interpretation

Powell

According to Powell, Madison's interpretive theory rests primarily on the distinction between the public meaning of a constitution and the personal opinions of the individuals who had written or adopted it. Using this as a criterion, he assigned different relative values to "the various sources of information to which constitutional interpreters might turn for evidence on 'the intention of the States'" (937). The text is the primary source from which intention is to be gathered, but it might be unclear. It was then proper to engage in structural inference and to consult the direct expressions of state intention in the resolutions of their ratifying conventions. The state debates, given evidentiary problems and the distinction between binding public intention and private individual opinions, could only be an "indirect and corroborative witness to the meaning of the Constitution" (938). Contemporaneous expositions of the document by its supporters were of some value, but these were useful "chiefly in shedding light upon the meaning of words and phrases that the fluidity of language might gradually change over time" (938). Last and least were the records of the Philadelphia convention.

Madison also assigned significant weight to "*usus*," the "exposition of the Constitution provided by actual governmental practice and judicial precedents" (939). This practice was strong enough to outweigh his own abstract opinion of the meaning of the text, as when he signed into law the second national bank. "For Madison," says Powell, "there could be no return to the unadorned text from interpretations that had received the approbation of the people. The Constitution is a public document, and its interpretation, for Madison, was in the end a public process" (941). Powell does note in a footnote, though not in the main text, that some constructions would so transform the nature of the federal compact that only a formal exercise of the amending power would justify them.

Berger

Berger denies that Madison distinguished between the public meaning of a document and the personal opinions of those who had written it.

(Madison's actual distinction, he says, was between the meaning of the document and the writers' recollection of it later, not their contemporaneous interpretation of it.) Madison's distinction between the "true meaning" of the Constitution and "the opinions entertained in forming the Constitution" was at most a reminder to use caution in relying on the views of the Philadelphia convention, since the ratification conventions were the authoritative voice of the people.

Powell's argument that contemporaneous expositions were of some value, but that they were to be regarded strictly as private opinions, useful chiefly in shedding light upon changeable language meaning, Berger considers "highly misleading" (326). Madison's own language is much more emphatic: "I entirely concur in the propriety of resorting to the sense in which the Constitution was accepted and ratified by the nation. In that sense alone it is the legitimate Constitution. And if that be not the guide in expounding it, there can be no security for a consistent and stable, more than for a faithful, exercise of its powers" (326).

Berger notes that Madison did regard the ratifiers as more authoritative—where their views conflicted with the framers. But he emphasizes that the framers represented the people too, having been appointed by their representatives. Moreover, frequently the ratifiers asked the framers who were in the ratifying conventions for explanations, thus approving resort to the framers' own explanations. Since most of the Constitution's provisions were not discussed by the ratifiers, why should the people be shut off from the explanations the framers had in mind?

Berger then collects some of Madison's own citations of the framers, in the *Federalist* and in four letters. He also criticizes Powell's use of a Madison letter to John Davis, which, according to Powell, shows that the interpreter must decide "the intention of those who framed, or, rather, who adopted the Constitution" by reference to "the meaning attached to the terms by '*usus*' [governmental and judicial precedent]" (937). Berger points out that Powell omits a key part of Madison's statement: "the intention, if *ascertained by contemporaneous interpretation* and continued practice, could not be overruled by any latter meaning put on the phrase" (329, Berger's emphasis). Thus, *usus* is tied to contemporaneous interpretation, which is tied to the intention of those who framed, or who adopted, the Constitution.

Powell also cites Madison's acknowledgement that his knowledge of the views of the Philadelphia and Virginia conventions was a possible source of "bias," for example, in the *Federalist*, which might be "sometimes influenced by the zeal of advocates" (329). But, says Berger, the representations designed to garner votes for adoption of the Constitution cannot be discounted by the advocates' zeal.

According to Berger, Powell has Madison elevating judicial "construction" over the author's intentions, when he says that laws are equivocal "until their meaning be liquidated and ascertained by a series of particular discussions and adjudications"—supposedly a restatement of the idea that the "intent" of a legal document "is the product of the interpretive process and not some fixed meaning that the author locks into the document's text at the outset" (910). But in fact, Madison was highly critical of judicial constructions that were unwarrantably broad, pointing out that avowal of such construction would probably have prevented ratification. Powell does not appreciate, says Berger, the incompatibility between these criticisms and Powell's "theory that Madison's judicial 'liquidation' of the text could serve as a vehicle of unfettered discretion" (334).

Berger likewise criticizes Powell for cutting off a quote without including Madison's advice to have recourse to extratextual sources of intent (i.e., the *Federalist* and the "debates in the State Conventions") (331).

Berger is willing to concede that Powell has "uncovered one interesting point," that is, Madison's willingness to accept the acquiescence of the people to a construction [Congress' power to establish a national bank] as settling that point (334). Much as Berger reveres Madison, he finds this argument flawed. First, more than Madison's private opinion is involved, since the Convention rejected the power. Second, that fact (the Convention vote) had not been revealed to the people. There can be no acquiescence to an unrevealed arrogation of power. As Hamilton pointed out, "[u]ntil the people have, by some solemn and authoritative act [amendment], annulled or changed the established form, it is binding upon themselves collectively. . . ." (334). Third, while Madison thought that judicial precedent served to "fix the interpretation of a law," he also distinguished between expounding the law and altering it. Precedents can fix interpretations of law, but they cannot repeal or alter laws. (Moreover, if Powell is right, then the fact that original intention won out in the revolution of 1800 and has ruled the roost ever since makes his whole article of no moment.)

Analysis

Again, one of the striking points of this exchange is the failure of Berger to note explicitly how much Powell seems to concede in his description of Madison. At numerous places in the article, Powell uses very absolute language excluding recourse to extratextual sources of intent. For example, he says that "Madison, one of the greatest of the Republican thinkers, excluded from his understanding of normative constitutional intent *any trace of* the historically ascertainable purposes and expectations of the Philadelphia framers" (945, emphasis added).

Yet according to Powell himself, among the aids in interpretation where the text is unclear "[l]ast and least in value were the records of the Philadelphia convention." The records of the convention are not, then, "utterly without value," but rather they are of less value than other sources (e.g., structural inference and state ratifying convention resolutions and debates).

Likewise, Powell argues in the introduction to the article that

> [t]his original "original intent" was determined not by historical inquiry into the expectations of the individuals involved in framing and ratifying the Constitution, but by consideration of what rights and powers sovereign polities could delegate to a common agent without destroying their own essential autonomy. Thus, the original intentionalism was in fact a form of structural interpretation. To the extent that constitutional interpreters considered historical evidence to have any interpretive value, what they deemed relevant was evidence of the proceedings of the state ratifying conventions, not of the intent of the framers. (888)

If one reads this closely, it bears a striking resemblance to the old saw about the criminal lawyer who tells the jury that he will prove two things: first, that beyond a shadow of a doubt his client was not present when the murder occurred, and second, that if he was present, the killing was in self-defense. Powell first completely rules out any historical inquiry, and second says that if historical inquiry was accepted, it was only in a certain form. All the evidence on the second point undermines the first.

Rather clearly on various occasions Madison pointed to the intentions of those who framed the document, and on other occasions he even more pointedly invoked the intentions of those who ratified it. Powell is perfectly correct when he argues that these arguments were secondary ones for Madison, inferior to the most important arguments, from the text itself (which includes structural arguments). But if he shows that these are secondary or supporting or confirmatory arguments for Madison, he undermines his contention that they have no status at all.[22]

Powell also pushes his point on *usus*, government practice and judicial construction, too far. Interpreters of the Constitution in early

American history do rely on such usage, but Powell subtly blends together two points that ought to be kept distinct. First, usage contributes to interpretation per se in some cases. For example, in *Gibbons v. Ogden*, Marshall notes that it has been the universal practice of American government from the beginning to treat navigation as a form of commerce. This usage illuminates the *general* understanding of the word "commerce" among those who wrote the Constitution and those for whom it was intended, and thus it contributes to an accurate ascertainment of the meaning of the Constitution. And in *Marbury v. Madison*, the practice of the government is cited to establish the general understanding as to when an appointment has been considered complete.

Second, usage, or more precisely, acquiescence in a precedent, can serve to settle the meaning of a constitutional term or provision. This is a point that goes beyond interpretation in the strict sense, to the question of authority: which understanding will prevail when "interpretation" leaves a matter controversial. In such a case, the good of the community requires that the point be settled (so that the law can have the certainty it requires). Madison argued that usage—not just judicial precedent, but the acquiescence of the nation as a whole—"a course of authoritative expositions sufficiently deliberate, uniform, and settled"— had determined the question on the national bank by the time the second bank bill was presented for his presidential signature.

He is not quite so absolute as Powell suggests, however. In his later defense of this position, he points out that "cases may occur which transcend all authority of precedents," though "they form exceptions which will speak for themselves and must justify themselves."[23] I take Madison to mean that acquiescence would not preclude resistance to gross usurpation and also (more controversially) to reopening questions about interpretations that undermine the essential principles of our government.[24] Madison, in that view, had come to see that Hamilton's interpretation of the necessary and proper clause—whatever its other abstract defects, in his opinion—had not in fact undermined the essentially limited character of American government. But that whole issue requires more lengthy discussion in a different place.[25]

Berger, for his part, does not accept this "one interesting point" that Powell has uncovered for him. Part of the reason reflects his own views of constitutional interpretation, which differ from Madison's. The first reason he gives for rejecting Madison's argument is that it is not just Madison's private opinion, but the explicit vote of the convention, that makes the national bank unconstitutional. But why didn't Madison think so? Two possible explanations are: 1) that Madison realized (on grounds

I pointed out above) that the Convention had made no such explicit decision on the matter and/or 2) that Madison did not consider a convention vote authoritative in the way that Berger does.

The second reason Berger gives for rejecting Madison's acceptance of precedent is that the convention vote had not been revealed to the people, and therefore the people could not acquiesce to this unrevealed arrogation of power (since that would require an amendment). But that seems to miss Madison's argument completely. Madison certainly thought that the Constitution did not give the power at issue to Congress (it *was* an arrogation of power)—that was true whether you placed emphasis on the convention vote or not (Madison does not). He is simply arguing that even wrong interpretations, if they are widely accepted in American political practice and are not "cases . . . which transcend all authority of precedents," can become "settled."

Berger seems to emphasize the fact that the vote was not revealed, but that is secondary to his real point, which is that it would take an amendment for the people to change the Constitution. (From what Berger says, it seems that even if the people had been informed about the convention vote at some time after the original ratification and had consented to the power anyway, he would not accept this consent.) More importantly, for Madison, given that the authority of the Constitution came from the people, through the ratifiers, as they understood its language, any "unrevealed" events at the convention itself were irrelevant.

I believe that Powell is correct that Madison did distinguish between the public meaning of a document and the personal opinions of those who wrote and ratified it. The example he gives involves Andrew Jackson's invocation of Madison's veto message of 1817. Madison said that "[t]he document must speak for itself, and [the] intention [of its author] cannot be substituted for [the intention derived through] the established rules of interpretation. . . . [W]hether the language employed [in the veto] duly conveyed the meaning of which J. M. retains the consciousness is a question on which he does not presume to judge for others" (Berger, 324). Berger attempts to read "intention" as referring, not to Madison's contemporary intention, but to Madison's "consciousness" years later. (So Madison is only saying that the interpretation of the document according to the usual rules—i.e., original intention—takes precedence over his understanding of the document years later.) But if that is so, why use the phrase that "he does not presume to judge for others"? There is no opposition here between Madison's original intention and his later understanding of it, as Berger suggests; in fact, Madison emphasizes that he "retains the consciousness" of that meaning; that is, he has the same opinion. Powell is right that Madison is saying something like the following: "I can't say that Jackson was wrong in citing my veto message simply because I understood the veto message in a different way. My personal understanding of the language of the veto is not dispositive—the veto message has to speak for itself—and whether Jackson misused it depends on whether he interpreted it correctly, according to the usual rules."

But the distinction between the public meaning of a document and the individual opinions of its authors does not make the latter irrelevant, as Powell would have it. The public meaning is the authoritative meaning, and it is collected chiefly from the text itself. However, extrinsic sources of intention are subordinate but legitimate factors in interpretation, especially insofar as they confirm a meaning arrived at by employing the ordinary rules of construction.

Berger is right, I think, to reject Madison's remarks warning about caution in using the *Federalist* on the grounds that it may reveal the zeal of advocates. (Caution is justified, but on a different ground: the *Federalist,* for all its authority, cannot automatically be assumed always to represent a unanimous or general understanding of the Constitution.) Perhaps Berger could have pushed further, asking why Madison employed this argument. I think that we will find a reason that also explains why Madison emphasized the state ratifying conventions so much, one that raises some questions.

In a letter to J. G. Jackson on 27 December 1821, Madison says he was always

> a votary of the principle of self-government: I was among those most anxious to rescue it from the danger which seemed to threaten it; and with that view was willing to give to a Government resting on that foundation, as much energy as would ensure the requisite stability and efficacy. It is possible that in some instances this consideration may have been allowed a weight greater than subsequent reflection within the Convention, or the actual operation of the Government would sanction. . . . But whatever might have been the opinions entertained in forming the constitution, it was the duty of all to support it in its true meaning as understood *by the Nation* at the time of its ratification.[26]

What gives one pause in reading these lines is the sense that Madison is worried that he may have gone too far in giving power to the new government and is relying on the sense of "the Nation" to bail him out. But how is one to know the "true meaning as understood *by the Nation*"? Perhaps the nation, under the leadership of men like Hamilton and Madison, did what he hints he himself did: give the government too much power. Hamilton might observe that this statement comes perilously close to the admission that the Constitution, if read as it was written, approaches closer to his than to Madison's views.

The objection here is not that Madison is on weak ground in giving greater authority to the state ratifying conventions. There is ample theoretical ground for that. What is problematic would be relying on some vague "spirit" of the state ratifying conventions to counter or limit a fair reading of the text itself. (Story's trenchant critique of Jefferson in his *Commentaries*, discussed above, raises this problem forcefully.)

As Berger would argue, however, this is an argument not against relying on state ratifying convention debates that clearly delineate a general understanding of a constitutional provision (where the text is otherwise doubtful), but against relying on bad or inadequate arguments from the ratifying conventions (ones that are alleged to show a general understanding, but do not).

Berger notes Madison's arguments against excessively broad construction of the Constitution. This does indicate that there are limits on judicial construction; in Berger's word, it is not "unfettered." (It is difficult to know exactly how fettered Powell considers the power, since he does not discuss it in detail. Some of his comments do cause me to share some of Berger's concern, however.) At the same time, Madison's criticisms of latitudinarian judicial constructions (which he phrased carefully—Madison did not want to needlessly offend Spencer Roane and his allies) do not necessarily deny judicial power to construe the Constitution. In fact, they may even implicitly concede it, arguing only that it has been exercised poorly on occasion.[27]

Berger's own discussion of Madison, while compelling on many points, is still unbalanced in certain ways. He has no trouble showing that Madison himself made use of certain historical materials, giving primacy to the state ratifying conventions but not excluding the records of the Philadelphia convention. But Berger displays little sense of the primacy of the text that is manifest in Madison's constitutional interpretation, especially during his public life.

The Marshall Court and Constitutional Construction

Powell

Marshall and Story applied traditional methods of statutory construction to constitutional interpretation, says Powell. For example, in *U.S. v. Fisher* Marshall says that the mind, in seeking to discover the design of the legislature, "seizes everything from which aid can be derived" (942). The various aids he referred to (indirectly) were consulting the act's title, preamble, and general scope and design, and considering the mischief and defect of common law the statute meant to remedy, other federal statutes, and the consequences of taking the act literally. Marshall placed most emphasis on close analysis of the wording and structure of the act. No one (Marshall or the attorneys in this case) suggested an investigation of congressional debates.

The Marshall Court's response to invocation of extratextual state intent was emphasis on the supremacy of the text, read in light of the Constitution's purposes as set forth in its Preamble. Powell sees in this an approach strikingly similar to Madison's, despite their different starting points.

> Both Marshall and Madison accepted the common-law understanding that the intent of a document is, at least in part, the product of the interpretive process; both accepted the authority of practice and precedent; and neither regarded the framers' personal intentions as a definitive or even particularly valuable guide to constitutional construction. (943–44)

Berger

While Berger does not have a section directly responding to this part of Powell's article, he does speak to Marshall's remarks in *U.S. v. Fisher* that the mind seizes on everything in seeking to discern the design of the legislature. Berger emphasizes that Marshall's words say *everything*. If he does not specifically mention legislative debates, that is because there were no legislative debates of Congress available until 1834.

It is hard to know whether Berger would accept Powell's contention that Marshall and Madison were surprisingly close on rules of interpretation. What is clear is that he would reject Powell's characterization of what Madison had in common with Marshall.

Analysis

Marshall does use the *Federalist*, and he also uses history on more than just one occasion. Powell notes *Barron v. Baltimore* (where Marshall appeals to the universal understanding of the history of the times that produced the Bill of Rights), but Marshall also appeals to history in *Fletcher v. Peck* (regarding the historical background of the contract clause).

Marshall does not limit the purposes in light of which the Constitution should be read to the Preamble, as Powell seems to, but then he does not cite legislative debates either. Berger is right that they were not available—but again, why not, if legislative intention in that sense was so important? Apparently, the founding generation was content to infer the purposes from the constitutional provisions themselves and, perhaps, from the general understanding of their purposes (if such a thing was available, as it was in *Barron* and *Fletcher*).

Another interesting source appealed to by Marshall that Powell does not mention is found in *Ogden v. Saunders*, where Marshall says that

> [w]hen we advert to the course of reading generally pursued by American statesmen in early life, we must suppose that the framers of our constitution were intimately acquainted with the writings of those wise and learned men, whose treatises on the laws of nature and nations have guided public opinion on the subject of obligations and contract. . . . We must suppose that the framers of our constitution took the same view of the subject, and the language they have used confirms this opinion.[28]

The mind does indeed seize upon everything. At the same time, Marshall, as he usually does, employs these as ancillary aids to confirm a reading of the text itself.

If common-law statutory interpretation allowed consideration of the mischief to be cured, what was the appropriate analogue for constitutional law? Isn't some examination of history (again, as in *Barron*) the plausible way of knowing more about the mischief? Powell seems to exclude extratextual sources of intent, and historical evidence as to the mischief seems to qualify as an extratextual source. But perhaps it could be considered as one of the ordinary common-law rules of textual interpretation regarding the "context" of the words. For that matter, practice and precedent are not "textual" either, but Powell considers them admissible. (Perhaps the practice of government can be considered under the common-law aid of "subject matter.") All of this suggests that perhaps the sharp distinction between "common-law" interpretation and "extratextual sources of evidence" can be overdrawn.

One thing Powell has to omit from the description of Madison's approach to interpretation, in order to stress the similarities between him and Marshall, is Madison's emphasis on the state ratifying conventions. While I believe that it is true that Marshall would accept evidence from these as subordinate factors in constitutional interpretation (part of the "everything" the mind draws on), he does not place as much reliance on such evidence as Madison does.

Conclusion

The foregoing analysis shows why neither Powell nor Berger gives an entirely accurate perception of the "original understanding of original intent," though each has a grasp of important facets of that "interpretive intention."

Berger places too great an emphasis on extratextual, historical sources of intent, failing to understand that the ordinary common-law intent was not primarily the subjective intent of the lawgiver. Nothing shows this more clearly than the relatively late development of legislative records, which is hard to explain if Berger is right about the emphasis placed on what the legislators said about their laws. Whenever there is more than one person constituting "the lawgiver," legislative intent is inevitably a somewhat artificial "construct." As Hamilton and Story observed, the one thing we know for sure about the intention of those who have given authority to the law (by ratifying it) is that they adopted the text before them. The text is therefore the single most important source of the intention of the law. On the whole, then, I believe that Powell is more accurate in his general description of common-law intent.

This general accuracy notwithstanding, Powell tries to create a rigid distinction between "common-law legislative intent," on one hand, and "historical" and "extratextual" sources of intent on the other, excluding the latter from constitutional interpretation. But his own description of early American law shows that it is impossible to exclude them so completely. Berger is correct that, when the text is unclear, one species of aid in interpretation is historical sources of intention. These sources must be treated with extreme caution—a fact that Berger never denies, but unfortunately does not emphasize sufficiently—because it is often difficult to know when they clearly represent the general understanding of constitutional provisions. But difficulty is not the same as impossibility.

My greatest concern about Powell's understanding—what makes me conclude that in the final analysis I may be closer to Berger, despite the greater formal similarity between Powell's description of interpretation and my own—arises from his formulation that the common-law legislative intent is a "product of the interpretive process" (910). According to that view, the interpreter "produces" or "makes" the intention.[29]

But, in fact, it is fundamental to interpretation, in the proper sense of the term, that the intention of the law is "discovered." That means that in some sense "it is already there." How did it get there? The intention or meaning of the law is inextricably intertwined with its being: they who made the law gave it its meaning or intention.[30] That is the most fundamental sense in which it is accurate to speak of "original intention."

In that sense, the original understanding of original intention was that the document derived its meaning from those who wrote and ratified it, and that meaning—as it is expressed in the document—is authoritative in constitutional interpretation. The ascertainment of the meaning is to be accomplished primarily by a careful interpretation of the text, according to the usual rules of interpretation. Those rules, which call for consideration of context, subject matter, effects and consequences, and the reason and spirit of the law, as well as the words themselves, allow for some consideration of extratextual historical sources of intent, done with the appropriate caution and generally to confirm a reading of the text itself—not as a substitute for it.

This still leaves other arguments against "original intention" jurisprudence, of course. To defend such a jurisprudence would still require a showing as to *why* the framers' "interpretive intention" should be accepted. Opponents are correct when they point out that an argument that appeals to original intention simply on the grounds that it was the original intention are circular and inadequate. I believe that such a defense of original intention jurisprudence exists, based largely on the need for a fixed Constitution and on the fact that the Constitution properly interpreted is a document worthy of the authority it has. But my primary concern in this chapter has been simply to show that Powell has not disproved original intention on its own grounds. In fact, a careful reading of his article actually lends it considerable support.

Part II

Twentieth-Century Judicial Power: Practice and Theory

4

How the Constitution Was Taken Out of Constitutional Law

In contemporary discussions, scholarly commentators routinely distinguish between different "modes" of judicial review, of which merely one form is "interpretive" or "originalist."[1] This trend represents both a gain and a loss in discussion of judicial review. It is a gain in that it straightforwardly acknowledges that modern judicial review is qualitatively different from the kind of judicial review described and defended in *The Federalist* No. 78[2] and *Marbury v. Madison*[3] and that this new form of judicial review requires a different kind of justification. It is a loss because it is a sign of the legitimacy, even the dominance, of "noninterpretive" or "nonoriginalist" review, which in most of these discussions is contrasted favorably with the "narrowness" (and often the lack of "sophistication") of the interpretive "mode."[4] This distinction among legal commentators has *not* become widespread in *public* discussions for obvious reasons: even those who favor judicial activism of various stripes know that a frank admission of the breadth of the modern Court's power would provide its opponents with a powerful weapon in the court of public opinion. This helps to explain the widespread unhappiness at the character of Court nomination battles such as those over Robert Bork and Clarence Thomas: there is a sense that, despite the political impact of appointments that all recognize, somehow the law should be above politics.[5]

In this chapter, I would like to explore in more detail how the new form of judicial review arose, not so much historically but in terms of the legal doctrines and notions of interpretation that were an essential part of the change.[6] Essentially, I want to ask: "How was the Constitution taken out of constitutional law?"

This assumes, of course, that, as I argued above in chapter 1, there was a time when the Constitution was "in" constitutional law, a time when constitutional law consisted of genuine attempts to provide a fair interpretation of the Constitution itself. This chapter will examine how advocates of "modern judicial review" have come up with techniques for taking a rather inconvenient Constitution out of constitutional law without destroying the public "myth of the Constitution," on which the legitimacy of judicial review is based.

The modern process of taking the Constitution out of constitutional law has two main steps. The first is to empty the Constitution of its (original) substantive content so that constitutional interpretation is no longer "restricted" by that content. The second step is to fill the vacuum created by providing ways of giving new content to the Constitution.

The First Step: Emptying the Constitution of Substantive Content

The first step in taking the Constitution out of constitutional law is to empty the Constitution of substantive content. This is necessary because practical political reasons make it impossible simply to repeal or drastically recast the Constitution, and because our political tradition has so closely tied the legitimacy of judicial review to the notion of interpretation and the enforcement of constitutional provisions. Thus, "getting around" the Constitution in constitutional law requires one to interpret the Constitution in such a way that what it really means is not binding on the interpreter.

It may be worthwhile to point out that "what it really means" includes knowing what it does *not* say as well as what it says. Insofar as modern constitutional interpretation manifests a dissatisfaction with the Constitution, that dissatisfaction often lies not in what the Constitution actually says but in what it fails to say. But to "find" something in the Constitution that is not actually there (say, a broader right to free speech than the one the framers placed there or a right to privacy, in the sense of "moral autonomy") is a form of misreading the Constitution.

The process of emptying the Constitution of substantive content itself involves two steps: first, severing the provisions of the Constitution from the political thought upon which they were founded; and second, raising the meaning of the Constitution's provisions to a high level of generality.

Severing Constitutional Provisions
from Underlying Theory

Proper interpretation of the Constitution (or any substantial piece of writing) requires more than simply "parsing out" words and sentences. An author conveys his meaning not word by word, but by putting many words together within a certain framework so that they express a larger idea. Thus, an interpreter must be able to ascertain this larger idea—the great "object" of a provision—in order to do the job of interpreting well. A failure (or refusal) to attend to the principles that the words and phrases are meant to embody makes "interpretation" impossible and sets in motion a process that deserves some other name. (In the context of judicial review, perhaps "judicial legislation" is the proper term.) I will give some examples of this "failure" from different sources, both outside of and within constitutional law.

One good example may be taken from the work of Woodrow Wilson.[7] He wrote two major books on American government: *Congressional Government* (1885)[8] and *Constitutional Government in the United States* (1908).[9] In the first piece Wilson roundly damns the American Constitution for being inadequate to meet the exigencies of modern government, because principles such as separation of powers prevent government from being "strong, prompt, wieldy, and efficient."[10] In the second work, while he still has some criticism for the Constitution, he generally praises the document because of its "elasticity and adaptability."[11] What happened between 1885 and 1908? The answer is simple: Wilson had developed a way to take the Constitution out of constitutional law. The one aspect of this transformation on which I would like to focus is Wilson's argument that the Constitution must be separated from the theory it was meant to embody.

Wilson argues that "the government of the United States was constructed upon the Whig theory of political dynamics, which was a sort of unconscious copy of the Newtonian theory of the universe."[12] But we have come, he says, to realize that government falls "not under the theory of the universe, but under the theory of organic life,"[13] and so we have substituted Charles Darwin for Sir Isaac Newton. Whig theory, therefore, is outmoded. It is at this point that Wilson severs the Constitution from the political principles on which it is based.

Fortunately, the definitions and prescriptions of our constitutional law, though conceived in the Newtonian spirit and upon the Newtonian principle, are sufficiently broad and elastic to allow for the play of life and circumstances. Though they were Whig theorists, the men who framed the federal Constitution were also practical statesmen with an experienced eye for affairs and a quick practical sagacity in respect of the actual structure of government, and they have given us a thoroughly workable model.[14]

He concludes that

the makers of the Constitution were not enacting Whig theory, they were not making laws with the expectation that, not the laws themselves, but their opinions, known by future historians to lie back of them, should govern the constitutional action of the country.[15]

In short, the Constitution "contains no theories . . . it is as practical a document as the Magna Carta."[16]

This process provided Wilson with what he needed. His long-range goal was to modify the constitutional separation of powers to provide a government adequate to modern exigencies. For Wilson, the great means to do this was through the expansion of presidential powers, because a strong party president could command public opinion (and hence the Congress) and thus achieve an informal fusion of powers. But this required overcoming the Whig theory, which was, in Wilson's words, only one "very mechanical"[17] interpretation of the framers' presidency. Wilson's alternative theory was not, in his mind, "inconsistent with the actual provisions of the Constitution"[18] because the president "is at liberty, both in law and conscience to be as big a man as he can."[19] Wilson's use of the word "actual" suggests, however, that he was departing (and knew he was departing) from the spirit behind the letter of the Constitution, the spirit that the letter was intended to embody.

This process of severing the Constitution from its theoretical roots, exemplified by Wilson, can be seen as well in Supreme Court cases such as *Home Building and Loan v. Blaisdell.*[20] While the Minnesota Mortgage Moratorium Law[21] was not identical with the laws the contract clause was specifically intended to prohibit, it was not far off.[22] Chief Justice Hughes's majority opinion tip-toes gingerly around the constitutional question, denying that the law is constitutional merely because there are emergency circumstances. But he says that:

there has been a growing appreciation of public needs and of the necessity of finding ground for a rational compromise between individual rights and public welfare . . . It is no answer to say that this public need was not apprehended a century ago, or to insist that what the provision of the Constitution meant to the vision of that day it must mean to the vision of our time. If by the statement that what the Constitution meant at the time of its adoption it means today, it is intended to say that the great clauses of the Constitution must be confined to the interpretation which the framers with the conditions and outlook of their time, would have placed upon them, the statement carries its own refutation.[23]

As Justice Sutherland notes in dissent, this argument goes beyond merely saying that the clause should not be applied as the framers would have *expected* it to be applied to their circumstances. It goes so far as to say that the *meaning* of the provision, not only its application, will vary with time.[24] In effect, the Court was simply saying that the framers were too solicitous of contractual sanctity, and that nowadays we know better than they and that it is sometimes necessary to impair contractual obligations. If the very meaning of a provision can be varied, it would therefore seem to be possible to take the Constitution out of constitutional law.[25]

Another way to modify, add to, or subtract from, constitutional provisions by divorcing them from their informing principles is to take advantage of the changed meanings of words. For example, the right to have the assistance of counsel originally meant that government could not prohibit a defendant's retaining counsel, although government had no duty to provide counsel, much as the free exercise right of the First Amendment meant that government did not have a right to deny free exercise, but was not obligated to finance it. In *Johnson v. Zerbst*,[26] the Court (not surprisingly, through Justice Black) simply ignored this foundation and used for its purposes an expanded, modern notion of "right" (as "entitlement"), and held that the Sixth Amendment obliges government to provide counsel for those who cannot afford it. Whether or not this is good policy (it seems obviously good to me), is it "interpreting the Constitution" (ascertaining its meaning) or is it adding to the Constitution (giving it new meaning)?

Finally, another way to put aside the thought on which constitutional provisions are based is to ignore the implications of one part of the Constitution in favor of other parts. What is the meaning of the Fourteenth Amendment's equal protection clause? Does it include equality of voting rights? By itself, perhaps, this might not be clear. But looking to other parts of the Constitution, it is clear that it does not. First, there is the Fifteenth Amendment, passed only two years later, which prohibits denial of voting rights on racial grounds—an amendment that would have been completely unnecessary if the Fourteenth had already guaranteed equality of voting rights. Moreover, in the Fourteenth Amendment itself, section 2 specifically foresees the possibility of such a denial of voting rights and-—instead of prohibiting it—provides an alternative disincentive.

Likewise, some argue that the cruel and unusual punishment provision of the Eighth Amendment prohibits the death penalty. Yet the Fifth Amendment implicitly acknowledges that a person may be deprived of life, as long as he is accorded due process of law.

I do not intend to address myself to the substantive *political* issues in these different examples. For the purposes of my argument, it does not matter whether the United States needs a president stronger than the one the Constitution provides or state governments need greater power to alter the provisions of contracts. Nor does my case rest on opposition to appointed counsel or equal voting rights or on support for the death penalty. The point is simply that one way to modify constitutional provisions with which one is unhappy is to divorce the provisions from the political principles on which they were based. It is worthwhile emphasizing, however, that the pressure to take the Constitution out of constitutional law is, at root, a dissatisfaction with the Constitution itself, a dissatisfaction that leads to a desire to modify or change the Constitution (by subtracting from it or adding to it) rather than to interpret it.

I would also like to note the importance that the concept of "adaptation" has played in the whole process of severing constitutional provisions from their underlying principles. Taken in a limited sense, adaptation might mean no more than taking the invariable general principles of the Constitution and applying them to new particulars. Equally narrow, it might mean that the legislature should have all the flexibility that the Constitution wisely accorded it to adapt the necessary and proper means to achieve the permanent objects of the national government to the circumstances of a given time. This is precisely the original meaning of the famous John Marshall quotation cited by Chief Justice Hughes in *Blaisdell*: "We must never forget that it is a *constitution* we are expounding . . . a constitution intended to endure for ages to come, and, consequently, to be adapted to the various *crises* of human affairs."[27]

But adaptation has come to mean much more than that. The notion of adaptation originally became prominent in early-twentieth-century constitutional law through Justice Holmes's dissents in economic substantive due process decisions. Justice Holmes might have objected to the Court's imposition of laissez-faire economic philosophy on the grounds that the due process clause applied only to procedural rights, but instead, he chose a quite different route. Conceding the principle of judicial power to review the substance of legislation under the due process clause, he argued that "a Constitution is not intended to embody a particular economic theory . . . it is made for people of fundamentally different views"[28] and that the Court should therefore defer to legislative action that adapts public policy to new economic ideas.

Justice Benjamin Cardozo likewise emphasized the adaptive side of such a view in *The Nature of the Judicial Process*[29] when he dealt with due process as a "concept of the greatest generality":

> Does Liberty mean the same thing for successive generations? May restraints that were arbitrary yesterday be useful and rational and therefore lawful today? May restraints that are arbitrary today become more useful and rational and therefore lawful tomorrow? I have no doubt that the answers to these questions must be yes.[30]

Justice Cardozo refers to this as a "fluid and dynamic conception," and contends that the "content of constitutional immunities is not constant, but varies from age to age."[31] "The courts, then, are free in marking the limits of the individual's immunities to shape their judgments in accordance with reason and justice."[32]

This emphasis on adaptation, change, and evolution originally occurred in a context in which judges were to *defer* to legislatures. In the hands of later judges, however, the notion of adaptability was easily molded to serve as the basis for judicial *overturning* of legislative decisions. But this notion of adaptation—that is, modifying or changing the principles of the Constitution rather than simply applying them to new particulars—is very different from the more limited idea of adaptation that Chief Justice Marshall espoused.

Making Constitutional Provisions "Great Generalities"

A second step in emptying the Constitution of substantive content is to raise the meaning of constitutional provisions to a high level of generality. If the Constitution can be made to mean anything "good," it can quickly be made to mean what the "interpreter" considers good. What the Constitution itself originally meant would pale beside what it could come to mean.

In order to argue that this involved a taking of the Constitution out of constitutional law, I will have to devote some space to showing that certain key constitutional provisions had to be *made* general, that is, they were not originally general, or at least not too general. Chief among these are the due process clauses, the equal protection clause, and the Ninth Amendment.[33] I have already (in chapter 2) described the "real meaning" of "due process of law," so I will briefly discuss the equal protection clause and Ninth Amendment here.

Equal Protection

Since the 1960s, the equal protection clause has challenged the due process clause as the preeminent source of constitutional litigation. The only surprise in this development, given the dominance of "modern" judicial review after 1937, is that it took so long to occur. The explanation for the delay, is that earlier judges were not willing to open a Pandora's Box, while the Warren Court had developed a strong enough sense of its own power that it was willing to do so.

Today the clause can be invoked by almost anyone who is treated "differently" and believes that such different treatment is arbitrary or unreasonable. Judges are then confronted with the duty to determine whether in fact there was a reasonable basis for the different treatment. The particular form of the test has varied: at the present time, the Court generally requires an "important government objective" and a "substantial relation" between the objective and the means chosen to further it.[34] As Chief Justice Rehnquist has argued, the present criteria provide a broad invitation for lower courts to constantly second-guess legislative judgments.[35]

Is there a more limited "traditional" interpretation of the equal protection clause that is superior to the vague generality it has become? I would argue that where the words themselves are not clear, one can avoid the temptation to convert them into vague generalities through the use of broader considerations, such as "subject-matter, context, and intent."[36] One interpretation that can be eliminated immediately is that the law must treat everybody equally. This interpretation strikes at the nature of law, because it is typical that laws create categories and treat people in different categories differently. The nature of the subject-matter thus precludes such an interpretation.

The context of the clause is section 1 of the Fourteenth Amendment. The Fourteenth Amendment as a whole was a "reconstruction" amendment, as the language of sections 2, 3, and 4 shows, and this confirms the universally acknowledged intent of the Fourteenth Amendment, which was to deal with problems of racial discrimination in the South, although *the wording* is not confined to race in the South. And yet the content of the amendment shows that not even all racial discrimination was precluded by the clause: it took the Fifteenth Amendment to prohibit racial discrimination regarding the right to vote. (Voting was dealt with separately in the Fourteenth Amendment—in section 2, not section 1.) This suggests (and the suggestion is clearly confirmed by historical evidence) that equal protection did not refer to all rights: it excluded at least the class of political rights such as voting. For what class of rights, then, does the equal protection clause guarantee equality?

The wording suggests something here. The clause uses the word "protection." In a general sense, any law "protects" someone or something, but in another normal usage "protection" connotes especially providing security of "life, liberty, or property" ("liberty" being understood in a limited sense, as in Blackstone: "[t]his personal liberty consists in the power of locomotion, of changing situation, or moving one's person to whatsoever place one's own inclination may direct without imprisonment or restraint, unless by due course of law"[37]). What I am contending the framers had in mind is that blacks, and whites sympathetic to blacks, should receive the same full protection that the law provides to others against murder, assault, kidnapping, theft, violation of contracts, and so on.[38]

This interpretation derives support from the wording of the Civil Rights Act, which the amendment was intended to "constitutionalize": to provide blacks with the "equal benefit of all laws . . . for the security of person and property . . ." Specific statutes to remedy state violations of this guarantee (i.e., their failure to enforce laws for the security of person and property equally on behalf of the newly freed slaves) were to be provided by Congress pursuant to section 5 of the amendment.

This interpretation squares with the implications of the Fifteenth Amendment and does justice to the wording of the clause better than any other interpretation. It also satisfies the essential criterion of harmonizing two aspects of context and intent more broadly defined. First, the amendment did not intend to change the role of the judiciary in American government: neither wording nor historical intent would support such a change. The rejection of judicial participation in a veto power over legislative proposals at the Convention of 1787 was firmly grounded in separation-of-powers reasoning: judges were to decide cases, not make law. Moreover, it should be remembered that judicial review is provided for in the Constitution only by implication and that the universal understanding of early Americans was that judicial review was warranted only in cases of clear or "manifest violations" of the Constitution.[39] No evidence suggests any intent by the framers of the Fourteenth Amendment to change these characteristics of judicial review. Thus, an interpretation of the equal protection clause as a broad delegation of power to the courts to enforce equality where, when, and in what ways they consider it reasonable to do so should be rejected in favor of a narrower view that would not so aggrandize court power.

Second, the amendment was not intended to eliminate or radically alter the nature of federalism and was certainly not understood to do so by the ratifying states. This matter is more complicated than judicial power because there was a clear intention to modify federalism in some important aspects, so as to permit federal intervention in the South to protect the interests of blacks and their white allies. Still, whatever the deficiencies of other parts of his opinion in the *Slaughterhouse Cases,*[40] Justice Miller was right to argue that

> the argument, we admit, is not always the most conclusive which is drawn from the consequences urged against the adoption of a particular construction of an instrument. But when, as in the case before us, these consequences are so serious, so far-reaching and pervading, so great a departure from the structure and spirit of our institutions, when the effect is to fetter and degrade the state governments by subjecting them to the control of Congress, in the exercise of powers heretofore universally conceded to them of the most ordinary and fundamental character; when in fact it radically changes the whole theory of the relations of the state and Federal Governments to each other and of both these governments to the people; the argument has a force that is irresistible, in the absence of language which expresses such a purpose too clearly to admit of doubt.[41]

These broad considerations counsel the interpreter to give a limited reading to the equal protection clause.

There is, then, a reasonable, relatively limited construction of the equal protection clause. The point of detailing the interpretation is to make it clear that a broad, "open-ended" reading of equal protection was by no means inevitable, even apart from the fact that it took eighty-five years for courts to see this "inevitability." Thus, one can say that the impact of the equal protection clause on constitutional law depends on the understanding of interpretation and judicial review that the interpreter brings to the examination of the clause.[42] The fact remains that one way to take the Constitution out of constitutional law—to make the key decisions in constitutional law turn on questions about which the

Constitution gives no guidance—is to choose an interpretation that raises a constitutional principle to its highest level of generality. When one interprets the equal protection clause to mean "no person shall arbitrarily or unreasonably be treated differently from others by government," and is willing to leave the decision as to what is "arbitrary" or "unreasonable" to the "interpreter," then for all practical purposes, the Constitution is itself irrelevant to the final decision.

Ninth Amendment

Part of the above argument concerning the equal protection clause was that the Fourteenth Amendment did not change the original constitutional intent of limited judicial power. In recent times, arguments have been made that the Ninth Amendment of the Bill of Rights contains one of the open-ended clauses used as a basis of modern judicial review.[43] But for the fact that this argument has been taken up by respectable legal commentators, it would be tempting to dismiss it as frivolous. A look at wording and historical intent should make the extremely limited character of the Ninth Amendment clear.

The amendment reads: "The enumeration in the Constitution of certain rights shall not be construed to deny or disparage others retained by the people." The wording is not "other rights shall not be denied."[44] On its face, the amendment simply supplies a rule of construction in interpreting the Constitution. It does this to offset another generally used rule: "an enumeration of powers or rights excludes a general power or right." This was the argument used against a bill of rights in *The Federalist*:

> I go further, and affirm the bills of rights in the sense and to the extent in which they are contended for, are not only unnecessary in the proposed Constitution, but would even be dangerous. They would contain various exceptions to powers not granted, and, on this very account, would afford a colorable pretext to claim more than were granted. For why declare that things shall not be done which there is no power to do?[45]

This is precisely the argument James Madison referred to in introducing the Ninth Amendment:

> It has been objected also against a bill of rights that, by enumerating particular exceptions to a grant of power, it would disparage those rights which were not placed in that enumeration; and it might follow by implication, that those rights which were not singled out, were intend-

ed to be assigned into the hands of the General Government, and were consequently insecure.[46]

Madison makes it clear that the danger with which the Ninth Amendment dealt was the possibility of the general government claiming powers that were intended to be reserved to the states. Nor is it an objection to this interpretation that the states reserved powers were protected separately by the Tenth Amendment.[47] After all, Madison did not think that the Bill of Rights was necessary—he proposed it and pursued its ratification in order to calm the fears of the Constitution's opponents.[48] The Tenth Amendment calmed those fears in one particular way, by stating explicitly what the original document had said implicitly: the federal government is limited to delegated powers. The Ninth Amendment simply was meant to calm them in yet another way: by stating a rule of construction to prevent a misinterpretation of what those powers were, keeping in mind that by rejecting the addition of the word "expressly" before "delegated" in the Tenth Amendment, the framers indicated that the "delegated" powers included *implied* powers.

Supporters for the open-ended view of the Ninth Amendment cite a letter from Madison to Jefferson in which he suggests that

> there is great reason to fear that a positive declaration of some of the most essential rights could not be obtained in the requisite latitude. I am sure that the rights of conscience in particular, if submitted to public definition would be narrowed much more than they are ever likely to be by an assumed power.[49]

They contend that the Ninth Amendment was the answer to this problem. There is not a shred of evidence to justify this assertion that it would result in an unbalanced shift of "open-ended" power to the judiciary. In fact, Madison was quite correct that the public definition, especially of the rights of conscience, would be narrower than he wanted it: the First Amendment religion clauses were not all that he would have liked them to have been.[50] But he thought that what he was able to get was better than nothing.[51]

The net result of basing most of constitutional law on vague generalities is to make the Constitution an empty formal document, possessing relatively little real content. To use an analogy, one can consider the Constitution to be a cup; its structure provides some vague contours for what is to be done, but its vitality as a document is derived from the contents of the cup and by who gets to pour things in and empty things out of it.

Second Step: New Ways to Give
Content to the Constitution

While severing constitutional provisions from their underlying theoretical foundations and raising them to a high level of generality go some way toward explaining how the Constitution was taken out of constitutional law, the task remains of describing how modern commentators substituted something new in its place. If constitutional law was no longer to be informed by the Constitution, but rather by "interpreters," what would be the methods for providing new content to the constitutional law?

I should reemphasize here that, even if one believes that some constitutional provisions are very general or even "open-ended," it does not follow that they should be used as a basis for judicial review. The original rationale for judicial review was the judge's duty to prefer the Constitution to a law that clearly violated it.[52] If there are "vague" or "open-ended" constitutional provisions, then a more traditional approach would leave the definition of their content to the political branches, because there is—virtually by definition—no clear conflict. If, to achieve modern judicial review, one must transform constitutional provisions into vague generalities, one must also necessarily transform judicial power.

I will focus particularly on two different methods used to achieve this transformation. First, constitutional interpretation was redefined as a "specification of constitutional generalities." Within these generalities, competing interests must be balanced. Second, a new, unwritten clause was added to the Constitution. This clause may be called the "judicial necessary and proper clause."

Redefining Interpretation

Interpretation normally means "ascertaining the intended meaning." In the context of judicial review, however, "interpretation" means not only the abstract construction of the words of the Constitution but also the concrete decision in a case as to whether there is an incompatibility between the fundamental law and a particular statute or governmental act. Given the modern interpretation of the Constitution as a set of "great generalities," which provides little or no guidance, how is the concrete decision made?

Another way of saying that the phrases of the Constitution are "great generalities" is to say that constitutional provisions are general rules that provide "presumptions." This re-formulation helps to explain how it is possible to raise *specific* constitutional phrases (for example, freedoms of speech, press, assembly, religion; the commerce clause; the contract clause; the takings clause) as well as general ones (for example, due process, equal protection) to a high level of generality.

If freedom of speech in the First Amendment meant "Congress shall make no law that in any way prohibits a person to speak or punishes him for doing so, simply because of what he says" (that is, if you read "no law abridging" to mean "No Law Abridging," as does Justice Black),[53] then the clause is general, but not a mere generality. It is general in that it applies to many cases of the same kind, but it is not a mere generality in that it has definite intelligible *content* applicable to all cases of this kind.[54] (The problem with this approach is that virtually no one—perhaps not even Justice Black—is willing to go the whole way, e.g., to eliminate libel laws entirely.)

If, however, freedom of speech means "there is a strong presumption against any governmental limitation on speech, so that no regulation of speech will be upheld unless the Supreme Court agrees that it is 'necessary,'" then freedom of speech is a vague generality.[55] It is a general rule, a presumption, but one whose form of application is determined by factors extrinsic to the Constitution.

In a similar way, the commerce clause, in regard to limitations on state regulation of commerce, can be defined as a general presumption in favor of a free flow of commerce, unless the Supreme Court determines that harms occasioned by the burdens on commerce are outweighed by legitimate state interests.[56] The contract clause can also be defined as a general presumption in favor of the inviolability of contractual obligations against state interference, unless the Supreme Court determines that there are reasonable grounds for permitting alteration of a contract by the state.[57] And so on.

Once this understanding of constitutional provisions is accepted, the function of the "interpreter" in constitutional law becomes that of the arbiter in a "balancing" process. Weighing competing considerations of broad public policy, the judges determine whether or not a given governmental action is controlled by the presumption embodied in the constitutional provision at issue. This balancing process is the typical modern form of "interpretation."[58]

The shift to "balancing" constituted a change in the very nature of judicial review. It was another step in the process of taking the Constitution out of constitutional law. The Constitution can only give the vaguest of guidance in this balancing process. The decision to be made comes down to a straightforward weighing of competing interests, similar to the legislative process. This similarity does not make balancing illegitimate in the eyes of proponents of this approach to interpretation and judicial review. After all, mainstream legal thought since the turn of the century (especially Justice Oliver Wendell Holmes Jr.) has argued that judging does not essentially differ from legislating—it is legislating in the "interstices" of the law.[59]

A corollary to the balancing process is the shift of emphasis in judicial decisions from questions of kind to questions of degree. This point can be made best by way of example from *McCulloch v. Maryland*.[60] Chief Justice Marshall suggested that one way to measure Maryland's taxing power was to limit it in accordance with the "original right of taxation": the right of the people within a state to authorize taxes upon themselves, their property, and objects brought within the state's sovereign jurisdiction.[61] One argument for this approach was that:

> If we measure the power of taxation residing in a state, by the extent of sovereignty which the people of a single state possess, and can confer on its government, we have an intelligible standard, applicable to every case to which the power may be applied . . . We are not driven to the perplexing inquiry, so unfit for the judicial department, what degree of taxation is the legitimate use, and what degree may amount to the abuse of the power.[62]

An intelligible standard (a question of kind of power) is preferable to a question of degree. Why is a question of degree "so unfit" for judges? The Constitution of its nature cannot provide guidance on such specific questions, because in order to survive the passage of time, it must be confined to the broad objects and goals of government. Questions of degree are contingent questions, based on continually shifting concrete facts that cannot be anticipated by the framers of a constitution.

But compare Chief Justice Marshall's approach to that of Justice Holmes, dissenting in a later case:

> It seems to me that the State Court was right. I should say plainly right, but for the effect of certain dicta of Chief Justice Marshall which culminated in or rather were founded upon his often quoted proposition that the power to tax is the power to destroy. In those days it was not recognized as it is today that most of the distinctions of the law are distinctions of degree. If the States had any power, it was assumed that they had all power, and that the necessary alternative was to deny it altogether. But this Court which so often has defeated the attempt to tax in certain ways can defeat an attempt to discriminate or otherwise go too far without wholly abolishing the power to tax. The power to tax is not the power to destroy while this Court sits.[63]

Modern judges feel no hesitation about deciding questions of degree. In fact, the dominance of the balancing approach makes such decisions the staple of constitutional law.[64]

A New "Necessary and Proper" Clause

A second method for giving new content to "constitutional" commands is to graft onto the Constitution a new unwritten clause: "The judiciary may make all necessary and proper laws for the effectual advancement of all rights contained in this Constitution." This trend is part of a general shift of the Court's function from protecting particular *constitutional* rights to a more general protection of noneconomic individual liberties. The Court has extended its protection of liberties beyond those specified by the Constitution itself by arguing that other, *unspecified*, rights are necessary to protect the substance of the rights that are specified.

An example of this reasoning is the exclusionary rule in Fourth Amendment search-and-seizure cases. The Fourth Amendment lays down a general principle that citizens shall be protected against unreasonable searches and seizures and specifies that warrants shall be issued only when certain conditions are met. There is no explicit statement one way or the other about the admissibility of unconstitutionally seized evidence, although the early common-law rule was that it was admissible.[65] The Court in *Weeks v. United States*[66] argued:

> if letters and private documents, can thus be seized and held and used in evidence against a citizen accused of an offense, the protection of the Fourth Amendment, declaring his right to be secure against such searches and seizures, is of no value, and, so far as those thus placed are concerned, might as well be stricken from the Constitution.[67]

The Court thus made provision for (legislated) an exclusionary rule in order to protect the specifically enumerated right to freedom from unlawful searches and seizures. Of course, even with the exclusionary rule, the right has been negated in practice: the unreasonable search and seizure cannot be undone. The question is more about the harmful effects of the unconstitutional act and the remedy for them, if any. The real issue is whether relief from the harmful *effects* of the unconstitutional search and seizure is part of the Fourth Amendment right.

The tightness of the link between the constitutionally protected right and the new right asserted in a particular case can vary substantially.

The potential for expansion of judicial power inherent in a loose connection can be seen in the Court's opinion in *Griswold v. Connecticut*,[68] where Justice Douglas outlined a theory of penumbral rights. These are rights that, although not specifically mentioned in the Constitution, can be found in it because "without those peripheral rights the specific rights would be less secure."[69] Thus, the "specific guarantees in the Bill of Rights have penumbras, formed by emanations from those guarantees that help give them life and substance . . . Various guarantees create zones of privacy."[70] While these rights are not "expressly included" in the Constitution, they may be "necessary in making the express guarantees fully meaningful."[71]

Note that, unlike the argument for the exclusionary rule, no absolutely necessary connection is asserted here between the specific right and the newly claimed right. The specific rights would only be "less" secure, and the peripheral rights only "help" give them life and substance. Such a doctrine of penumbral rights inevitably permits considerable judicial extension of original constitutional rights.

The right of privacy, created in *Griswold*[72] and extended in *Roe v. Wade*[73] to strike down abortion laws, is an example of this trend. The right to "privacy" in these cases is actually a right to autonomy, to do what one wants to do, and as such could be applied to strike down virtually any limit on what a person wants to do, although the Court will limit this broad right to those cases where it feels strongly enough (and believes that it has sufficient support among intellectual elites and the citizenry) that government should not be involved.

The "judicial" necessary and proper clause has also been used in other procedural-rights cases. For example, the Sixth Amendment right to counsel is a right that holds "in all criminal prosecutions." This would suggest that a defendant has a right to the assistance of counsel during trial and perhaps during the legal proceedings leading up to the trial, that is, after "prosecution" has begun. But the court extended that right to preprosecution circumstances in *Escobedo v. Illinois*,[74] on the ground that

> a Constitution which guarantees a defendant the aid of counsel at . . . trial could surely vouchsafe no less to a defendant under interrogation by the police in a completely extrajudicial proceeding . . . Anything less . . . might deny a defendant "effective representation by counsel at the only stage when legal aid and advice would help him."[75]

In effect the Court is saying that the same general reasons that make counsel necessary in a criminal prosecution also make it necessary before the beginning of a prosecution. The Court, therefore, expanded the constitutional right to counsel "in all criminal prosecutions," by grafting onto it an added right to counsel even before the prosecution of the defendant has begun. As a matter of policy, that may or may not be objectionable. Certainly, however, it is adding a new right over and above what the Constitution itself provided.

A similar way to expand constitutional rights is to substitute for the words of the Constitution new words that possess wider or narrower meanings. Starting from one word with a particular meaning, one could interchangeably employ a different word that includes the meaning of the first but also includes something else. Thus, one can "build" on original constitutional rights and begin to include new rights, which are linked to the old ones by a common concept. On this point Justice Black has some notably accurate observations:

> One of the most effective ways of diluting or expanding a constitutionally guaranteed right is to substitute for the crucial word or words of a constitutional guarantee another word or words, more or less flexible and more or less restricted in meaning. This fact is well illustrated by the use of the term "right of privacy" as a comprehensive substitute for the Fourth Amendment's guarantee against "unreasonable searches and seizures." "Privacy" is a broad, abstract and ambiguous concept which can easily be shrunken in meaning but which can also on the other hand easily be interpreted as a constitutional ban against many things other than searches and seizures.[76]

Finally, there is a similar way to add to the Constitution by building on ambiguous precedents to extend a provision beyond its original meaning. For example, in *Skinner v. Oklahoma*,[77] the Court struck down a law requiring sterilization of criminals after commission of a certain number of specified crimes. The Court said that it was essential to view with "strict scrutiny" legislation dealing with "one of the basic rights of men," one that is "fundamental."[78] At the same time, however, the Court explicitly denied that it intended thereby "to re-examine the scope of the police power of the States."[79] Two decades later in *Shapiro v. Thompson*,[80] however, the Court cited *Skinner* as a precedent for the proposition that it is unconstitutional to impinge upon the exercise of a constitutional right without a showing of a *compelling state interest*.[81] What had been a common-sense observation of the seriousness of a particular and unique case became a precedent for a complete reformulation of (and restriction on) the state police power. Likewise, the Court's offhand reference to the "necessity" of vaccination in *Jacobson v. Massachusetts*[82] was turned into a justification for substantial restriction on the state police power in *Bates v. Little Rock.*[83] Over time, accretions to original constitutional meanings can expand (or contract) the meaning substantially.

To the extent that the judiciary can add a new right if judges believe that such a new right would further the ends sought by specific constitutional rights, the judiciary has been granted new powers that the Constitution originally left to the legislative branch. To this extent, the Constitution has become much less relevant to the content of constitutional law.

A Note on a Different Quarter

In this chapter, I have dealt with what I would call the mainstream modern movement to take the Constitution out of constitutional law.[84] It is worth noting that, paradoxically, there is a danger of taking the Constitution out of constitutional law from a very different quarter: that of "strict constructionists" such as Thomas Jefferson. What characterized his thought was an excessive emphasis on history:

> On every question of construction, carry ourselves back to the time when the Constitution was adopted, recollect the spirit manifested in the debates, and instead of trying what meaning may be squeezed out of the text, or invented against it, conform to the probable one in which it was passed.[85]

Jefferson does not discuss how one is to ascertain the "spirit manifested in the debates" on the ratification of the Constitution. In the bitter political struggles of the 1790s, Federalists and Republicans both claimed to represent the true "spirit" of the Constitution. Some claimed the "spirit" was a dissatisfaction with the Articles of Confederation because of its weakness, and a desire to establish a more energetic and stable government,[86] while others claimed it was a spirit of jealous liberty, intent on preserving republicanism against any monarch or consolidated government.[87]

It is hard to resist the impression that Jefferson identified the spirit of the people in the ratification debates with his own political principles. Moreover, the appeal to the spirit is ambiguous in another way. When considering the question of, for example, establishing a national bank under the necessary and proper clause, would Jefferson have the interpreters ask, "what did the people in the ratification debates understand by 'necessary and proper'?" or would he have them ask, "what would they have thought of a national bank?""? Would he appeal to their understanding of constitutional principles or would he speculate about how they would have applied them to concrete cases?

In thus deemphasizing the text of the document vis-a-vis the (alleged) spirit of the ratification debates, Jefferson may have been trying to undercut the legitimate construction of the document itself. The nature of this process could result in substituting history—or an interpreter's skewed version of it—for the Constitution itself.[88]

As my analysis in chapter 3 suggested, Raoul Berger, author of *Government by Judiciary: The Transformation of the Fourteenth Amendment*,[89] can at times be charged with the same error. I am, however, generally more sympathetic to Berger's reliance on history in *Government by Judiciary* because he was dealing with the arguably ambiguous words of the Fourteenth Amendment. Where wording is ambiguous, I think there is a stronger ground for relying on historical intent, as gathered from historical research, and not merely on the text of the document itself, in order to confirm the appropriateness of deferring to the political branches (which is normally appropriate in cases of genuine ambiguity). I would not go as far as Berger did, however, in making that kind of historical research *the* norm for constitutional interpretation. I would, again for reasons discussed in chapter 3, particularly disagree with his insistence that the expectations of the framers, known in ways apart from the constitutional text, are as authoritative as if they were written in the text.

This by no means undercuts all of Berger's arguments, because many of them concerned not merely what the Fourteenth Amendment's framers "expected" in the way of specific applications, but the actual *principles* the framers were embodying in given provisions. Still, I think that Berger did overemphasize the historical approach and underemphasize the fair reading of the document in his general discussion of interpretation.

Despite Berger's valuable historical research on the intention of the framers of the Fourteenth Amendment, which shed great light on many questions, it cannot be said that he conclusively established that intention on all points. Some of his conclusions were unassailable. The Fourteenth Amendment was not intended to deal with political rights, for example, voting.[90] Others are, I think, wrong: the equal protection clause is not limited to discriminatory legislation alone, but extends to discriminatory enforcement (for example, selective nonenforcement) of laws.[91] To other questions, there are only less clear-cut answers.

An example of the last category is school segregation. Berger presented some solid evidence that segregated education was not intended to be prohibited by the Fourteenth Amendment: direct statements by a few individuals in debate on the Civil Rights Bill, indirect statements opposing "social equality" for blacks, removal of a "no discrimination" clause from the Civil Rights Bill (because it was too broad), the practice of Northern states in providing for or permitting separate schools, maintenance of segregated schools in the District of Columbia, segregation in the Senate gallery, and public and congressional references to the establishment of schools for blacks.[92] This evidence is not *determinative*. One cannot assume a one-to-one correspondence of the Civil Rights Bill and the Fourteenth Amendment in all respects. One cannot automatically conclude, from the statement of certain individuals, the opinion of the whole Congress or of state legislatures (as Berger ably showed about the incorporation of the Bill of Rights, in regard to remarks by the floor leaders in both houses).[93] The overwhelming focus of the Congress on providing a basis for congressional (not judicial) enforcement of rights[94] might explain why contemporary segregative practices (in states, the District of Columbia, the Senate gallery) were not eliminated simply by passage of the amendment and had to await future action by Congress. The early practice of government after ratification of the amendment, including passage of civil rights bills based on a broader reading of the Fourteenth Amendment than Berger's, cannot be completely dismissed as after-the-fact extensions of its meaning, since traditional canons of interpretation give some weight to such practice as an indication of intent.[95] Some people used the term "civil rights" in a very limited (Blackstonian) sense of "security of life, liberty, and property," as Berger showed, but others used it more broadly. For example, Berger cited Representative John A. Bingham to the effect that "civil rights include and embrace every right that pertains to a citizen as such," including "political rights."[96]

Still, even if his own case is not air-tight, Berger was quite right that the position of his opponents is virtually indefensible. The strongest of these arguments was the possibility that section 1 of the Fourteenth Amendment was meant to be "open-ended," to "expand with the future." But as Berger showed, the case for this is very weak. For example, if "equal protection" was meant to be "open-ended," how could its supporters so definitely rule out the possibility that it guaranteed political rights such as voting, as they did over and over again?[97]

Berger's historical case is overwhelmingly the stronger. But rather than rest the case simply on historical grounds, he would have done well to rely not only on history, but also on the limits of judicial review (some of which he discussed in Part Two of his book).[98] Where the basis for legislative action (or inaction, for that matter) is a reasonable constitutional opinion, judges should defer to the legislature.

If Berger had not relied so much on historical intent, then he might have avoided certain common misinterpretations of his work. For example, Berger did not say only that the framers of the Fourteenth Amendment did not have school desegregation *in mind* when they wrote the equal protection clause, or that they would not have *expected* that clause to require school desegregation. He said that there was a definite understanding of the general principle embodied in the words "equal protection of the laws" (namely, that persons are guaranteed equality with respect to state laws for security of life and property), and that this general principle does not properly extend to the requirement of school desegregation. By relying so much on historical intent, Berger opened himself up to a charge (sometimes legitimately) that he was substituting obscure historical research for the Constitution itself. In view of the genuine contribution of much of his work to a proper understanding of the Fourteenth Amendment, that was unfortunate.

Conclusion

The Constitution has, to a very great extent, simply been taken out of constitutional law. Of course, the discussion does not end here. One might accept all that I have said and applaud this tendency.[99] In a way, the more important question is whether the Constitution *should* be taken out of constitutional law or put back in. We turn now to that question by examining some of the arguments on behalf of a more activist judiciary that have been put forward recently by several well-known legal commentators: Laurence Tribe (with Michael Dorf) and Harry Wellington.

5

The Result-Oriented
Adjudicator's Guide to
Constitutional Law I:
Laurence Tribe and Michael Dorf

In the 1960s it was difficult to find outstanding books that articulated the foundation for and gave a defense of broad judicial activism—with very little discussion it had simply become the ruling dogma of the legal academy. Perhaps the most important theoretical book of that period was Alexander Bickel's *The Least Dangerous Branch*, which provided a rudimentary rationale for post-*Marbury* modern judicial review, but endeavored earnestly to prevent it from becoming "judicial activism." The measure of this work's failure was the plethora of influential law review articles providing various theoretical grounds for much broader judicial activism from the late 1960s into the 1970s. At that time, judicial activism seemed utterly dominant in the intellectual world, even as Republican presidents made appointments that reined in the Warren Court. In the mid-1970s, Raoul Berger came to symbolize the threat to judicial activism with the publication of his *Government by Judiciary*, a book almost universally attacked by the legal intelligentsia. Yet this book, together with the political conservativism dominant during the Reagan years and the public reaction to some judicial decisions (especially *Roe v. Wade*), shaped subsequent legal discussion. In the early 1980s, John Hart Ely and Jesse Choper defended forms of judicial activism that claimed to recognize greater constraints on judicial power, though at this same time, Michael Perry and especially Ronald Dworkin continued to preach a more unabashed activism.[1] The battle took on new dimensions with the confirmation hearings for Robert Bork, which were followed by his own attack on judicial activism in *The Tempting of America* and with an attack from the left on *all* constitutional theory, in books such as Mark Tushnet's *Red, White, and Blue*.

As we entered the 1990s, proponents of judicial activism seemed to be rallying. The specter of an increasingly conservative Supreme Court certainly made a contribution, although in some cases that had the effect of providing liberals with a sober second thought about judicial activism.[2] Perhaps judicial activists were simply tired of having to make obeisances in the direction of what they saw as the prevailing conservative tendencies (much as Mario Cuomo/Paul Tsongas/Tom Harkin liberal Democrats tired of apologizing for liberalism in the face of a string of electoral defeats at the presidential level). The election of Bill Clinton, which brought prospects of more liberal judicial appointments, certainly reinforced hopes for a resurgence of judicial activism.

Enter Laurence Tribe and Michael Dorf and Harry Wellington, ready to resurrect the unabashed judicial activism of the glory days of the Warren Court. Despite an occasional bow to the need for limits on judicial review, the central message of their books, *On Reading the Constitution* and *Interpreting the Constitution*, is that modern, activist judicial review is simply an inevitable and altogether desirable aspect of "Our Common Law Method."

The Argument

Laurence Tribe's and Michael Dorf's *On Reading the Constitution* starts with a survey of ways *not* to read the Constitution, which is largely a whirlwind tour of contemporary theories of judicial review, with their bite-sized critiques. There is no way of returning to the founding, they say, despite the efforts of Garry Wills, Raoul Berger, and Edwin Meese, because the originalist view is internally inconsistent and incapable of dealing with the elaboration of doctrine and precedent that has occurred since the founding. The principles are the same, but they must be applied to a changing reality. Returning to the source, "we find an invitation not to linger too obsessively in the past" (12).

But reading the Constitution is not an exercise in wish fulfillment for the reader either, though attention to the text cannot eliminate judicial choice (*pace* Richard Posner). Ronald Dworkin's enterprise, despite its insights, is too unbounded, as are approaches such as Michael Perry's that seem to rest on vague assertions about "the essence of the American spirit" (17) (and Tribe and Dorf refuse to accept Henry Monaghan's similar characterization of Tribe). The Constitution is not totally indeterminate, nor can it properly be determined only by the reader's view of the good society. People can be without "faith in the timeless, the universal, the unquestionable," and still "*know* that slavery and murder are wrong, even if they cannot derive these truths from first principles" (19).

Constitutional interpretation must avoid the twin fallacies of "disintegration" and "hyper-integration." Dis-integration involves reading one part of the Constitution without considering other parts. Supporters of the death penalty do this when they note the implied acceptance of the death penalty in the due process clause without giving separate weight to the guarantee against cruel and unusual punishment. Mark Tushnet does it when he wants to read the Constitution to advance socialism, because he exalts the equal protection clause only by denying parts of the Constitution that affirm private property rights. Those who deny weight to the Tenth Amendment as a limit on federal power, because it only guarantees states' residual powers, forget that the presuppositions behind the original meaning of the Tenth Amendment have been altered by the Seventeenth Amendment.

Hyper-integration consists in seeing a single, unitary vision—a seamless web—underlying the Constitution. Even apart from the presence of slavery in the original document, which should make us hesitate, we must acknowledge that the Constitution has an "undeniably plural and internally divided nature" (25), which is not a sad reality, but a strength. We cannot argue that constitutional amendments are unconstitutional. We cannot follow John Hart Ely in reading some things out of the Constitution in order to pursue a pure representation-reinforcing, democracy-protecting judicial review. Nor can we, with Jesse Choper, pursue individual rights so strongly that we rule out judicial review in federalism and separation of powers cases. Richard Epstein's "sadly singleminded vision" of the Constitution as the protection of property will not do, nor will David Richards's more elevated and lofty, sympathetic and humane view (28). Resisting hyper-integration will make us worry less than critical legal scholars about the "internal contradictions and anomalies" of "liberal constitutional scholarship" (29). There is no need to reduce to a single theme all aspects of the Constitution. Inconsistency (even with democracy) is "hardly earth-shattering" (30).

The second chapter provides us with a middle path—not "an overarching theory of constitutional interpretation," but a sketch of "some acceptable approaches to the enterprise" (31). What do we learn from two centuries of that enterprise? Judicial ingenuity is indispensable, and our most regrettable decisions have often come from mechanical, wooden, and insensitive interpretation (e.g., *Dred Scott*). No formula can eliminate the need for judicial choice. The "best way to achieve wisdom in constitutional interpretation is to subject all constitutional arguments and decisions to constant analysis and continuing critique . . . The Constitution is . . . a text to be interpreted and reinterpreted in an unending search for understanding" (32–33). It channels choice without eliminating it.

Choice is often necessary even in easy cases, where the text is supposedly clear, for example, the prohibition of bills of attainder and the Nixon papers case. The First Amendment (a specific provision, at least relative to others such as due process) gives rise to cases like *Arcara v. Cloud Books* (where police closed an adult bookstore on the grounds of the sex acts being committed there). That Tribe and Dorf (First Amendment liberals) agree with the Court "conservatives" in upholding the closing of the shop, against the Court "liberals," is an illustration of "how honest and conscientious readers of a quite specific constitutional provision, engaged in the process of genuine interpretation, can reach entirely opposite conclusions, regardless of their overall philosophical leanings" (37).

What, then, of parts of the text that are less precise? Tribe and Dorf conjure up a hypothetical involving an act of Congress prohibiting state laws allowing home rule to municipalities, and then dance through analysis of various federalism cases, including *Usery* and *Garcia*. After twitting "strict constructionist" justices such as Rehnquist for inconsistency in their reliance on something as nebulous as the "tacit postulates" of the constitutional system, they ultimately rely on the republican guarantee clause to ground a right of states to choose home-rule arrangements. The lessons they draw from this discussion are four: 1) relying on an amendment written so that it cannot plausibly apply (the Tenth) won't do; 2) relying on an overall, unstructured system of tacit postulates won't do; 3) searching the Constitution for other applicable texts is an available option; 4) but the text on which we settle must be able to support the weight we would make it bear.

Tribe and Dorf then shift to another hypothetical in order to discuss the search for unenumerated rights. Suppose a local ordinance enjoins families to eat at home, alone, at least once a month, and precede the meal with a moment of thankful silence. They lead the reader through a preliminary discussion of the establishment clause and free speech issues and finally arrive at the core issues, which involve substantive due process, privileges and immunities, and the Ninth Amendment. The latter is used as a ground for rejecting the argument that substantive due process is too unclear to ground a constitutional right: that would be to "disparage" an unenumerated right. One legitimate method of constitutional interpretation is to seek unenumerated rights by drawing on other parts of the text, coupled with history. The First, Third, and Fourth Amendments suggest a tacit postulate of the document with a textual root: "consensual intimacies within the home are presumptively protected as a privilege of United States citizens" (60). This provides a ground for striking down the hypothetical ordinance, as well as for defending the Court's privacy decisions and the dissent in *Hardwick* (the homosexual sodomy case).

Finally, Tribe and Dorf apply this approach to the hardest case of all, *Roe v. Wade*. The privacy interest of the woman is clear, but there is the asserted state interest in protecting the unborn. Ultimately, Tribe and Dorf feel that it is necessary to rely on the equal protection clause to find sufficient grounds for the decision (since the law does not require men to use their bodies to save the lives of others). They do, however, criticize *Roe* for the unnecessary breadth of the decision; it would have been preferable to follow the slower, common-law method of case by-case formulation and reformulation. Judges should deal with such troubling cases with caution and humility, and we must "urge one another, along with the judges who bear a special responsibility in constitutional matters, to engage in reasoned conversation with as open a set of minds as we can possibly muster" (63). Indeed, we should welcome these divisions as an opportunity for dialogue within the Court—a dialogue made necessary by the fact that "the Constitution *itself* embodies a multitude of irreconcilable differences" (64).

The third chapter takes up the question of how the Constitution channels judicial value choices. Looking at the Constitution alone (as Robert Bork suggests) is not enough. If only flat contradictions are unconstitutional, then hardly anything will be unconstitutional. What is the middle ground between the literal text and judges' subjective values? Tribe and Dorf suggest that we identify the central value of a clause by trying to "locate that clause within the overall structure of the rest of the Constitution—to ask whether the practices that are either mandated or proscribed by the Constitution presuppose some view without which these textual requirements are incoherent" (69–70). One way of doing this is to look at the framers' overall philosophy. For example, the legal realist view of property rights (that they are merely creations of the law) is incompatible with constitutional provisions such as the takings clause, which presume that property rights can be prepolitical, reflecting something like a Lockean view of property. But text and framers' philosophy are rarely dispositive. More commonly, the elaboration of constitutional values proceeds from prior decisions. Why is precedent so important? "Perhaps the best answer that can be given is an institutional one: the Supreme Court, as a court, is most properly trusted to read cases, especially its own cases" (72). This is not an easy task. To illustrate it, Tribe and Dorf turn to the question of identifying fundamental rights.

The question of whether a particular right is fundamental will usually turn on another question: at what level of generality should the previously established right, and the right currently claimed, be described? For example, is *Griswold* properly characterized as a right to contraceptives or a right to a variety of procreative decisions? Abortion cases will turn on the answer to that question. Tribe and Dorf develop this issue largely through a discussion of *Bowers v. Hardwick*. Is the case about "a right to homosexual sodomy," as the majority says, or about "the right to be let alone," as the dissent argues? How does one choose between competing abstractions?

Harlan's opinion in *Poe v. Ullman* is taken as a model. It looks at the connection of rights in the Bill of Rights and infers unifying principles at a higher level of abstraction. "[I]f constitutional decision-making is to be in any sense 'rational,' then one must seek rationalizing—that is, unifying—principles to link disparate decisions" (78). The *Hardwick* majority seems radically reductionist in its rejection of the need for unifying principles, between areas of child rearing and family, marriage, and procreation. (One cannot offer protection of the traditional nuclear family as the underlying principle—it would not explain *Eisenstadt* and *Moore*, and there is no plausible connection with constitutional text, structure, or history.) But if there is no reliance on more general unifying principles, then there is no limit on judicial subjectivity in deciding cases.

The problem with the task of securing unifying principles is that there is almost always more than one. This is true even for originalists like Bork, since they must identify intent at some particular level of generality. Bork, for example, has to avoid the most specific level of intent in order to save *Brown v. Board of Education*. "[T]he interpretation of words, structure, and history can usually 'fairly support' a wide variety of conclusions. The value-laden *choice* of a level of generality remains" (80).

The fourth chapter is an excursion into other disciplines—literature and mathematics—to see whether they can provide perspective on what is unique about interpreting the Constitution. Tribe and Dorf take up Dworkin's image of writing a chain novel, noting that novels can have different possible endings (as Dickens's *Great Expectations* did, for example). The judgment about which ending is best is necessarily a judgment based on values external to the text itself. The same is true of constitutional interpretation. (For example, *Roe v. Wade* is consistent with *Eisenstadt*, but not dictated by it.) On the other hand, some endings can be ruled out—that is, completely *non sequitur* endings— not so much by logic as by widely shared aesthetic judgments. Likewise, the internal structure of prior cases and widely shared values rule out some formulations of a fundamental right (e.g., if *Griswold* had gone the other way, that would have ruled out *Roe*). The difficulty arises when appeal is made to values that are not widely shared, as occurs in virtually any interesting case.

Having shown how law is like literature, Tribe turns to an influential argument of the mathematician Lakatos, to show how it is unlike math. Lakatos argues that mathematics is not an accumulation of proven truths, but a process by which proofs are made more rigorous as they are subjected to counterexamples and criticisms. Tribe uses the example of the theorem that the sum of the angles of a triangle is 180 degrees. How does one respond to the counterexample of a triangle drawn on the surface of a sphere? There are three approaches: 1) "monster-barring," wherein one simply denies that "triangles" include enclosed areas on the surface of a sphere, 2) "exception-barring," an ad hoc maneuver in which one modifies the proposition to exclude triangles on the surface of a sphere, and 3) "lemma-incorporation," by which one specifies that the proposition is true for all triangles where Euclid's Fifth Postulate holds, thus specifying the domain of validity of the original proof.

Monster-barring in law includes making a distinction without a difference (e.g., limiting *Flast v. Cohen* to cases involving the taxing and spending power, to distinguish *Valley Forge Christian College*, which arises under Article IV). Exception-barring includes relying on the holdings of previous cases while ignoring their rationales (e.g., the way the majority opinions in *Morrison v. Olsen* and *Oregon v. Smith* treat precedents). But there is no lemma-incorporation in law—that is where the analogy breaks down. Math proceeds from assumed unprovable postulates, whereas legal arguments turn on the truth or falsity of the preliminary assumptions.

The final chapter starts out with a lengthy critique of Justice Scalia's *Michael H.* footnote 6, which is an attempt to eliminate the levels of generality problem. Scalia argues that, insofar as substantive due process arguments turn on societal traditions, the appropriate level of generality is "the most specific level at which a relevant tradition protecting, or denying protection to, the asserted right can be identified." But historical traditions, Tribe and Dorf argue, are even more subject to manipulation than legal precedents. For example, does the establishment clause embody a deeply rooted tradition of separation of church and state, such that religious displays on public property are unconstitutional? Tradition here is conflicted (e.g., a Massachusetts establishment that lasted until 1833 and a Virginia religious liberty statute from before the Constitution). Even if there were a consensus, that would not help. The absence of laws encroaching on a right does not indicate the fundamentality of that right, nor would the presence of positive laws encroaching on a right negate its fundamentality (otherwise, a pattern of government violations of a norm would justify continued violations).

Moreover, historical traditions, like rights, exist at various levels of generality. Jefferson's religious liberty act resonates with Enlightenment ideals, but historians have shown that the political impetus for the act came from religiously fervent nonconformists. So there is a tradition of toleration in Virginia's positive law, but also doubt as to whether there was such a tradition in Virginia's social attitudes. Likewise, there was a nineteenth-century American tradition of harmony between government and religion (especially Christianity), but we cannot assume that the Constitution is whatever the majority practices, since that would make it a dead letter.

> History provides ambiguous guidance both because historical traditions can be indeterminate, and because even when we discover a clear historical tradition it is hardly obvious what the existence of that tradition tells us about the Constitution's meaning. (100)

As Scalia's writing on originalism shows, he is aware of the difficulties with it, but prefers it to subjective, illegitimate, nonoriginalist modes of interpretation. He might respond: "better some ambiguity than to abandon the historical enterprise entirely." But he fails to answer the question of how we know when to reject a historical pattern or understanding, which he concedes we must do at times (e.g., with respect to practices of early American history such as public flogging and hand-branding). But this applies to a "most specific level of tradition" approach as well as to originalism.

Moreover, how do we measure "specificity"? Are positive laws more or less specific than social attitudes? Are social attitudes on one subject (say, gender) more or less specific than those on another (e.g., religion)? In *Michael H.*, Scalia says that if there is no societal tradition respecting rights of natural fathers of children conceived adulterously, then the Court should consult traditions regarding natural fathers in general. But why not consult general traditions regarding children adulterously conceived?

How does one measure specificity in a case like *Roe v. Wade*? If there is no dispositive tradition regarding the right of women to control their reproductive freedom when that results in the destruction of a fetus (as the Court argued), then what is the next most specific tradition? A tradition regarding women's reproductive freedom in general? A tradition regarding rights of the fetus (e.g., laws against feticide by someone not the mother)? One simply has to choose, since there is no way of measuring specificity here.

Scalia's formulation is already a considerable abstraction. On the facts of this case, he could have asked more specifically about traditions regarding the rights of a natural father of a child conceived in an adulterous *but long-standing* relationship, *where the father has played a major role in the child's early development*. Since it is doubtful there is a tradition that specific, what should be abstracted away? Should we abstract from the father's relationship with the mother and child, as Scalia does, or should we abstract from the adulterous character of the relationship with the mother, as Brennan does?

Scalia knows that his approach would severely curtail the Supreme Court's role in protecting individual liberties (as his *Cruzan* opinion shows). He says that this is no problem, since most of our protection comes from the equal protection clause anyway. But equal protection does not protect unpopular liberties. Laws forbidding homosexual sodomy or flag-burning apply to everyone, but they would only restrict the actions of the minorities that want to engage in those activities. If Scalia does not focus on the literal statute, but on differently situated individuals (so that homosexual sodomy receives the same treatment as heterosexual vaginal intercourse), then he would be back to a high level of generality, which he does not accept. There is no room in Scalia's equal protection for nontraditional liberties.

Finally, Tribe and Dorf argue, this tradition-bound method does not require judges to control their biases, but permits them to import them surreptitiously. Like original intent according to Justice Brennan, it is "arrogance cloaked in humility." In another footnote in *Michael H.*, Scalia criticizes the two-step approach of identifying a fundamental liberty interest and then balancing it against state interests, arguing that the state's possible justification be incorporated into the definition of the liberty. But unless the state interest is absurd, this would render the liberty so specific as to seem insupportable or at least radically disconnected from precedent. (*Roe* becomes the right to destroy a fetus, *New*

York Times v. Sullivan becomes the right to libel a public official, the *Mapp* exclusionary rule becomes a right of the criminal to suppress the truth, and so on.) Were Scalia's suggestion only a plea for a sliding scale, it would be harmless, but Scalia's hostility to balancing makes this a dubious explanation. Combining the two footnotes, Scalia would start from the most specific tradition *and* one that has the state interest built in from the start, with the result that a liberty to frustrate various state policies could not count as a liberty deeply rooted in tradition. That approach would be a tool for overruling all the Court's individual rights decisions, or (more likely) a method to be deployed selectively, allowing judges to define rights more or less abstractly according to their own views of how important the rights are.

The final section of the book argues that legal thinking, the method of the common law, requires the even-handed application of general principles to concrete situations. Principles must be abstract (distinct from intuitions about specific fact situations). The call for more abstract principles (while it can be dangerous when principles are applied to fields for which they were not crafted) is on the whole a source of progressive pressure, pushing us to check our practices against our principles. A philosophy that refused to generalize would restrict the Declaration's "all men are created equal" to propertied men or free men or white men or all three in conjunction. In a perfect world ("if men were angels"), generalization of rights would be done by elected legislatures, but "the framers of our Constitution understood that this is not a perfect world, and thus, like it or not, judges must squarely face the task of deciding how to define our liberties" (110).

What are the checks on judges' making subjective judgments? There is the requirement that fundamental rights be connected to the constitutional text. And there is the test of whether the asserted level of generality provides an appropriate description of already-protected rights, without reference to newly asserted rights. Judges must first determine what concerns actually underlay the prior decisions, and only after selecting the appropriate level of generality to describe those concerns should they test the asserted specific right against that abstraction. This does not eliminate judicial value choice, but it does channel it. Scalia's position is a form of judicial nihilism, since it assumes that there is no way to read prior cases on their own terms so as to discern rationally the level of generality at which a right was recognized.

The method of the common law assumes that judges have the tools to do this. A too-abstract right will be recognizable as such whenever its enunciation requires us to ignore much of what was said in cases that allegedly established it (e.g., a right to privacy used to justify selling narcotics or assisting an otherwise healthy individual to poison himself). The boundaries of this private sphere undoubtedly "are difficult to ascertain, and are fluid through time" (115). But "to marshal this uncertainty in support of a jurisprudence that allows traditions of intolerance to insulate intrusive government activities forever from constitutional scrutiny is to question much more than the enterprise of fundamental rights: it is to question law itself" (115).

Tribe and Dorf bemoan that even progressive scholars increasingly hesitate to generalize fundamental rights (citing Cass Sunstein's shift of focus from due process to equal protection). Whatever its status as a matter of advocacy and strategy, this shift is dubious as a matter of constitutional theory. There is a basic choice to be made: between emphasizing the conservative functions of both clauses or their potential as generators of critique and change. The choice must be justified extratextually, but it should be implemented in ways that draw as much guidance as possible from the text. The model is Justice Harlan's *Poe* dissent: a moderately conservative orientation toward generalization, with an effort to seek unifying structures for specified rights in an intermediate level of generality drawing heavily upon textual points of reference.

The Constitution's text—in the First Amendment's protection of peaceful assembly and in the special solicitude for the home in the Third and Fourth Amendments—points toward generalizing in the direction of intimate personal association in the privacy of the home rather than generalizing in the direction of freedom of choice in matters of procreation. That is why *Hardwick* is so egregiously wrong, why *Roe* is a much closer and more difficult case, and why a right to use a sperm bank would be a bold leap, and a right to enforce a surrogacy contract (against a woman who has changed her mind and wishes to keep her gestational child) is inadmissible.

The Defective Critique of Originalism

Tribe and Dorf refer to originalism on numerous occasions, but their comments are generally unoriginal, consisting mostly of standard citations and bald assertions. Deciding what a "speedy" trial is, they say, is as subjective as saying that Fourteenth Amendment "liberty" includes the right to have sex without children. The exact line between "speedy" and "not speedy" may be grey, but there is a world of difference between that and the privacy cases. The clause is not just "liberty"—it is deprivation of liberty "without due process of law," so having sex without children is not in the Fourteenth Amendment at all.

Historical traditions are difficult to specify, as the case of religion shows, they say. But that is one area where the legal tradition is rather clear. The fact that Thomas Jefferson and Isaac Backus both supported religious freedom does not indicate that we have a conflicted tradition as far as constitutional law is concerned. It only means that the meaning of the First Amendment religion clauses should be able to embrace them both, along with still others. As Gerard Bradley has shown recently (again), nonpreferentialism—not a "high wall of separation"—is the clear principle of the establishment clause.[3]

Tribe and Dorf try to hang the albatross of *Dred Scott* around the neck of originalism. That decision, they say, resulted not from judicial creativity or ingenuity, but from an overly mechancial, wooden, and insensitive interpretation. But even if Taney's opinion in *Dred Scott* was "originalist," one cannot evaluate originalism on the basis of a poor originalist decision (as Lincoln showed *Dred Scott* to be). And the key principle of *Dred Scott* was a distinctly nonoriginalist reading of the due process clause, the harbinger of future nonoriginalist Court decision-making.

Rehnquist is twitted because, though a "strict construction" justice, he employs "tacit postulates" in a federalism case. I happen to think that Rehnquist was wrong to exercise judicial review in *Usery*,[4] but only a crabbed view of originalism (which is convenient, rhetorically, for nonoriginalists) makes it incompatible with the notion of "tacit postulates." "Strict construction," in the sense of construction faithful to a fair reading of the text, is not a kind of Jeffersonian *narrow* construction that refuses to look beyond the literal words of the text to its structure and implications. The test is whether the alleged tacit postulates can be shown to be necessary implications of the document, understood as a whole, and whether there is sufficient clarity for judges to exercise judicial review. I think that *Usery* fails on the latter standard, but that is not because it involves tacit postulates per se.

Perhaps the most important defect in Tribe and Dorf's understanding of originalism is their assumption—in common with most other critics—that originalism requires that there be a single, clear meaning to all constitutional provisions. Any uncertainty about meaning defeats the case for originalism. Originalism, however, is really a twofold doctrine. First, it holds that the Constitution is generally intelligible and with effort its meaning can be understood—its meaning is not simply and inevitably in the eye of the beholder. Second, it holds that in the absence of a clear meaning—since language cannot be perfect and the framers did not intend to provide rules for all possible future circumstances—the conditions for the exercise of judicial review do not exist.

This second aspect of originalism is derived from reflection on the foundations of judicial review. Judicial review is an implication of the Constitution, fairly read (notwithstanding Bickel and subsequent critics of *Marbury*), but it is an implication with a definite form: judges should prefer the Constitution to an act that is incompatible with it. That presumes that the meaning of the Constitution is *known*. As soon as one makes a successful argument that a constitutional provision, even after careful interpretation, is ambiguous, the conditions of judicial review have been eliminated.

Tribe and Dorf, like most contemporary scholars, tend to take for granted the modern definition of judicial review—a judicial power to define vague phrases of the Constitution and to strike down laws in light of those definitions. Such a definition has no textual support and no support from study of the intention of the founders, that is, no support in the Constitution itself. Yet Tribe and Dorf can ritually invoke the founders: "The framers of our Constitution understood that this is not a perfect world, and thus, like it or not, judges must squarely face the task of deciding how to define our liberties abstractly" (110). You can study the founders for as long as you like, but you will not come across that distinctively modern understanding of judicial review. Of course, it seems unlikely that Tribe and Dorf really care whether that notion comes from the founders; if so, they ought to forgo the rhetorical benefits of invoking them.

Originalism, they rightly see, will result in rare exercise of judicial review, what they call judicial abdication of the responsibility to defend individual rights or severe curtailing of the Court's role in protecting individual rights. But the duty of the Court to defend constitutional rights is not a duty to create them, and unfortunately, there is little in Tribe and Dorf, despite efforts to deny it, to make possible such a distinction. If the Court fails to fulfill such a role, it is not failing to live up to its constitutional duties, but only failing to live up to Tribe's and Dorf's preferences for expansive judicial review. Unlike the Constitution, however, Tribe and Dorf's preferences cannot claim to have authority by means of the explicit consent of the people.

Standardless Constitutional Interpretation

The distinction between dis-integration and hyper-integration, as they describe them, is worthless. It is really something of a *tour de force* to describe as dis-integration an interpretation of the cruel and unusual punishment prohibition that takes into account the implied acceptance of the death penalty in the due process clause, that is, an interpretation that refuses to isolate the two clauses and deny their coherence, that *integrates* them. And if Tribe and Dorf can isolate and deny the implications of the due process clause for the Eighth Amendment, why can't Tushnet isolate the takings clause from the equal protection clause in his pursuit of socialism?

Tribe and Dorf's critique of hyper-integration, for example, as applied to Ely, is quite solid. Unfortunately, it is also applicable to their own interpretation of the Bill of Rights. If imposing a single unitary vision on disparate constitutional provisions is problematic, what are we to make of a constitutional right to intimate association in the home that results from a vision attributed to such provisions as the right peaceably to assemble and to petition the government for a redress of grievances, and the right against quartering soldiers in a home in peacetime? One only wishes that one could be present to hear the reaction of the members of the First Congress if someone had informed them that by the Bill of Rights they had created a right to homosexual sodomy. The Constitution, in the hands of Tribe and Dorf, is a thing of wax. They say, after all, that "the Constitution *itself* embodies a multitude of irreconcilable differences" (64). But they have shown no such thing. Irreconcilable differences only appear when new meanings are invented and attributed to the document. (For example, the much-discussed incompatibility between the establishment and free exercise clauses is a result of modern decisions that changed and expanded their meanings.) Some differences among the framers had to be compromised, of course—slavery being the most obvious. But compromises are not necessarily incoherent, involving irreconcilable differences.

The nebulousness of Tribe and Dorf's Constitution comes across nicely in rhetorical excesses such as: "the American experience teaches that the best way to achieve wisdom in constitutional interpretation is to subject all constitutional arguments and decisions to constant analysis and critique" (32) and "[f]undamentally, the Constitution is, rather, a text to be interpreted and reinterpreted in an unending search for understanding" (33). What are Tribe and Dorf's standards for "wisdom" and "understanding"? As faithful progressivists unwilling to believe in a "static" Constitution, they can give only the vaguest and most formal criteria, which are of little real use. After all, "the very *meaning* of the thing we call 'the Constitution'. . . [is] a reality partly reconstructed by each generation of readers" (9).

One of the most consoling parts of the book for me was the following passage:

For instance, if a mother tells her son, "always do the right thing," we would not think it honorable for her son to ignore her words entirely merely because their intended meaning is not crystal-clear. Rather, we would say that in delivering a somewhat vague message, the mother left to her son the task of applying a general principle to concrete unexpected circumstances. The dutiful son would strive to do the right thing, knowing that he will sometimes falter, but knowing also that if he simply abandons the effort to implement his mother's wishes he will surely fail. So too, judges, legislators, and other officials sworn to uphold the Constitution would be derelict in their duty if they were simply to ignore those parts of the document whose meaning is not crystal-clear to them. (53)

Why consoling? For years I have used this exact analogy in class to describe modern constitutional interpretation and judicial review, always with the fear that I was setting up a straw-man case. And now, behold, I am vindicated. "Always do the right thing," we are told, is a message that is not "crystal-clear"; it is a "somewhat vague message"! Crystal-clear? Somewhat vague? Let's be more blunt: if the framers of the Constitution wrote the document to give *that* message to their successors, their enterprise was a fatuous one. All they would have been doing was to delegate power blindly to . . . of all people, in a democratic republic, unelected and not very accountable judges.

Of course, Tribe and Dorf do not propose that this judicial power go without checks. They make an effort to show that there are some genuine constraints on it. But that effort is an abject failure. Take, for example, the following constraint:

the test should be whether the asserted level of generality provides an appropriate description of already-protected rights without reference to the newly asserted rights . . . the Court must determine what concerns actually underlay the prior decisions; only after the Court has selected the appropriate level of abstraction at which to describe those concerns should it test the asserted specific right against that abstraction. (111)

And, we are told, "a too-abstract right will be recognizable as such whenever its enunciation requires us to ignore much of what was said in the cases that allegedly established it" (114).

Apply this to the authors' own advocacy of a privacy right. The privacy cases, as they describe them, move from 1920s decisions such as *Pierce* and *Meyer* to *Griswold* (vindicating Harlan's dissent in *Poe v. Ullman*), *Eisenstadt*, *Roe v. Wade*, and *Bowers* (actually, the *Bowers* dissent). Does this progression of cases meet the criteria established by our authors? Even putting aside the 1920s cases (whose foundations were deeply intertwined with the property-rights jurisprudence of the time), can it be contended that the succession of cases demonstrates the supposed constraints? Harlan's dissent in *Poe v. Ullman* was profoundly traditional in one way: it connected the privacy right to the sanctity of marriage. (It also explicitly says that homosexuality, among other acts, is not immune from criminal enquiry, belonging to a category "which the law has always forbidden and which can have no claim to social protection.")[5] And Douglas carries over this emphasis into *Griswold*, which concludes with an effort (somewhat lame, in my opinion) to wax rhapsodic on marriage. And yet the Court in *Eisenstadt* finds that marriage is not only not an essential part of that right, but in the equal protection context of that case, *it doesn't even provide a legitimate ground for classification under a rational basis test!* (Later, in *Carey v. Population Services International*, we will discover with Justice Rehnquist that the due process clause "enshrined in the Constitution the right of commercial vendors of contraceptives to peddle them to unmarried minors through such means as window displays and vending machines located in the men's room of truck stops.")[6] If this is a legitimate progression that respects "what concerns actually underlay the prior decisions" and does not "ignore much of what was said in the cases that allegedly established" the right, then criteria that allow such a progression are useless as constraints. The same applies, *a fortiori*, to the extension of the right to abortion and homosexual sodomy.

Another constraint is that the judicially discovered rights must have some textual link with the Constitution. What are the constitutional foundations for a right to homosexual sodomy? They turn out to be the First Amendment's right "peaceably to assemble, and to petition the Government for a redress of grievances," the Third Amendment's guarantee against soldiers being quartered in house in peacetime, or otherwise than by law in wartime, and the Fourth Amendment's guarantee against unreasonable search and seizure. Is this constitutional analysis or a game of free association of ideas? The fact that the Constitution has some guarantees relating to the privacy of the home is no authorization to add to the Constitution new ideas with some ties to the home (as well as public hospitals and bathhouses) about which the Constitution says absolutely nothing. If you want to add another right to the Constitution that is not already there, just do it—but why mangle the notion of interpretation by applying it to such a process?

The answer is clear, of course. It is necessary to maintain, among the general public especially, the illusion that judicial power to negate laws is tied to the Constitution and is not simply an act of judicial will. True, the bloom is already off the illusion to some extent, especially after the Bork and Thomas confirmation processes. But few proponents of judicial activism have the fortitude to dispense with what is left—a prudent judgment, I think, from their perspective.

But the Constitution itself, we hear, tells us in the Ninth Amendment not to disparage unenumerated rights—and therefore it should be no obstacle to judicial enforcement that a right is not enumerated? First, textually, when the question at issue is whether such-and-such is a right or not, the absence of judicial power to mandate it is not necessarily a disparagement. It would be so only if the judiciary had a monopoly on establishing and protecting rights. But the legislature has the power to pass legislation to protect rights. Second, this argument exemplifies the usual amnesia about the constitutional foundations of judicial review: judicial review involves striking down acts that violate the Constitution (and not a Constitution that can be reconstructed from time to time, apart from Article V's requirements for amendment). No constitutional prohibition, no judicial review. For judges *not* to do what they are *not* authorized to do is no disparagement.

Third, and most clearly, Madison made the purpose of the Ninth Amendment "crystal-clear," and it had nothing to do with judicial identification of unenumerated rights. In his speech introducing the Bill of Rights, Madison cites Hamilton's argument in the *Federalist* (No. 84) that enumerating rights will provide a handle for "the doctrine of constructive powers": it will provide a plausible pretence for the federal government to claim power in areas where power is not limited by enumerated rights. Madison acknowledges that an enumeration of rights might be taken to disparage other rights, because "it might follow by implication, that those rights which were not singled out, were intended to be assigned into the hands of the General Government, and were consequently insecure."[7] The Ninth Amendment's rule of construction, then, was to limit the construction of federal powers. What an irony that those who employ it today have used it precisely to aggrandize the powers of the federal government, but in the judicial rather than the legislative sphere.[8]

While criticizing *Roe v. Wade* for its unnecessary breadth, and indicating that it is a "troubling" case involving "tragic choices," Tribe and Dorf try to strengthen it by adding an equal protection component to its rationale (men aren't forced to use their bodies to save lives, so women shouldn't be either). What else can be said about such cases? "We can urge one another, along with the judges who bear a special responsibility in constitutional matters, to engage in reasoned conversation with as open a set of minds as we can possibly muster" (63). Indeed, we can welcome the opportunity for dialogue it provides, "the open ventilation of conflicting views on the meaning of the Constitution" (64).

Is that the way Tribe and Dorf would have reacted to *Dred Scott* or *Plessy v. Ferguson*? Reasoned conversation is always to be valued, of course, but the more important thing that "can be said" about such cases as *Roe v. Wade* is that judges should keep out of them, for they have no authority to overturn laws that in no way violate the Constitution, but are merely inconsistent with a tortured reading imposed on it contrary to any fair rules of interpretation. As for their equal protection argument: it would take a much less tortured reading (although one that I would concede cannot legitimately provide a basis for judicial review) to say that the laws may not refuse to protect fetuses—incipient human beings—from a destruction that it would not allow to be visited upon men or women after birth.

Tribe and Dorf criticize Justice Scalia for "judicial nihilism," because he refuses to engage in the generalizing of constitutional principles they recommend. That is to lack the faith that "judges possess the requisite tools to make principled distinctions in the selection of levels of generality in defining fundamental rights" (114). What Scalia is doing, I suspect, is making the best of a bad situation: assuming that the votes are not present to eliminate the doctrine of substantive due process (as a fair reading of the Constitution would require), he is trying at least to tame it, to prevent it from being the blank check for judicial creation of rights. If he cannot eliminate ambiguity entirely, he can at least substantially limit its use. Is this a lack of faith in judges' capacity to make "principled distinctions in the selection of levels of generality in defining fundamental rights"? It is more radical: it stems from a position that would simply deny judges the power to define fundamental rights, otherwise than by finding them in the document itself by fair interpretation.

And if Scalia needs evidence to show the dangers of "principled generalization of rights," he will not have to look far to find evidence: in this respect, Tribe and Dorf will be a welcome addition to his library.

6

The Result-Oriented Adjudicator's Guide to Constitutional Law II: Harry Wellington

Another clarion call in defense of a significant role for the courts in defining and fleshing out our national values came from the highly respected former dean of Yale Law School, Harry Wellington. Like Tribe and Dorf's book, Wellington's *Interpreting the Constitution* can be viewed as a response of mainstream legal liberalism to the attack on activist judicial review identified most closely in the political world with Edwin Meese and in the world of legal scholarship with Robert Bork, Raoul Berger, and other (not altogether identical) originalists. In my view, it is also like Tribe and Dorf's book in its failure to provide a satisfactory defense of modern, activist judicial review.

The Argument

Harry Wellington's *Interpreting the Constitution* is intended to tell us how "public values" function (and should function) in the elaboration of constitutional provisions, especially due process and especially in regard to the controversial issue of abortion. At another level, it is a book, accessible to the general reader but of interest to scholars, about the process of adjudication and particularly the role of the Supreme Court in constitutional interpretation.

The first two chapters of the book focus on the nature of constitutional adjudication. Cases have two aspects: they resolve present disputes, and they also regulate the future (for parties not involved in the case). The fact that some people are regulated without participating in the case is troubling. It would be less so if law were clear, but that would require it to be static, which is both impossible and undesirable. Given the rapid social, economic, and technological change and the limited ability of legislatures and agencies to cope with it, we must rely on adjudication to change the law over time.

What, in adjudication, is the functional substitute for the access to representatives and electoral accountability that theoretically exists in the legislative process? Courts can distinguish earlier cases to limit their regulatory consequences, and legislatures can usually revise the regulatory effect of judicial opinions. But because legislatures are so busy, and because some cases are grounded on the Constitution and are not subject to judicial review, courts feel freer to override some decisions.

For the parties in later cases, is the ability to distinguish previous cases a functional equivalent of participation in the previous ones? Ultimately, Wellington says "yes." He starts from the ideal that like cases should be treated alike. This doesn't always happen, of course, but there is a strong commitment to the ideal, judges strive to achieve it, because of the nature of the judicial process, and they are reasonably successful. The judicial process is adversarial, and lawyers on both sides are hedged in by the conventions of the legal profession. (These are not static, but they do provide for "an interpretive community.") Moreover, at the appellate level, cases are argued before several judges, with disinterested discussion and negotiation among them. Therefore, adjudication protects parties subject to prior decisions (though strangers to them) in two ways: first, where the interpretive conventions of the legal profession determine that precedents are weak, regulation can be changed; second, where precedents are strong, disputes will be settled by the ideal of like cases being treated alike.

Trouble remains, though: perhaps the conventions of the legal profession are insensitive to some of the many groups making up the American polity as, for example, the law has in the past been insensitive to the perspective of women. This imposes an obligation on the legal community to be increasingly open and diverse. The downside of this is that a more diverse community will bring more perspectives on what is alike in possibly distinguishable cases, and the law will be more ad hoc. This makes law harder to use for planning purposes and settling disputes, and it means an apparent increase in judicial discretion, which bothers some people. But laws made by judges must in the end be "politically digestible," and if a judge is disinterested, then disciplined discretion in reshaping the law is not an evil.

Wellington turns to a special case of adjudication in the second chapter: judicial review. *Marbury v. Madison* is supported though not required by the language of the Constitution, its structure, and the differing functions of the three branches. Nonetheless, the debate over judicial review has continued. Congress cannot be a fair judge of its own power and so the Court assumes the role of umpire. But, as Bickel argued, what is unconstitutional is not self-evident, but a policy issue that someone must decide. Bickel's alternative justification of judicial review was that the Court is the institution best equipped to be the pronouncer and guardian of our nation's enduring values.

Why the continuing anxiety over judicial review? Bickel located its source in the countermajoritarian problem, the undemocratic character of judicial power. But Wellington downplays this issue, arguing that our political system includes many undemocratic aspects (the Senate, the impact of wealth, incumbency, the unelected bureaucracy, etc.). Moreover, judges are more capable of a disinterested perspective. Thus he concludes that judicial review is countermajoritarian, but that makes it not an oddity but a regular feature of our political landscape.

The real source of the anxiety, says Wellington, is the apparent finality of judicial review. But this anxiety can be calmed in several ways. Not only is statutory interpretation (which we readily accept) often more final than it looks, but judicial review is often less final (e.g., as when it focuses on process rather than substance). And no case, at the time of its decision, is final: the decision can be eliminated if it is a mistake and politically indigestible. Moreover, judges are constrained in their value determinations by norms generally applicable in adjudication.

In the third and fourth chapters, Wellington turns to flawed modalities of constitutional adjudication: original intent and "representation-reinforcing" judicial review and judicial restraint. The essential questions are: what are the sources of law, what is a good argument, and what counts as a justification for judicial review? These, in turn, point to consideration of authority (by what right does the Court use a particular interpretive method?) and control of the judiciary (how can the other branches of government and individuals regulated by the court keep the justices in their place?).

Wellington says that the real difference between "interpretivists" and "noninterpretivists" (a false distinction, since all are involved in interpretation—the question is over the sources of law) is not interpretive at all. It is about the nature of American constitutional adjudication—an institution, not a text. Originalists like Robert Bork argue that, when the text is not clear, the questions of authority and control are answered by reading the text in light of original intent.

Wellington argues that originalism is shaky with respect to both questions. First, the question of authority: The founders were deeply divided about most matters, including constitutional interpretation (Wellington here cites H. Jefferson Powell's article). The authority of the text does not extend to the original intention of the founders as a gloss on the text. Evidence suggests that the records are rather unreliable. Constitutional interpreters do not have eighteenth-century minds, the founders themselves had many minds, and what we know about them has been filtered through many other minds.

Another problem for originalism is its consequences. The founders were deeply attached to the protection of property—a protection that modern government has reduced substantially. The founders' ideas about the relation between liberty and property were rooted in the founders' different environment; today's environment calls for a different relation. One might want to reconcile the two by saying that a discussion with the founders would bring them around to the twentieth-century view. But the important point is that there is no fit between originalism and contemporary legal practice.

Wellington argues that originalism rests on two broad and interrelated sets of ideas: the first concerns the certainty of language and methods of discovering its meaning, and the second concerns the allocation of institutional responsibilities between legislative bodies and courts. Originalists are optimistic about the founders' ability to capture complicated ideas precisely in words and about the existence of what we know is missing, a definitive historical record to resolve linguistic ambiguity (which is purposefully pursued in the drafting process). Moreover, there is widespread evidence that the meaning of texts such as the Constitution are never fixed, because they are rich with meanings and with competing accounts of the past attributable to new information and fresh perspectives of increasingly diverse historical and legal professions.

Originalists see a sharp difference between making law and applying it, and if this line is blurred they "contend that courts should keep clear of any action that constitutes an assumption by judges of the drafters' prerogatives—although it is hard to imagine how they could do so, since judges must act" (55).

Wellington offers his own nonoriginalist perspective. First, he is very skeptical about situations where a committee has written the text to be interpreted (which involves negotiation, major problems left unresolved, and open-textured language). "[P]urposeful ambiguity is to legislative drafting what the fastball is to major league baseball. I doubt that it is even coherent to talk about the intention of a class consisting of the framers at Philadelphia and the ratifiers at the state conventions" (56). If he did search for it, he knows that almost certainly it would not reveal itself with sufficient clarity to be the authoritative source of the meaning of the text. Finally, he rejects the sharp distinction between making and applying law. The legislative and judicial processes differ, but they are part of a common enterprise of governing the future wisely. Because of the difficulty of producing a text that controls (over time and in a changing world) the outcome of concrete cases dealing with all aspects of the relation of governments to their constituent parts and of governments to individuals, lawmaking is an inevitable and authorized function of adjudication.

Just as originalism fails on the question of authority, so does it fail on the question of controlling judges. Originalists worry (more than most Americans) that if judges are not limited by text and history they will convert their personal preferences into law and bring about dramatic social and political change through constitutional interpretation. Wellington engages in an extended discussion of the jurisprudence of Justice Hugo Black to show that originalism does not prevent judges from converting their personal preferences into law and that originalism can be used to bring about dramatic change through constitutional interpretation.

Chapter 4 deals with forms of judicial review that eschew substantive questions. Wellington argues against John Hart Ely that finding a "process malfunction" requires determinations of values. For example, striking down malapportionment requires a theory of political fairness (especially given the Senate) that requires value determinations. And judicial cures for process malfunctions may likewise require judicial value determinations, as in the case of *New York Times v. Sullivan*, which requires weighing substantive values of speech and reputation. Ely might respond that the Constitution adopts "participational values," but the fact is that (as Ely concedes) it does not adopt only these. "Yet if we have judicial review, the First Amendment, for example, must be elaborated. And as I have just demonstrated in discussing *New York Times v. Sullivan*, this requires judges to make substantive value judgments" (69).

Wellington thinks that the desire to limit judges to participational values arises from a rather idealized conception of nonjudicial decision-making. An understanding of the limits on democracy elsewhere (e.g., the House is not really electorally accountable, given the power of incumbency and money) makes judicial value determinations acceptable.

Finally, the type of judicial review exemplified in the *Carolene Products* footnote requires judges to engage in a task far removed from adjudication. They must engage in "stratospheric philosophizing" as they understand, develop, invent (whichever is the right word) "the American system of representative democracy" (70–71)—a rough equivalent of an open-ended constitutional convention.

Other approaches share the same hesitations of participational judicial review (e.g., theories that limit judicial review to certain areas, such as Jesse Choper's restriction of it to protecting individual rights, putting questions of federalism and separation of powers off-limits). And finally, there are those who would limit judicial review by across-the-board judicial restraint, most notably Justice Felix Frankfurter and his teacher James Bradley Thayer. Thayer rested his argument on the nature of judicial review, which is always after the fact. If the framers had intended a broader scope for judicial review, they would have provided for earlier intervention, for example, in the form of a council of revision. Wellington confesses that he does not understand this argument, seeing no relation between the time of review and its limited scope. Indeed, time and a specific case give the judges a different perspective, which is an advantage—one that would be sacrificed by strong deference to Congress. Thayer's case is strong only when it rests on the views that judicial review is a deviant institution and that there are no sources of law for interpreting the Constitution except the personal values of the interpreter. Both those views, however, are wrong.

Having dealt with flawed modalities of constitutional adjudication, Wellington turns in chapters 5 and 6 to the correct approach, "the common-law method." He recalls the basic points about adjudication made earlier, arguing in summary that

> [i]n practice law changes, after negotiation within a court, because of the judges' skeptical receptivity and reserved openness to the claims of various groups—claims shaped and presented by lawyers using legal arguments and trying to win cases. This is the way all law develops through adjudication, including constitutional law. (82)

Constitutional law (because of its frequent finality, the relative difficulty in changing it, and its failure to be a model of pure reason) is different and requires a special justification. Wellington's effort to locate the Court's interpretive strength starts with Bickel's distinction between the practical aspects of government action and "values we hold to have more general and permanent interest" (83). These latter values are a source of legal principles, weighed in the adjudicative process and changing over time. They form a "public morality, the ethical principles, the ideals and aspirations that are widely shared by Americans— even as their application is deeply contested" (84). Legislatures are often insufficiently attentive to these principles. Courts have a special role, requiring the legislatures to "articulate the principles used to elaborate text in the past, principles that often acquired their weight in public morality and that must be reinterpreted in terms of a contemporary understanding of that morality" (85). (An example of change is the prominent place for equality in more recent women's rights cases.) When the attention of the legislature has been primarily on formulating a program, judicial review should be robust (without a presumption of constitutionality).

The weight of public morality as a source of law (relative to other sources such as language, precedent, structure, and history) is determined by the court in the creative adjudicative process. Through a constructive reworking of the materials, the participants in that process make law, constrained by the methodology and substantive conventions of the adjudicative process. Public morality is not always decisive for the court (sometimes, as in the flagburning cases, other factors take precedence), but it plays a role even in cases where other sources of law predominate, since it can affect whether cases are "politically digestible." In the area of substantive due process, public morality is the "workhorse of interpretation" (88).

Wellington turns to this area, starting with the observation that a statute inspired by the desire to control population, that forbade intercourse between the tenth and twentieth days after menstruation would be unconstitutional even on Thayer's "clear mistake" standard. The statute in *Griswold* was more complicated, its goal being to regulate morality and its means being less offensive to public morality. Judicial review was appropriately robust in this case, since the statute was an old one (1879) and public morality had changed.

The state sponsors marriage as an institution, and part of that institution is its intimacy, which is a barrier to a detailed code of official behavior. This liberty creates obligations between husband and wife *and* between the couple and the state. The statute in *Griswold* would result in personal degradation if enforced, and it was contrary to one of the major reasons for marriage. In mid-twentieth-century America, an increasingly important part of marriage is the growth and nurturing of love, one aspect of which is the pursuit of sexual gratification, which is undermined by fear of unwanted pregnancy. The shift in public morality, the movement of the romantic and sexual relationship to the core of the marital institution, now demands liberty in the practice of the sexual act, and the Connecticut act was arguably an unconstitutional condition on the privileges that flow from a state-supported institution.

The state in 1965 would break its moral obligation if it tried to ban marital intercourse, or tried to regulate the frequency of it or the day or time of place when it was permitted. This statute, though less drastic, was still "in sharp conflict with the entire concept of the marriage relationship," given its potential impact on the love life of the married couple: dramatically reducing pleasure because of the fear of unwanted pregnancy and thus imposing a major strain on the relationship. The decision striking down the law was supported by data about contraceptive practice in the state, since the law was not enforced against married couples—if it had been, the legislature might well have changed the law. This was better evidence of public morality than an 1879 statute.

Should we worry about the overtones of *Lochner* in this case? Not much. Other cases in that era concerned personal rather than economic liberty (*Pierce, Meyer*) and have not been overturned. And what was wrong with *Lochner* was not that the Court gave some weight to liberty of contract, but that it was more weight than an appeal to public morality could justify.

The sixth chapter applies this common-law method that relies heavily on public morality to "the tragic problem of abortion." Wellington identifies the principle in *Roe* as the right to control what happens in and to one's body. (A non-abortion-related example would be the unconstitutionality of a statute that forbade removing gall bladders except to save a life.) The abortion right has nothing to do with a right to the death of the fetus.

Wellington cites Judith Jarvis Thomson's example: you are kidnapped and you are hooked up to a famous violinist with a kidney problem, who will die if you are unplugged (during the next nine months). Must you accede to this? An appeal to our attitudes and practices says that the answer is no. This is at least indistinguishable from pregnancy resulting from rape. The weight of the right to control your body does vary with time (nine months or nine minutes) and the nature of the violation (pregnancy or vaccination). Your position would be different if you had agreed to be hooked up. But a pregnant woman has not really given consent that way (she may have taken precautions against conceiving, but they are not foolproof; and sexual intercourse is not voluntary in the way going to the opera is).

The fetus, moreover, is not like the violinist. Common attitudes attribute a greater right to life to someone who has been born than to a fetus. Even Texas would accept the death of the fetus to save the life of the mother, though we would not accept the idea of killing a newborn infant if it were necessary to obtain something to save the mother's life. And we would not be surprised by those who favor aborting deformed fetuses but oppose infanticide of deformed infants. Since we accept the principle that a woman who has been raped needn't carry the fetus to term, can we compel a woman who has taken thalidomide and may have a seriously deformed fetus to do so?

These observations are examples of how, "for the Court and the lawyers arguing before it, reasoning from these commonly held attitudes should be an important method for interpreting the values—the public morality—that are a source of law" (107). This same approach, however, is also related to the state's interest in potential human life, and "there is bound to be a tragic conflict between them" (107). He concedes that he is not able to justify the sweep of *Roe* this way, though he indicates a hope that someone else may be able to do so.

The Court was right not to defer to the legislature's decision to limit abortion. Yet if the statute in *Roe* was old, other statutes struck down by that decision (e.g., the one in *Doe v. Bolton*) were relatively recent. The history of the statute's enactment is another ground besides the date of the statute for diminishing the weight of legislative decisions regarding public morality (e.g., the impact of a narrow, well-organized interest group). Where legislative history is not available, the Court can reconstruct it by taking note of commonly held attitudes and reasoning from them. If abortion legislation departs from this analysis, then the Court should discount legislative interpretation of public morality. (While this means that Texas's statute was too restrictive, however, it also "means that *Roe v. Wade*, when decided in 1973, went too far.") "The Court should defer to the legislature when it is in doubt, but not when it is confident about its conclusions" (109).

If *Roe* went too far when it was decided, it should not necessarily be overruled. Precedent is important. More importantly, overturning *Roe* would lead to great diversity in state legislation, with a disproportionate impact on poor women, in the form of the probable increase in deaths caused by back-alley abortions.

Webster v. Reproductive Health Services means that *Roe* is at least unstable. O'Connor argues that the state's interest in protecting potential life exists throughout pregnancy. But Wellington contends that this does not mean that the Court was wrong to choose viability as the line in *Roe*. Most of us do attach more value to life later in pregnancy (and that attitude is likely to be reinforced with the advent of the RU-486 pill). And the principle that supports a woman's right to abortion (a right to decide what happens in and to her body) must influence judgment about what constitutes a sufficient interest to defeat that right. Wellington criticizes O'Connor for separating these issues, arguing that viability is relevant in considering the extent of state power over the abortion right. White also comes in for criticism for doing the same, and for arguing that viability is a function of medical practice and technology, which Wellington says is simply wrong, since viability before twenty-three or twenty-four weeks "does not seem to be in the medical or technological cards" (119).

Wellington moves on to a consideration of *Bowers v. Hardwick*. White mischaracterized the right in *Roe* as the right to decide whether to beget or bear a child, when in fact the woman's right is one to decide what happens in and to her body. For the Court to describe the principle in terms of a set of applications already decided is not true to the process of adjudication, nor to the principle of treating like cases alike. *Roe* and *Bowers* rest, in fact, on the same principle. The principle may have different weights in the two cases in regard to public morality. Before *Griswold*, for example, Hardwick surely would have had to lose.

The right place to begin is with *Griswold*'s principle regarding the privacy rights of married couples (a principle that is even stronger now, after the Bork confirmation process). Subsequent decisions extended this right to single people, as evolving law reflected (and perhaps influenced) changing social attitudes. It is likely today that a sodomy law would be held unconstitutional in the case of married couples and unmarried heterosexuals. (That would depend on the weight the Court assigned to legislative judgments that sodomy is immoral and the actual lax enforcement of the crime when committed in private.) If the Court was unsure about whether the law applied to unmarried heterosexuals, then it should never have heard the case. Judicial ambivalence on public morality requires judicial restraint. But if the Court would uphold the right of sodomy for unmarried heterosexuals, it could make it a crime for homosexuals "only if the Court determined that it was permissible under the equal protection clause for a legislature to draw distinctions in a criminal statute that turned on nothing but raw prejudice" (122). (AIDS—the only possible justification for the law that Wellington considers—can be dealt with by less drastic means.)

The last two chapters deal with "the politics of the indigestible." The common-law method explains the role of the Supreme Court better than originalism or *Carolene Products* review, and has the advantage of building into law change that takes into account contemporary substantive values. But what is the constitutional substitute for legislative revision of statutory interpretation? Not constitutional amendment or control of appellate jurisdiction, but separation of powers and the American people. Wellington takes Meese's side (in his Tulane speech) in arguing against *Cooper v. Aaron* and its claim of judicial supremacy (though he disagrees with Meese's argument that the distinction is "between the Constitution and constitutional law").

The Court can be overruled when it makes a mistake. There are two types of mistakes: those based on the policy consequences of the decision and those based on public morality. How does one know whether these mistakes have occurred? Cardozo's "test of experience" suggests that consequences be tested by social science. Wellington is hesitant about basing constitutional law on this because of the limits of social science investigation, which typically fall short of clear conclusions. As for mistakes about public morality, the criterion is likely to be the community's reaction to judicial decisions. Of course, there will be reaction whether the Court is right or wrong: "turmoil, resistance, and threats from other governmental entities, from private groups, institutions, and individuals" (140). This provides a "rich political dialogue, one that may give the Court the information it needs if it is to know whether it has made a mistake" (141).

The standard response to the Court is accepting the authority of its decisions as regulation. But this is not the only response. Jefferson, Lincoln, and Jackson all denied that it was necessary for politicians to leave constitutional interpretation to the judicial department (though Wellington says that it is permissible). Judges must obey (or resign), but nonjudicial officers may openly disregard a Court decision as regulation, as Lincoln did. This is most strongly justified when the source of law has been public morality, and the official strongly believes that the Court has made a mistake. Public morality is, after all, an interactive concept.

Another arena in which the issue of public morality can be fought out is the appointment and confirmation process. The president can nominate people of like views, and the Senate can focus on the same issues that the president properly addresses. This process, along with attempts at Court-curbing legislation and the public forum—learned and popular journals, newspapers, TV, political platforms, parades, and rallies—is part of the "background noise" that the Court hears, trying to separate the wheat from the chaff.

The role of ordinary Americans (nonofficials) includes scholarly critiques, action to bring about legislation, and action to bring about litigation (e.g., sit-ins at lunch counters as part of the civil rights movement). And "we must be tolerant of competing views of various groups about constitutional meaning . . . for a public morality must be as inclusive as possible and adjudication needs its substitutes for the access and accountability that theoretically exist where regulation is by legislation" (155). So we must vigorously protect the speech we hate, and the state must not be harsh in responding to peaceful civil disobedience.

Of course, bombing abortion clinics is not tolerable. But many anti-*Roe* activities have been acceptable: state legislative activity, peaceful picketing and counseling at abortion clinics, punishing pro-choice legislators at the polls, pressuring public officials to use views about abortion as a litmus test for appointments, and presidential calls for constitutional amendment, and other rhetoric calculated to undermine *Roe*.

Even demonstrations in Washington aimed directly at the Court are an entirely proper (though possibly politically unwise) part of the dialogue that constructs public morality. This form of dialogue has risks. First, it may undermine our belief in law. But it is also a risk—a form of mendacity—to persist in seeing the Court as an apolitical institution. And we can retreat from that older orthodoxy without abandoning ourselves (with critical legal scholars) to nihilism. Second, there is always the possibility that peaceful protest will lead to violence. This is unfortunate, but inevitable.

Court justices are fallible, but the public usually acquiesces in, if not approves of, their regulation. Even when those decisions are seen as mistakes by most Americans, they are usually easily digested and become law. When the decisions are not accepted, then the Court's decision will last only as long as it is politically digestible. Public attitude, however, will be affected by the Court's decision, which is derived from public values but also shapes them. It is this complex and robust dialogue that ultimately makes final the meaning of our fundamental law.

Legislative Adjudicators

Wellington starts from a position that assumes the need for a legislative judiciary. Rapid change and the limited capacity of the legislature, he says, mean that law cannot be static or clear and must be changed over time through the adjudicative process. But even were there a need for judicial legislation in areas where law is subject to legislative revision, this judicial legislation would not be necessary in the area of judicial review. Rapid change often leads to desire for change in the law, but often what the change should be is controversial, and Americans have traditionally (and rightly) been reluctant to permit change without the requirement of consent by the people's representatives. The contention that there is a "need" for judicial legislation in constitutional matters often comes, not surprisingly, from those who have failed to obtain the legislation they want or have failed to stop legislation they do not want. Such allegations of "need" ought to be viewed with some skepticism. In fact, most claims on behalf of judicial activism have relatively little to do with "rapid change," though that rhetoric taps a kind of thoughtless historicism that is widespread today.

But judicial power is constrained by the adjudicative process, Wellington tells us. His confidence is based on the "interpretive community" that exists among lawyers. He does worry a bit about whether the legal profession is diverse enough; for example, in the past the views of women have not been represented, and still today those who are deviant or cannot afford lawyers are not heard. Perhaps he has in mind people like evangelical Christians and advocates of traditional morality, whose voices are much less likely to be heard at prestigious law schools than those of radical feminists and homosexuals—but one doubts whether his worries about the diversity of the legal profession extend quite that far to the "right."

Like most contemporary constitutional commentators, Wellington is extremely casual about the textual foundations of judicial review. Marshall's position receives some support from the text, but is not required by it. So he cheerfully joins Bickel's quest for a new foundation for judicial review, accepting Bickel's suggestion that it lies in the courts' superior capacity to deal with our "enduring values." The nation's enduring values are, it would seem, too important a matter to leave in the hands of the legislature, which is the branch of government most accountable to the people, since it tends to be too oriented toward immediate interests.

But if judicial review is undemocratic, that should not be a cause for alarm, says Wellington. As such, lack of democracy is not an oddity in our political landscape but one of its regular features, since most other parts of the political system are not all that democratic either. Just think of the Senate, the power of wealth, incumbency, seniority, lobbyists, and unaccountable bureaucrats. But Wellington passes over the fact that these other parts of government may still be much more democratic than the Court. Perhaps incumbents are successful not only because of the franking privilege, but because most representatives avoid like the plague political positions to which their constituents—often even less than a majority of them—are hostile. Nor does it seem to matter that the people explicitly consented to the Senate's disproportionate representation. Of course, he might respond, they also consented to the Supreme Court and even to judicial review. But what *form* of judicial review did they consent to? The judicial review in *Federalist* No. 78 has little to do with that of Bickel or Wellington. My guess is that Wellington would not accord significant weight to that factor, on the grounds that law changes over time and the absence of consent in 1787 has very little relevance today. It is consent enough that there has been no successful popular opposition to legal developments that have produced the expansive modern judicial power.

Turning to modalities of constitutional adjudication, Wellington argues that it is not really a case of "interpretivism" against "noninterpretivism," since we are all interpreting a vague, open-textured, and ambiguous text. What divides us is a dispute not about interpretation, but about the nature of American constitutional adjudication; it is a debate about an institution, not a text.

Wellington is half right here, in an important way. The dispute is basically *not* about interpretation, but the reason is very different from the one Wellington offers. It is because the kind of constitutional adjudication that Wellington and other "non-originalists" favor is not interpretation in the sense that judges were intended to exercise. It is a form of judicial legislation in which judges balance allegedly vague constitutional presumptions against asserted state interests of various sorts. "Interpretation" versus "noninterpretive judicial legislation" says it exactly right, and that is why Wellington is correct that the battle is not about interpretation, but rather about the power of the court.

Wellington on Originalism

Wellington's critique of originalism is fairly standard. He cites H. Jefferson Powell on the framers not intending originalism and describes originalism by emphasizing the search for extrinsic sources of intent, rather than the careful interpretation of a text, supplemented by history (when it is clear) to confirm a reading of the text.[1] But, says Wellington, the constitutional language is unclear, the records are unclear, and the history is unclear. Even if a clear meaning were available, it would not be desirable, since there is no real fit between the thought of the founders and today's constitutional practice (e.g., they placed more weight on property rights and less on liberty independent of property).

This critique misses the mark. First, the text is not as unclear as he alleges. For example, the due process clause is not, as he contends, a vague generality, but a simple guarantee of the standing law on legal procedure.[2] The First Amendment is a guarantee against prior restraint. The establishment clause is a prohibition of preferential treatment of a religion or religions.

But let us concede for the moment, for the sake of argument, that the text *is* unclear in a given case (privileges and immunities and equal protection might be among the better examples). Why assume that the judges have authority to give meaning to concededly ambiguous provisions? The fundamental rationale for judicial review was the need to strike down acts that violated "the manifest tenor of the Constitution," as Hamilton put it in *Federalist* No. 78. The originalist claim is that any genuine ambiguity in the Constitution removes the essential condition for judicial review.

Such a view is almost incomprehensible to Wellington. He argues that when the meaning of the law is blurred, the "courts should keep clear of any action that constitutes an assumption by judges of the drafters' prerogative—although it is hard to imagine how they could do so, since judges must act" (55). Why is it hard to imagine that, in cases of judicial review, judges act by deferring to the legislative judgment that has as much textual support as the judges' preferred interpretation? Not only is this easy to imagine but it is a view much more consistent with the principles of a democratic republic.

Second, there is the claim that the records of the Federal Convention and the ratifying conventions (as well as the First Congress) are unclear in details. But how many constitutional questions turn on the kinds of points that are uncertain in the records? More importantly, when the records are unclear, they simply should not be used.

Third, is the history unclear? Sometimes it is, in which case it does not help—judges simply return to the text and if that is unclear, defer to the political process. But much of the allegedly unclear history is not unclear at all. For example, the religion clauses clearly have a nonpreferentialist meaning, and the Fourteenth Amendment was clearly intended to have no effect on voting rights.[3]

The crowning touch of Wellington's critique of originalism is an extensive discussion of Justice Hugo Black to show that originalism does not constrain judges: it permits them to transform their personal preferences into law and it permits them to bring about dramatic social change. But Black, most scholars would admit, was an extremely eccentric originalist. Anyone who reads the constitutional provision that representatives shall be elected "by the People" as a *textual command* "that as nearly as practicable one man's vote in a congressional election is to be worth as much as another's" does not have strong credentials as an originalist.[4] Wellington's critique only shows that Black is a *poor* "interpretivist."

Wellington's rejection of James Bradley Thayer's argument for self-restraint is revealing. Wellington confesses that he does not understand Thayer's argument, which he characterizes this way: the scope of judicial review is related to the judicial nature of the power the Court exercises, and "this judicial nature meant that the constitutionality of a statute was generally not considered by the Court for some time" (73).

Thayer's argument, however, is not based simply on the timing of review. It involves a more comprehensive understanding of the nature of judicial power ("[t]he courts are revising the work of a co-ordinate department, and must not, even negatively, undertake to legislate"), which is itself based on a broad understanding of separation of powers and republicanism. Wellington does not come close to considering Thayer's real argument. Wellington's understanding of judicial power simply denies the fact that the exercise of judicial review is not an ordinary judicial power, but a very different kind of power: the exercise of a kind of "political administration." In this he is a child of legal realism, steadfastly insisting on the political character of all law—at least until faced with the logical implications of that in critical legal scholarship, at which point he retreats.[5]

One of the starting points of Wellington's description of his own common-law method is that Marshall "committed the Constitution to the one department of government that many students of law would say finds its authority in the ideal of a rigorous adherence to principle" (79). He then goes on to describe a method that demands anything but a *rigorous* adherence to principle, leaving judges with enormous discretion to adjust the law to fit their political preferences, a discretion that often results in frankly ad hoc constitutional law.[6]

Judicially Defined Public Morality

Wellington's low opinion of the legislature, and especially of its capacity to consider enduring public values in its legislation, leads to a very "robust" judicial review indeed. Judges should not presume the constitutionality of legislation in cases where legislative attention has primarily been on formulating a program (e.g., its 1988 antidrugs program). Even if legislatures have considered the broader public values, judges should not presume constitutionality in cases where the law is an old one (e.g., the nineteenth-century law at issue in *Griswold*; it is less clear, of course, whether this standard would lead Wellington to a skeptical evaluation of immediately post-Civil War enactments expanding civil rights). Even if the law is not an old one, judges should not presume constitutionality when the legislative history shows that a narrow, well-organized interest group is responsible for the law. (The difficulty of identifying such key interest groups, however, goes unremarked by Wellington. For example, applying this norm to abortion, it seems likely that Wellington would have in mind "narrow, well-organized" pro-life groups rather than, say, "narrow, well-organized" feminist groups.) If legislative history is not readily accessible, legislative deference still may be unnecessary because the court can "reconstruct" legislative history by "tak[ing] note of commonly held attitudes and reason[ing] from them" (109), striking down legislative interpretation of public morality that departs from the insights of this judicial analysis.

Does this all amount to *ignoring* the legislative contribution to public morality? "Perhaps, but this is a matter of degree" (109). The court "should defer when it is in doubt, not when it has confidence in its conclusions" (109). A fair reader would have to conclude that, if Wellington is trying to portray judicial review based on public morality as constrained in any significant way, these criteria completely undercut such an argument. They leave the judges free to strike down virtually any legislative enactments they seriously dislike.

The Court discerns public morality through a "creative" process, a "constructive reworking of materials," constrained, of course, "by the methodological and substantive conventions of adjudication" (86). There is always the—presumably, for Wellington, unsettling—possibility that public values might lead to politically conservative decisions—for example, the flagburning decisions[7]—but that concern should be allayed by the fact that public morality is only one source of law, whose weight is determined by the Court. Language, as well as "structure, precedent, and history" (88) (all those factors Wellington showed to be so indeterminate in his critique of originalism) can also control. Apparently, they are clear enough to be "presumptive vetoes" in some cases, for example, "legislation aimed at restricting speech, interfering with religion, and distinguishing among people on the basis of their race." (Whether the latter category includes affirmative action we are not told. Somehow, it seems unlikely.)

But public morality is the "workhorse of interpretation" in the area of substantive due process. Wellington exemplifies this by a look at *Griswold v. Connecticut. Griswold* was rightly decided because it was based on a more accurate perception of public morality than the Connecticut statute. Public morality, in this case, demanded that the state not undermine a major reason for marriage, for its anticontraception law created a fear of pregnancy, which undermined "the pursuit of sexual gratification" that is "a vital aspect of love" (91). In this case, the nonenforcement of the statute was better evidence of public values than the law.

The refusal of the legislature to repeal the statute was of no weight, apparently, though in 1965 it might have been taken as a residual ambivalence in public values, an ambivalence that likely would have been eliminated, along with the law, very soon after *Griswold*, which was a truly unnecessary decision. Justice Stewart's dissent rightly objected to the overruling of what he called "an uncommonly silly law." Why it appeared so silly to him is unclear. It may be that he meant the law was so out of touch with public values that it was silly even to try to enforce it, since laws cannot be imposed with complete disregard for social mores. (Stewart's comment, on this interpretation of it, I consider defensible.) Or he may have been saying that the values represented by the law were themselves silly. I suspect he had both reasons in mind.

In view of the fact that Justice Stewart's comment is almost universally unchallenged, perhaps it is worthwhile at least raising some questions about it. While the law was ineffectual in the absence of social mores to support it, there are reasons to question such a dismissive attitude toward the substance of the law (i.e., in a society where the mores supported it, it might not be as outlandish as it seems to most Americans). A disinterested observer might note that contraception has been part of a broad change in cultural mores respecting marriage, family, and sex.[8] Some of the observations such an observer might make about the current state of these matters are: abortion (at best "a tragic problem," as Wellington describes it) is frequent; no-fault divorce has permitted the break-up of a large percentage of marriages and the impoverishment of many of the successor households; the number of illegitimate pregnancies has risen to undreamed of heights, first in the inner-city but now also in the suburbs; an extraordinary percentage of American children spend much of their childhood without two parents; many of those with two parents spend much of their time with inferior care-givers; pornography is widespread and extremely profitable; and sexual assault has risen dramatically. Such an observer might even give some attention to the assertion that society would be much better off if women, who have a greater natural propensity to understand sex as "self-giving" rather than "taking" or mere self-gratification, could educate men to that view (a daunting task, to be sure) instead of focusing on a more egalitarian distribution of sexual gratification, as some feminists seem to. This self-giving dimension of sexuality might even be fostered most effectually when sex is tied to children, who represent the couple's joint self-giving and who constitute a permanent responsibility that conditions what Wellington calls the pursuit of sexual gratification.

One obvious response to this is that correlation of current pathologies with the spread of contraception does not prove causality. True enough, but it does suggest the possibility of an underlying connection—and this should make observers free of the prejudices of our own age hesitate about calling the law silly, at least on substantive grounds. They might then believe that such a law would be unfortunate where mores do not at all support it, but they might lament that change in the mores. Whether current American attitudes toward sexual gratification are compatible with a stable two-parent family (the benefits of which an increasingly wide range of Americans recognize[9]) remains to be seen.

Needless to say, I am not contending that judges ought to make constitutional decisions on the basis of this argument, since these ideals are embraced nowhere in the Constitution. And unlike abortion rulings, the Court's decision in *Griswold* did reflect emerging societal attitudes. The blame for the not silly but tragic contemporary mores regarding marriage, family, and sex can only in part be attributed to the Court.

Returning to Wellington, however, he says that we should not let fears related to *Lochner* inhibit such decisions: the problem with *Lochner* was not the Court's assertion of its right to base decisions on public morality but merely that they happened to get public morality wrong in that case.

Roe v. Wade was also correctly decided, according to Wellington's common-law method. His effort to "understand *Roe* on its own terms" proceeds by attributing to *Roe* a fundamental principle—namely, "a woman's right to control what happens in and to her body"—that is not the explicit one *Roe* relies on. *Roe*, as Wellington recognizes, moves pretty directly from a generalized privacy right to a right to abortion—and does so rather casually, basing the right on *either* the Ninth Amendment or—the Court's preference—Fourteenth Amendment due process. The absence of any more substantial reasoning is what compels Wellington to supply his principle in order to "understand *Roe* on its own terms."[10]

Wellington then continues by taking note of "commonly held attitudes and reasoning from them." Where are these commonly held principles derived from? Wellington gives us hypotheticals and then he tells us what "we," or at least most of us, think about them. For example, he gives us Judith Jarvis Thomson's example of being kidnapped and hooked up to a famous violinist. Must we accede to this arrangement? He says that "no is the only answer that can be defended by an appeal to our attitudes and practices" (104). Evidence? Apparently that is not necessary, for he gives none. But what would most Americans actually *do* in such a situation? They would think that it was unjust that someone put them in that situation, but would they therefore assume that they were free to pull the plug? There is considerable doubt in my mind about what "our" attitudes are. If the hypothetical tracks the typical pregnancy example closely—that is, if my being connected to the violinist somehow is compatible with my living a fairly ordinary life—I find it altogether plausible that many, if not most, Americans would consider it wrong to pull the plug.

But let's alter the example a bit and make the famous violinist a helpless little child. And let's specify that the child is there as the result of an action that the person hooked up to it could foresee as at least a possible—even if undesired—result of his own action? (Even if sexual intercourse is not voluntary in the way that going to a baseball game is, as Wellington says, can this exempt a person from accepting responsibility for consequences he or she foresees as possible—however reluctantly?) Would "we" or "most of us" feel free to pull the plug in that situation?

How can Wellington know? By what authority does he blithely assert his answers? Even if he took a scientifically valid poll, what would that tell us about the decisions that people would make if they were actually in the situation of seeing a human being hooked up to them and knowing that pulling the plug was a death warrant? In the final analysis what we know is that Wellington—and perhaps those with whom he most frequently associates—would make the decisions that he tells us "we" would.

One of the "commonly accepted attitudes" Wellington tells us about is that "we are not apt to be surprised or to think it madness if a person favors the abortion of a badly deformed fetus and at the same time opposes infanticide" (106). But that kind of reasoning is not far removed from those who would say that "we" oppose infanticide in general, but would not think it "madness" to favor infanticide of deformed infants.

Why does Wellington start with the right to control one's body as a commonly accepted principle and dwell on the various attitudes that are associated with it? Why is so little time spent on the commonly accepted attitudes about unborn children? Some would argue that refering to "unborn children" loads the question, when that only applies to late-term fetuses—how could it refer to a zygote? And yet when a couple very

much wants to conceive a child and even knows the time of conception, isn't it a "commonly accepted attitude" to regard that as "our
child," even from the very beginning of pregnancy? Who among those
not unhappy with their pregnancy talks about "products of conception"
and who among them regards a newly conceived child as merely "part
of my body"? Yet none of these commonly accepted attitudes receives
any attention, much less substantial weight, in Wellington's analysis.
Indeed, the interest opposed to the "woman's right to control her body"
is mentioned, but given no careful consideration or discussion at all.

Another typical reflection of that myopia appears when, after Wellington's concession that *Roe v. Wade* went too far for public morality
in 1973, he constructs an argument for maintaining it anyway on equal
protection grounds: turning the matter back to the states results in diversity in state legislation, and that would have a disproportionate adverse impact on poor women. But another way to phrase the same
argument—one that Wellington does not mention—is that such diversity has a disproportionate adverse impact on the fetuses of nonpoor
women, and a disproportionately favorable impact on the fetuses of poor
women. (This is so even if we take into account the specter of "back-
alley abortions": from the fetus's perspective—notably absent in this
whole discussion—whether they are destroyed in a back-alley or a hos-
pital or a clinic hardly seems to matter.)

Wellington criticizes Justice Sandra Day O'Connor's separation of
the abortion right from the judgment about the interest that would defeat it. At the risk of using a long quotation, I want to give the reader
Wellington's complete argument on this point:

> The principle that supports a woman's right to an abortion must itself
> influence judgment about what constitutes a sufficient state interest to
> defeat the woman's right. Put more generally, the concept of a compel-
> ling state interest is related to the nature of the right it trumps. Justice
> O'Connor, however, seems to think otherwise. It would appear that she
> sees the state interest and the woman's right as discrete. This might be
> analytically clear, but it is substantively wrong.
>
> If the woman's right to an abortion included the right to demand the
> death of the fetus, viability would be irrelevant. It would, as Justice
> O'Connor insists, be a totally arbitrary point within the nine months of
> a pregnancy. But the woman has no such right: the death of a fetus
> from abortion is a consequence of the woman's having exercised a right
> based on and coextensive with the principle that she may decide what
> happens in or to her body. Thus, while it is not inescapably true that
> the state should be prevented from regulating before viability, it is in-
> escapably true that viability is relevant in considering the extent of state
> power over the abortion decision. (115–16)

That is the sum total of the argument. Despite considerable effort to understand it, I find this passage very puzzling. What does Wellington think he has proved by it? It may show that there is no right to an abortion after viability, but I don't see how it says anything at all about abortion before viability—unless there is an assumption being smuggled in that life begins at viability, which doesn't appear to be Wellington's argument. (If I do figure out what the argument is, I would like to take a shot at doing the reverse: namely, insist that the very definition of the abortion right somehow be related to the state's interest in protecting incipient—not "potential," since that loads the question too much—human life.)

Wellington's critique of *Bowers v. Hardwick* is equally unsatisfactory. He says that the Court misstated the principle in *Roe* as "the right to decide whether or not to beget or bear a child" (which is closer to what *Roe* does say than the principle Wellington attributes to it), and substitutes his own "right of a woman to decide what happens in or to her body" (which *Roe* does not talk about). Starting with the more general principle, Wellington argues that, just as *Griswold*'s principle was extended to single people in *Carey*, so it is likely that a right to marital sodomy (which he assumes would be upheld) would be extended to single heterosexuals. The Court, he thinks, was uncertain about the likelihood of the latter development, and so it should have refused to decide the case. But once it took the case, the ideal of deciding like cases alike would make it difficult to declare homosexual sodomy a crime. Wellington's reasoning is: permitting criminal punishment of sodomy "would be possible only if the Court determined that it was permissible under the equal protection clause for a legislature to draw distinctions in a criminal statute that turned on nothing but raw prejudice" (122). One can hear the roar of applause from an audience of liberal academics, but . . . where's the substantive argument? It is no *argument* simply to dismiss your opponent's position as "raw prejudice." The opposing argument is simple: homosexual acts are immoral, because they involve the pursuit of sexual pleasure outside of a heterosexual union. You may not agree with that argument—I confess that I don't find it as persuasive as it would be if we (at least) substituted "marital relationship" for "heterosexual union." But as a moral proposition, it is no more "raw prejudice" than "people should not hurt other innocent people," "it is wrong to be cruel to animals," or "we owe our descendants a decent environment"; it is certainly as good as "it is legitimate to starve comatose patients or seriously deformed children to death." The only thing that explains the satisfactory character of Wellington's argument for Wellington, as far as appears here, is his own opinions (what some might even call prejudices), perhaps because they are widely shared by the people he knows. Unfortunately, Wellington is right that the Court not only reflects public values but shapes them, and so larger numbers of people are coming to share his opinions these days. But that is no argument for his model of constitutional adjudication, since he has not established why the Court should have the *right* to disproportionately shape future public values.

Advocates of constraints on judicial power should agree with at least one of Wellington's arguments: if we really think a decision is terrible, we are allowed to try to overturn it. The power of judges to take certain minority opinions and make them law for the nation is constrained and counterbalanced by the opportunity of those who lose in the court to overcome all the checks of the ordinary political process in order to defeat that minority opinion and make authoritative a different (even majority) opinion. But this is a pretty minimal concession. Recall that early-twentieth-century liberals were upset about not only specific court decisions but also the breadth of judicial power during the *Lochner* era—and they were not particularly comforted by the fact that, someday, in some circumstances (like the Great Depression decades later), they might be able to turn things around.

To his credit, Wellington defends the argument of Edwin Meese, the former attorney general, that the other branches of government may not be bound by a Court interpretation of the Constitution. Meese, Wellington rightly points out, was only saying in his Tulane speech what Lincoln and others had said before him: that Court decisions do not always serve as a rule for the future actions of other branches of government. But less graciously, Wellington quickly undercuts that concession by commenting that "Meese is no Lincoln" because "he doesn't quite get it right when he insists that 'the necessary distinction [is] between the Constitution and constitutional law'" (133). The fact is, however, that Meese gets Lincoln exactly right on that score. Lincoln's constitutional argument is quite traditional in character—it bears no resemblance to modern constitutional approaches. For example, his critique of *Dred Scott* does not accuse it of being "overly mechanical, wooden, or insensitive" (as Tribe and Dorf characterize it): Lincoln says it's a *wrong* interpretation of the Constitution. There is no talk in Lincoln about judges having authority to "fill in the gaps" of the Constitution, or "adapt" it to the times, or give clarity to its "ambiguities." His distinction, like Meese's, is precisely between the Court's decision (constitutional law) and the Constitution.

Conclusion

What is it that Wellington's book, and Tribe and Dorf's and others like
them, sound like? As one reads them, one has the feeling of being in a
room with very intelligent lawyers who are both very frank and supreme-
ly confident about their ability to "adjust" the Constitution to establish and apply the "principles" they consider to be both important for
the nation and embedded in its tradition in some vague way. Especially given their sincere commitment to the national well-being, this group
is somewhat puzzled and irritated that such a big fuss is now being
made over the foundations of such power; lawyers and scholars have
known for so long that judicial power necessarily is political, and it
does, after all, work out rather well. Those who question not merely
modern readings of particular constitutional provisions, but the right of
the Supreme Court (guided by the legal fraternity) to make authoritative decisions based on something other than the meaning of the document as originally given are regarded as either unsophisticated,
eccentric, or insensitive to the modern panoply of rights that can obviously be protected in no other way.

I recognize that representative democracy has its problems. The people are not always "wise, virtuous, and competent to manage their own
affairs," contrary to the republican assumption noted by Chief Justice
Gibson in his dissent in *Eakin v. Raub*. That is one reason the founders
set up a system in which the people are constrained to act through representatives and can be limited by judges enforcing a clear written law.

But whatever the defects of republicanism, reading books such as
these is enough to tempt one (only "tempt," mind you) to become a rag-
ing populist. The idea of being ruled by a legal aristocracy—or
perhaps oligarchy is the word, one based on legal education rather
than wealth—may sound attractive to lawyers and those who typically influence or agree with their opinions (e.g., intellectuals, jour-
nalists, and other members of the "new class"). But if these arguments
for "principled" judicial review are the best they can come up with, how
unfortunate are the people over whom they have such extensive, so little constrained, such unauthorized, and finally—despite all the talk of
principle—such unprincipled power.

7

Grand Theories and Ambiguous Republican Critique: Mark Tushnet on Contemporary Constitutional Law

Tribe and Dorf and Wellington provide what might be called typical "liberal" defenses of judicial activism. In some leading law schools today, such liberals find themselves on the "right wing," due to the relative absence of conservatives and the powerful presence of legal scholars who adopt more radical approaches to law (including constitutional law), such as the Critical Legal Studies Movement and feminism. In this chapter, I would like to examine a leading example of such a radical approach: Mark Tushnet, the author of *Red, White, and Blue*.

   Tushnet approaches the subject of constitutional law with the concerns of an intellectual historian and a cultural critic. His analysis of constitutional law and constitutional commentary has two main parts, both of which use as their framework the tension between the "liberal" and "civic republican" elements of American political life. Part one of *Red, White, and Blue* describes various "grand theories" of judicial review and shows why all are inadequate (separately or in combination). Judicial review has an integral role in the liberal intellectual program, but theories of judicial review can be coherent only at the price of invoking republican assumptions that undermine the argument for judicial review. Part two contains an analysis of different areas of constitutional law that attempts to show how constitutional doctrine "constitutes" or shapes and defends important social institutions. (This doctrine embodies the structural presuppositions about the nature of American society shared rather broadly across the American political spectrum.)

The revival of grand theory in the 1980s, Tushnet argues, occurred partly to defend Warren Court results that seemed tenuous with the emergence of a more conservative Burger Court, but more deeply to shore up liberal legal theory in its crisis of legitimacy. Each grand theory identifies problems at the edges of the existing system, but in the end is an attempt to maintain the basic outline of liberal legal theory. That there is a crisis of legitimacy is demonstrated simply by the fact that no grand theory commands widespread assent, each one only serving as grounds for new critiques and yet more grand theories.

The series of critiques of "grand theory" in part one of *Red, White, and Blue* are often quite trenchant, but in this chapter I want to focus my comments on one segment that I find less so: his discussion of interpretation and originalism. While I view original meaning as an *alternative* to "grand theories" of judicial review—precluding the need for them—Tushnet treats it as just one more inadequate theory, for reasons that I find unpersuasive.

Tushnet's analysis of Court doctrines in various areas of constitutional law, in part two, also contains many valuable insights, especially in regard to the ways that supposedly "neutral" liberal law is quite politically "constitutive." Here, too, however, I am more concerned with raising questions about the political theory that provides Tushnet's framework. In particular, I want to 1) suggest inadequacies in Tushnet's notion of civic republicanism, which contains a healthier dose of liberalism than Tushnet's description would suggest; and 2) argue that a certain blend of liberal and republican elements is what the founders of our regime (successfully) sought and that, on the whole, it has been a successful regime—though it is now endangered by contemporary liberalism (including liberal elements in Tushnet's own intellectual framework).

Tushnet's Critique of Interpretation

In this first section of my comments on *Red, White, and Blue*, I will respond to Tushnet's criticism of the position with which I most identify, which he calls "nostalgic originalism." Tushnet deals with this approach especially in his critiques of originalism in chapter one and of conservative theory in the appendix to chapter four.

Tushnet divides "the almost self-consciously unsystematic theories invoked by conservative popularizers and publicists" into two groups: simple anticonstitutional majoritarians and nostalgic originalists. I will deal with both (though I belong primarily to the second category) because the two categories overlap: on the originalists' views, judicial review would be rather rare and therefore critiques of majoritarianism would apply to them in great measure.

Tushnet's critique of simple anticonstitutional majoritarianism is threefold: they are anticonstitutional, noncomparative, and inconsistent. Majoritarians' anticonstitutionalism could be defended, he says, but only if there were some concern for alternative means of preventing popular or legislative tyranny—a concern notably absent from contemporary conservative majoritarian thought. What would be required is the development of a republican concern that citizens subordinate their private interests to the public good.

"Nostalgic originalists" are not fairly subject to that aspect of Tushnet's criticism of majoritarianism, since they do display precisely that concern. Their originalism does lead them to conclude that legitimate judicial review will probably be rare (as it was before the Civil War), and therefore they do look to the ordinary political process as the chief arena in which to protect liberty. The most important mechanism implicit in the original American constitutional system for protecting liberty was, of course, the extended republic—the fact that society would contain such a multiplicity of interests that no one group could dominate and oppress. The framers added other "auxiliary" precautions as well, such as separation of powers, federalism, and a quite limited form of judicial review.

But those who are most oriented toward the founders rely, like them, not only on the institutional mechanisms that the founders created within government, but also on some measure of citizen character. This is not the "virtue" of Montesquieu's small republic, which requires a degree of subordination of private to public interests that cannot be expected in a basically liberal regime, but it is a genuine concern for aspects of morality especially important for political life. It is reflected particularly in the founders' concern for religion and public morality, not at the level of the federal government, but in the various states and localities.

Respect for the rights of others and a sense of obligation to perform public duties (which overlapped considerably with the moral precepts of Christianity) were considered essential elements of a healthy republic, as Washington's Farewell Address emphasized. These moral teachings were an essential part of ordinary education (as the Northwest Ordinance of 1787 suggested) and to a significant extent they took the form of a public morality in the states' common law, backed up by the unwritten mores of society. Originalists today defend a view of constitutional law that would make it possible to maintain the place of religion in the public square and to foster a public morality.

Tushnet believes that it is nostalgic to seek a return to the alleged "good old days", since the dynamic of capitalism has undermined that past. Nor were those good old days all that great, in his view. But originalists think that the roots of religion and morality grow deeply enough in human nature to survive capitalism and that religion and morality can take healthy forms. Every real-world regime, of course, creates problems for religion and morality in some way, since each one has its own dangerous tendencies, and capitalism is no exception. And religion and morality have frequently been abused to justify injustices. But what is unwarranted is a deterministic assumption that the decline and/or abuse of religion and traditional morality in a capitalist society is necessary and irreversible.[1]

Tushnet says that contemporary conservative majoritarianism is non-comparative; that is, it is not intelligently result-oriented. Will majorities support the program of today's conservatives? Tushnet doubts it.

But originalists, at least for the short run, have principled objections to result-orientation. Their focus is primarily on the legitimacy of the decision-making process—rooted in consent[2]—rather than its results. They do believe that in the long run a good process is more likely to yield good results or avoid bad ones. Originalists consider that plausible, partly because they have a higher opinion of the limitations inherent in the political process of an extended republic. (And most states today are diverse enough to provide similar protections.) Presumably, then, they would argue that majorities (or, more precisely, their representatives) are not systematically more likely to decide wrongly than judges, and in fact are less likely to do "extreme" things. Originalists also believe that federalism and decentralization provide something of a safety valve (providing diverse communities in which to live). This often means that the national political process is unable to do many things that might benefit society, but that is regarded as a worthwhile trade-off to limit its power to do bad things. Behind this lies the conservative view that the status quo (with incremental change thereof), with all its faults, provides for a pretty decent government (relative to likely alternatives) and should not be jeopardized for speculative gains.

Finally, Tushnet argues that conservative majoritarianism is inconsistent, in that conservatives are sometimes perfectly willing to use courts for their own purposes, as in the protection of property rights.

But not all conservatives do so. I would be perfectly willing to join Tushnet in a criticism of such conservative activism.

Tushnet concludes his critique of majoritarianism by suggesting that liberalism might benefit from seeing the importance of majoritarian processes. But he asserts that conservative majoritarianism cannot both remain conservative and pay attention to the social conditions under which majoritarian opinion is formed.

But although some conservatives are insensitive to how opinions are formed, some are not. "Cultural" or social conservatives pay considerable attention to the formation of citizens, emphasizing the place of religion and traditional morality in providing a framework for a healthy political community. Tushnet simply thinks that they are wrong about the possibility of forming citizens well in the ways they would employ.

Nostalgic Originalism

This leads to Tushnet's critique of nostalgic originalism itself. He notes, rightly, that this is a way of preserving majoritarianism (at least substantially) while retaining constitutionalism. But this is "nostalgia for a past which never existed and is now forever lost" (171). The use of the framers' views by political scientists like Walter Berns, Harry Clor, and myself, is "tendentious and empty." It focuses only on the intention of the framers of 1789, with a little bit of Lincoln thrown in, as if the Fourteenth Amendment did not change the Constitution because it was written by men of lesser stature. Modern conservatives' account of the framers' thought bears little resemblance to what they actually thought, but rather is a construct of what they would have thought if they had been as sensible as today's conservatives. In a footnote, he says that these (mostly) "Straussians" insist that the Court should enforce natural rights, but then specify these rights in an unconvincingly narrow way.

Tushnet is short on analysis here and rather heavy on name-calling. It is disappointing that he does not consider it worthwhile even to discuss seriously the views of scholars such as Martin Diamond and Herbert Storing, as well as the others named.

Nostalgic originalists throw in some Lincoln and ignore the Fourteenth Amendment? Where did the Fourteenth Amendment come from, anyway? When Lincoln gets "thrown in," doesn't that say something about the key purposes of the Fourteenth Amendment? Of course the Fourteenth Amendment changed the Constitution, but how much? The

framers of that amendment generally saw their task as one of clarifying and extending something implicit in the original principles of 1789,
but they certainly did not intend to write a blank check for judicial social engineering, as the Fourteenth Amendment is often regarded today.

Straussians insist that courts enforce natural rights, but specify them
in too narrow a fashion? First, not everyone in that group insists that
courts enforce natural rights in the absence of constitutional provisions
that protect those rights. The focus is less on judicial protection of natural rights, in fact, and more on the protection of rights through the
ordinary political process. Courts should understand the purposes or
"objects" of the various constitutional provisions they interpret, and that
involves an understanding of the natural-rights philosophy of the founding. The only example Tushnet gives is a citation to Gary Jacobsohn's
The Supreme Court and the Decline of Constitutional Aspiration,
which says, according to Tushnet, that courts should protect property
rights, but fails to indicate any awareness of the complexity of the idea
of property. But the cited pages do not argue that courts should protect property rights nor do they discuss property rights per se in detail—they simply criticize Ronald Dworkin's failure to take property
rights seriously.

To paraphrase what Tushnet says about conservative constitutional
theory: the question of what the framers' views were is an important
one; Tushnet's discussion of it might have been interesting but it isn't,
because he does not discuss but merely asserts.

Language and Historical Knowledge

Tushnet's deeper criticism of the conservative originalist position is that
conservatives treat the critique of originalism as a debate over the meaning of language, but fail to deal with the more important aspect of the
critique: namely, that the meaning of all language depends on existing
institutional arrangements, and a stable constitutional meaning requires
stable institutions. But change, whose explanation is a weak point in
conservative social theory, is a fact of life. Changed institutions lead
to changed language. This "is especially poignant for conservatives who
support a dynamic capitalism whose chief characteristic is unconcern
for tradition and existing institutions except insofar as they serve
present interests" (173).

Originalism is thus nostalgic in two ways. First, an understanding
of the past is an essential requirement of its view of interpretation. But
modern scholarship makes it clear, Tushnet says, that the past can be

understood only through the hermeneutic method, which requires that one "enter the world of the past." And the hermeneutic method also denies the possibility of discovering determinate intentions in the past, since what one brings to a reading of the past inevitably affects one's understanding of it. Thus, originalism is nostalgic in the sense that it relies on a theory whose premises have been demolished almost completely.

Second, originalism is nostalgic because conservatives support a political/economic system of capitalism that destabilizes the stable society toward which they nostalgically look back. The transformation of society through the dynamic growth of capitalism has led to changes in institutional arrangements that yield differences in the meaning of language. Nor is it likely that the shared conceptions of a community that must be present for language stability can be found or constructed in a capitalist society. According to the republican tradition, this is because such conceptions are possible only when there is substantial equality of wealth and access to material resources and common experiences (e.g., confrontation with scarcity).

Tushnet's critique relies heavily on the epistemological views most prevalent or fashionable among contemporary intellectuals (i.e., positivism or historicism, in their various forms, such as deconstructionism). Conservative originalists, of course, would deny that more traditional ("realist") epistemological views "have been demolished almost completely." They would maintain, in fact, that epistemological realism is the only adequate foundation of human reasoning. Let us look more closely, then, at Tushnet's critique of originalism on these grounds.

The first step in the argument against originalism is that it "must rest on an account of historical knowledge more subtle than the view that past attitudes and intentions are directly accessible to present understanding" (32). As an example, Tushnet points to the different accounts of the original intention regarding "establishment of religion." Until recently, the reigning orthodoxy was that the First Amendment reflected Madison's and Jefferson's strong separationist views. Rehnquist's account in *Jaffree* offered an alternative, conservative account of original intention as the prohibition of any preferences for one or more religions vis-a-vis others, that position being compatible with support for religion in general. Tushnet offers three kinds of arguments against Rehnquist's view: historical ambiguity, inference from limited evidence, and social change.

On historical ambiguity, Tushnet first cites Leonard Levy's careful study of original intention, with its very different conclusions. He then makes the more radical argument that the framers' thought "was located within their entire world-view, their—to us—confusing blend of the liberal and republican traditions" (34). Because that conceptual universe is so different from ours, we cannot simply cite what they thought about one matter and insert it into a body of law that makes sense in our terms.

The originalist response to the first point is simple. Levy is wrong in his interpretation, and Rehnquist is right.[3] As Gerry Bradley has shown in his *Church-State Relationships in America*, the key to understanding the religion clauses of the First Amendment is to see that it had to "satisfy," in some limited sense, the very different views of various groups in the founding era described by Tushnet, Levy, and others—to seek a kind of least common denominator. The nonpreferentialist reading of the First Amendment, far better than any alternative, explains how people of very diverse views could have supported the amendment, as they did.[4]

The second point raises two separate questions: whether we can know what the founders thought and whether we can or want to follow it. On the former point, Tushnet asserts, without offering evidence, that because the founders' conceptual universe was different in some very important respects from our own, we are unable to understand it. He treats what is sometimes a genuine obstacle in historical knowledge—the effort necessary to penetrate someone else's "conceptual universe"—as if it were an absolute bar. On the question of whether we can or want to follow the founders' thought, we must ask why it is impossible or (apart from a particular partisan position on these issues) undesirable to follow the founders in their nonpreferentialist position? Many Americans think that is precisely the proper constitutional understanding of the clause. It is certainly true that we must look not just to isolated instances of what the founders thought, but rather to the whole. But conservative originalists are puzzled as to why this somehow makes originalism "impossible." As far as we can see, the real underlying thought is simply that many contemporary intellectuals don't like the founders' views and would like to change them through the courts.

The second argument against Rehnquist is the problem of inference from limited evidence. The evidence he relied on, says Tushnet, might equally support other rules (e.g., nonpreference among Christian denominations or even some kinds of preferential aid). But conservative originalists have no problem agreeing that interpreters can erroneously infer conclusions on the basis of evidence that is inadequate to support their generalizations. That is a factual question. What they would simply deny is that such errors are necessary or that they apply to Rehnquist's position on the establishment clause, as supported by the best historical research on the subject (especially as to the prevailing meaning of "establishment" at the time of the founding).

The third argument is that of social change. Institutions such as the Thanksgiving Proclamation meant one thing to the framers' society ("a deeply felt belief that God had chosen to look after the United States in a religiously meaningful way") and have another meaning to us (turkeys and football games—mere ritual). Moreover, once society contains denominations that have religious grounds for rejecting government aid, the concept of nonpreferential aid to religions becomes incoherent.

One response is that Thanksgiving may be more than "mere" ritual to many Americans (rituals may have an important significance, even for those who participate relatively unreflectively). Another is that Americans are certainly free not to employ their constitutional power to give nonpreferential aid to religion if social change has made them disinclined to do so (and to amend the Constitution to take away that power, if social change is that broad). Finally, nonpreferential aid does not become preferential simply because some denominations have religious grounds for rejecting all aid, any more than religious freedom could rightly be called a hollow shell simply because we do not permit some religious believers to practice human sacrifice. The views of the believers themselves (as to government aid or human sacrifice) do not become the norm by which the impartiality of government action is judged.

It is true that preferential aid might disguise itself as nonpreferential aid and that it is a factual question whether a given practice is truly nonpreferential. It is also true that an absolutely pure equality of all religions is impossible, as the example of human sacrifice shows, and as is visible in our choice of "In God We Trust" as opposed to "In the gods we trust" on our coins. Nonetheless, we have a tolerably accurate idea of what the framers understood by the principle of nonestablishment and have few practical problems conforming to it.[5]

Tushnet concludes that "[i]n resolving historical ambiguity, drawing inferences from limited evidence, and taking account of social change, originalist judges have as much room to maneuver as nonoriginalist ones" (36). If by this he means that judges are not constrained if they read history badly, draw incorrect inferences from limited evidence, and change the meaning of the Constitution to suit newer ideas, then of course he is correct. (In fact, that is not a bad description of Justice Hugo Black, however unintentionally or sincerely he did those things.) But that is only to say that if you "do originalism" badly, the results will be bad. Tushnet has not, however, shown why it is necessary to be an incompetent originalist.

But the problems are even deeper, says Tushnet. The originalist project requires the discovery and use of unambiguous historical facts,

whereas the historian finds ambiguity. (Tushnet uses Jefferson's stand
on free speech as an example.) Moreover, in employing certain supplementary evidentiary rules to attain clarity, originalists distort the historical inquiry.

Does the originalist project require discovery and use of unambiguous historical facts? It does, in part. Nevertheless, the originalist position is perfectly compatible with the possibility of ambiguities in the
Constitution and the historical record. Originalists argue that judicial
review should be employed only in cases of clear violations of the Constitution, as it was understood by those who wrote it and those for whom
it was written. Where the meaning of the document is unclear, constitutional decisions should be made through the ordinary political process. (That might involve a separate theory of constitutional
decision-making for such cases—an interesting project, but not one that
must be resolved here.) Originalists concede that judicial review would
be rare under these circumstances (which is why they feel compelled
to answer arguments against majoritarianism, even though they are not
pure majoritarians).

But constitutional language and history may be less ambiguous than
is customarily assumed. Jefferson's position on free speech was not as
"jumbled" as it seems today. He interpreted the First Amendment in a
"federalist" form: it precluded all laws abridging the freedom of speech
on the grounds that such issues were reserved to the states. At the state
level, he accepted the legitimacy of sedition laws in principle, but would
have left the matter to prudence. That is not simply a "jumbled set of
responses," but rather a coherent position (although I believe it is a
wrong one for reasons set out in the minority report on the Virginia
Resolution, believed to have been authored by John Marshall).[6]

Tushnet argues that ambiguity leads originalists to adopt supplementary evidentiary rules. These may play a role in promoting accurate re-
constructions of the past, but they may also embody independent policy
judgments. For example, one could adopt a preference "for a 'special'
kind of intent—the kind exhibited on relatively formal occasions and
expressed in relatively formal terms—rather than the 'private' intent of
letters and the like." This would be "to make a policy judgment that
expressions of opinion on relatively formal occasions ought to be giv-
en special weight" (37).

But that preference would not, in fact, be a policy judgment. It is
justified by the nature of the intent for which one is looking. We want
to know what the general understanding of the document was: the intent of those to whom it was proposed and who ratified it (gave it the
authority it possesses, in a government based on consent of the gov-

erned). This requires that it be "public" rather than merely "private" (although the latter may be of some limited use to know—or more likely confirm—the former). Of course, the possibility always exists that some supplementary evidentiary rules will be used to smuggle in a policy preference. Originalists acknowledge that could happen, but would simply say that it should not—it is illegitimate. Such policy preferences would, as Tushnet argues, improperly "deflect attention from the political and intellectual contexts in which the Constitution was developed." But those contexts do not necessarily, as he asserts, "introduce all the ambiguities that lawyers must ignore." They may not be ambiguous. And if they are, then originalists would not try to create a spurious clarity, but would simply argue that the necessary conditions for the exercise of judicial review are lacking, leaving the issue to the ordinary political process.

Tushnet argues that "originalists presume that they can detach the meanings the framers gave to the words they used from the entire complex of meanings that the framers gave to their political vocabulary as a whole and from the larger political, economic, and intellectual world in which they lived" (39). But they needn't presume that. They can argue that *some* of the vocabulary they used (always within its context, for that is the way we understand words) is consistent with our own usage and/or tolerably clear in its meaning—clear enough for the practical purposes of adjudicating a particular case—and that where it is not, the resultant ambiguities should be resolved through the democratic process.

The second step in the overall argument against originalism is that the more plausible account of historical knowledge is the view of hermeneutics: that "historical understanding requires an imaginative transposition of former world-views into the categories of our own" (32). Tushnet raises doubts about the easy assumption of originalists that "past intentions are determinate and identifiable" by comparing the two approaches. According to hermeneutics, interpreters must enter the minds of the subjects from the past, see the world as they saw it, and understand it in their own terms. (So far, so good, the originalist would say.)

He then gives as an example, amazingly, Justice Brandeis's concurrence in *Whitney v. California*, in which Brandeis gives his famous panegyric on the founders and freedom of speech. Tushnet concedes that Brandeis's "reconstruction" of the framers' world-view was "partial and largely unsupported by specific references to what any framer actually said" but alleges that it "does in the end bring us into the framers' world." "It matters not very much that their views on specific aspects

of governmental design may have differed in detail from Brandeis's reconstruction; what matters is that they designed a government that com-
ported with their sense of a world in which civic virtue reigned"
(40–41).

To say that it is "partial" is an understatement. It is a thorough distortion of what the framers believed, overstating one aspect of their
thought and completely ignoring another. Tushnet's pooh-poohing of
differences of "detail" cannot justify this distortion. The framers valued freedom of speech, but in the narrower form that they intended it,
as allowing for suppression of seditious speech, either by the federal
government—the Federalists—or by the states—the Republicans. That
qualification is not just a question of detail. It means that Brandeis's
portrayal of the framers is fundamentally misconceived. If this is what
the hermeneutic method gives us, it is simply an excuse for distorting
history in the service of contemporary preferences. Tushnet accuses originalists of looking at parts, not the whole, but then seems to opt here
for a method that creates a spurious whole by ignoring clear-cut parts.

But Tushnet goes on to argue that the hermeneutic method—the best
method for reconstructing the past—involves not only reconstructing the
world of the past, but doing so "creatively." Tushnet's example this time
is *Brown v. Board of Education*. The framers of the Fourteenth Amendment might have told us that the amendment did not outlaw segregation in the public schools. For them, public education was "a relatively
new and peripheral social institution designed (say) to civilize the lower
classes" (42), while freedom of contract (which the Fourteenth Amendment *did* protect from racial discrimination) was extremely important,
as the foundation for individual achievement. The hermeneutic method
would say, therefore, that public education in 1954—by that time a central institution for the achievement of individual goals—is "the functional equivalent not of public education in 1868 but of freedom of
contract in 1868" and therefore *Brown* was rightly decided. Originalists must require judges to find functional equivalences, if they wish
to use history meaningfully, but when originalists do so they reintro-
duce the discretion they wish to exclude.

The originalist must respond, of course, by refusing to adopt such
a nebulous theory of functional equivalences, which is simply another
way of bumping up the level of generality of the discussion, to avoid
being bound by the substantive content of constitutional provisions.[7]
Being aware of what the founders hoped to achieve by the Fourteenth
Amendment is important for interpreting the amendment, but it is not
an authorization to alter it (by trying to achieve that goal in another
area). Moreover, even if the amendment were ambiguous, so that it were

not simply a case of "altering" it, its general purposes would not justify reading it in a controversial way in order to strike down laws or issue judicial commands.[8]

Tushnet is right to point out that the Fourteenth Amendment was
written before the modern social welfare state and that this complicates
the application of the amendment's general principle to phenomena
(such as universal public education) not regularly a part of the framers' political world. But for the conservative originalist, this difficulty
or uncertainty is only another argument against employing judicial review in this case and in favor of resolving it through the ordinary political process. Tushnet himself, it should be noted, despite his use of
this example against originalist theory, seems skeptical about deciding
such issues through judicial review, and might well prefer leaving them
to the political process—but a transformed one.

Tushnet goes on to point out that functional equivalency is indeterminate. Many alternative hermeneutic accounts of *Brown* are possible.
But this is only one instance of the deeper problem. When we immerse
ourselves in the framers' mental world, we can understand it better, but
the understanding we achieve is "only one of a great many possible re-
constructions of that segment of the past, a reconstruction shaped not
only by the character of the past but also by our own interests, concerns, and preconceptions" (43).

It is true, abstractly, that there is no perfect reconstruction of the
past, human knowledge is never perfect. But for purposes of constitutional interpretation, the conservative originalist argues that the framers' world can be sufficiently illuminated to give us a generally clear
view of the basic principles they wrote into the Constitution. (For example, Leonard Levy's reconstruction of the framers' understanding of
free speech is much closer to the truth than Brandeis's rhetoric in *Whitney*, which is more like a reconstruction of John Stuart Mill's world.)
Some ambiguities in those basic principles remain, and much uncertainty may remain in applying those principles to concrete new situations
over time. But these ambiguities and uncertainties do not undermine a
conservative originalist approach to judicial review. They are simply
part of the stuff of political and social life that needs to be dealt with
through the political institutions established by the Constitution. Nor
does the conservative originalist offer any guarantee that the ordinary
political process will produce the right answers. He only says that such
a political process is likely in the long run to do a better job (i.e., better than a broad form of judicial review not tied to a clear reading of
the Constitution) because it requires a greater degree of consent and that
requirement (for a great variety of reasons) is preferable to alternatives.

Tushnet's concluding argument is based on an examination of the "originalist approach" of *Dred Scott v. Sandford*. Chief Justice Taney put himself back into the world in which the Constitution was framed and adopted and found that the black race was of an inferior order and that its members "had no rights which the white man was bound to respect."

Tushnet concedes that more could be said to blur the clarity of this originalist decision, since there were more conflicts over slavery and the status of free blacks in 1789 than Taney admitted. "But when all the evidence is assembled, what we make of it will depend on the past that we choose to identify." The problem with originalism is that it "attributes our choices to people in the past and so displaces our responsibility for reconstructing our society on the basis of the continuities we choose to make with our past" (45).

But originalism does no such thing. It certainly displaces the right of *judges* to have a disproportionate role in "reconstructing" our society on the basis of the continuities *they* choose to make with our past (and Tushnet has made clear in other parts of his book how broad that range of choice is). Originalism would make it more difficult for us today to change certain choices made in the past—that is the point of constitutionalism, after all.

But originalism also leaves much to our choice. For example, Americans chose Lincoln as their president, knowing that he advocated a position intended in the long run to eliminate slavery, on the basis of his articulation of the principles enunciated by the founders. They have chosen over time—too slowly and with too many fits and starts, and sometimes by dubious means—to pursue the ideal of racial equality before the law that Lincoln and most of the founders rightly saw implicit in the Declaration of Independence. (Taney's originalism was sincere, but he did a bad job of ascertaining original intent in *Dred Scott*.) And Americans today must continue to make choices to realize that ideal more effectively—perhaps sometimes even by rejecting programs that are put forward under its banner. Conservative originalism is not the theory that displaces that responsibility. It is judicial activism today that seeks to displace "our" responsibility by transferring it to judges.

The hermeneutic school that is the basis for Tushnet's critique is one contemporary form of radical historicism, which claims that all human knowledge is decisively conditioned and shaped by the circumstances of the observer. Human beings never get beyond their own somewhat distorted (or, less pejoratively, somewhat "creative") perceptions to reality itself.

If this viewpoint is carried to its logical conclusion, then there is no way of saying that any perception is superior to another one, since they are all personal creations, and there is no Archimedean point from which to judge the superiority of one to another. But then, if carried to this point, the very possibility of human *knowledge* seems to be destroyed, since we are all locked effectively into our own individual, self-created visions of reality. (In such a world, perhaps only a requirement of self-consistency would be a ground for criticizing anyone's perception; and, to the extent that even consistency is regarded as a "choice" rather than a requirement intrinsic to human knowing, not even that would work.)[9]

A less radical form of historicism admits that there are grounds for saying that at least some perceptions are "better" (more accurate) than other perceptions. If our access to and description of reality is never complete or perfect, there seems to be at least some contact with something beyond our own perceptions, some contact between our own perceptions and reality. But if that is the sum of the critique—that some perceptions of reality are better than others—then the epistemological realism upon which conservative originalism (at least my "nostalgic" variety) is based can hardly be said to be "almost completely demolished," as Tushnet suggests.

The claim that human beliefs *can* be conditioned by historical circumstances (always are, to some extent, e.g., in their formulation of the questions) is not a particularly new observation. One of the most interesting aspects of classical political philosophy is its insight into the profound influence of the "regime" in shaping citizens and the way they view the world. And, in fact, students of classical thought would join Tushnet in some of his acute observations about the influence of a supposedly "neutral" liberalism on the way of life of citizens in a liberal regime. But this claim is different from the claim that it is simply not possible to discover determinate intentions through historical research. In fact, the structure of the most persuasive arguments against the possibility of discovering historical "truth" reflects a contradiction: they take given accounts of history that claim to be true and show their shortcomings powerfully—but the power of the critique turns on skill in historical analysis, the ability to show the untruth of the given accounts, and the greater truth of others.

An example of this is the traditional legal-realist account of U.S. constitutional history in its various forms. The legal realists argue that, with varying degrees of subtlety, all judges are "politicians in robes," denying the traditional assertion that it was possible and desirable for judges to be "mouthpieces of the law." Legal realists made persuasive cases that certain decisions were wrong (or at least not compelled by law, as was alleged) as a matter of legal doctrine and therefore had to be explained in other ways, especially by the judges' underlying political views. But in showing that the decisions were "wrong" (or at best "optional"), they implicitly accepted the possibility of right decisions: in principle at least it was possible for judges to be true mouthpieces of the law.

That is why I defend the approach to constitutional law espoused by John Marshall—an approach that assumes the goal of judicial "objectivity"—without being bothered by the fact that someone may be able to persuade me that in a such-and-such a case, (say, *Dartmouth College*) Marshall decided an issue "wrongly," that is, not in accordance with the Constitution properly understood. That would only be to employ Marshall's method better than he did himself in that particular instance.

That is why careful legal realists must confine themselves to the apparently—at first glance—less radical contention that judges such as Marshall have not so much made clearly "wrong" decisions as they have made many decisions that are only one "possible" decision among many. And this argument must be based on more than just the observation that many people disagreed with Marshall about many cases. It would have to show that Marshall's arguments were consistently inadequate—which many have claimed to show, but unsuccessfully, in my opinion.

Destabilized Institutions and Meanings

Conservative constitutional theory is also nostalgic, according to Tushnet, because it looks back to a stable society whose institutions have been destabilized by capitalism. But a society without stable institutions will not have the stable language meanings that make originalism possible.

There is much truth in the observation that pure capitalism, in which economic efficiency is the sole consideration, requires such a high degree of mobility that it does foster change at a rapid rate, and this mobility and change can undermine the stability of human institutions. But I don't think that capitalism can be shown to have destabilized American institutions so much as to make originalism merely nostalgic.

For the record, American institutions may have been destabilized much less by our economic system and its tendencies than Tushnet suggests and much more by quite different factors, by intellectuals who have been unhappy with American political and economic institutions. (Religion, to take one case, an essential part of the founders' "package" of political institutions, may have been undermined more by intellectuals' pride than by capitalists' avarice.)

The destabilizing influence of capitalism has been mitigated by several factors. First, American capitalism has never been pure. Throughout American history, the concern for economic efficiency has always been qualified by many other concerns, such as religion, family, and the bonds of other intermediate associations. Second, some aspects of capitalism may be destabilizing. These include the desire for perfectly mobile resources, including human beings who may be uprooted and moved to niches where they will be more useful, and the willingness to alter political institutions to accommodate new economic circumstances, which may be seen as one source of the nationalization of American political life. But capitalism may also have contrary stabilizing tendencies, such as the desire to avoid disruptions that inhibit economic efficiency, which may lead to efforts to keep labor happy, even at some cost to pure efficiency and mobility; the attachment to property and the broad distribution of it characteristic of capitalism, which may mitigate class conflict, a key source of political instability; a preference for incrementalism rather than dramatic change in order to provide a more stable and therefore less risky environment for investment.

Thus, together with tendencies toward instability, there are others that may promote stability. Tushnet is sensitive to many of the tendencies of capitalism, but by downplaying some of the cross-cutting tendencies he may lapse into an excessive economic/social determinism.

A better model for dealing with regime tendencies is found in Alexis de Tocqueville. Tocqueville was also sensitive to the tendencies of democracy (and capitalism) in America, and he recognized that some of these tendencies were not attractive. His study of America was based on his belief that, within the broad flow of historical circumstances determined by the democratic revolution, it was possible to achieve better or worse forms of democracy. He sought to identify and secure the better form by highlighting certain aspects of democracy that offset the dangerous tendencies and perhaps by encouraging the partial retention in democracy of certain elements of previous (nondemocratic) regimes. Nevertheless, he recognized that there would be an inevitable price to be paid for the advantages of democracy, and he argued that, overall, this price was worth paying. Likewise, I think it is possible to offset some of the less attractive tendencies of capitalism by appealing to countertendencies within it and to other, noncapitalist tendencies, making the price to be paid a tolerable one.

The key question for us here is whether, when taking into account these factors that limit the destabilizing tendencies of capitalism, the resultant system still produces so much change that it becomes impossible to maintain a sufficient community of language meaning to sustain originalism. I am not persuaded by anything that Tushnet says—most of his discussion of capitalism's destabilizing influence is very general—that capitalism has brought such drastic changes. In the area where the strongest such case might be made—the nationalization of American economic life—the confines of the commerce clause seem to be flexible enough to accommodate the very substantial change that has occurred. Nor am I convinced that a proper reading of constitutional restrictions in this area (e.g., the contract clause) would be baneful. The substantial change that capitalism has brought over time seems to me to be compatible with a community of language meaning that makes originalism possible. Of course, there are many—intellectuals in particular—who are not happy with the Constitution in important respects and would like to change it. But their dislike of our form of government is not an argument that originalism is impossible because insufficient agreement on the meaning of language makes us unable to know what the Constitution was intended to mean. And the adequacy of our agreement on language is enhanced if we recognize that the Constitution was not intended to settle all issues and that the general language of the document, as well as its ambiguities, can and should be "specified" in the normal political process.

Tushnet's critique notwithstanding, then, it is possible to "interpret" the Constitution, arriving at a relatively clear view of its principles. This makes it possible to exercise judicial review in some (few) relatively clear cases, making judicial review "worthwhile." But Tushnet is right to say that such a form of judicial review would be of relatively limited use with respect to the problem of legislative tyranny. That is what I believe the framers thought, too. More important than judicial review, in their institutional design, was the extended republic, the separation of powers, and federalism.

Tushnet argues that such a set of institutions won't work anymore, without traditional republican elements (or their equivalents) that have been destroyed by a system that emphasizes private property and a dynamic economy. He is right that traditional republican elements are necessary. But I think he is wrong in seeing them as dead. These elements have not been destroyed but wounded (and more by anticapitalist liberal intellectuals than by capitalists).

Both Tushnet and I are unhappy about the present (though he much more radically than I) and wish to deal with its problems in ways that seem implausible under current conditions. He argues that current economic conditions of capitalism undermine the framers' original design (which was also seriously deficient even insofar as it "worked," e.g., in resting on a substantial restriction of the franchise), and he opts for a vaguely described future that he concedes to be "utopian" in important respects. I opt for what he calls "nostalgia," that is, I would like to see the essential elements of the framers' design restored (not necessarily all its details) despite current conditions of intellectual life (the continuing onslaught of modernity and postmodernity) that make such a restoration seem implausible. But this brings us well into the second aspect of Tushnet's book that I would like to discuss in more detail, namely, its discussion of liberalism and republicanism.

Liberalism and Republicanism in Tushnet

Much in Tushnet's critique of liberalism is very insightful. Perhaps most important is his sensitivity to the formation of (supposedly) "individual" preferences by social institutions. And with respect to constitutional law, he argues persuasively that once "plain meaning" is lost and the liberal tradition takes off on a search for a new "grand theory" of judicial review, the attempt to restrain judges will be a failure. But, overall, Tushnet's criticisms of liberalism, drawn largely from aspects of republican political theory, leave us with more questions than insights.

The matrix for Tushnet's analysis is the tension between liberal and republican political theory. In particular, he draws on a strand of contemporary scholarship that argues that the founding was dominated not just by liberal, Lockean thought but at least equally by the civic republican tradition. The liberal tradition stressed self-interest, governmental neutrality regarding the question of the good human life, and liberty, while the republican tradition emphasized community, the need for public institutions to shape private character, and equality. Tushnet rightly sees that these traditions in America vary largely in their emphases, with a good deal of overlap, but in the end he bases his critique on their incompatibility. Perhaps he argues, as Tocqueville seems to, that the mixed regime, for all its apparent benefits, will not work.[10] Social institutions are more dynamic than conservatives (and nostalgic originalists) admit. Attempts to combine different political principles are bound to break down due to change. As we have seen, special emphasis is placed on the dynamic and antitraditional character of the capitalist economic system.

The question, it seems to me, is whether Tushnet underestimates the possibility that our regime can endure as a mixture of principles. The balance of the different principles involved can vary over time, but it

need not move inevitably or irreversibly in one direction. A healthy capacity to be somewhat inconsistent may be a key virtue in a political
community like ours.

Tushnet's skepticism about such a capacity may partly reflect the fact
that he lives and works among intellectuals, who tend to be very uncomfortable with acknowledged inconsistency. Most legal intellectuals
today are either striving to purify liberalism of its "inconsistencies" or
are trying to get rid of liberalism altogether (with or without some workable alternative in mind).[11] His skepticism may also reflect a habit of
intellectuals to be deterministic, to take past and present trends and
project them to their logical consequences.[12] They tend to say, retrospectively, that history turned out the way it did because it had to (and will
continue to), downplaying the element of human choice. (In this respect,
Tocqueville takes a kind of middle position, arguing strongly for the
irreversible character of the historical movement toward democracy, but
at the same time writing a book so that his readers can help to choose
a better form of democracy rather than another that is worse.)

Tushnet's analysis seems to result in some rather black and white
observations. For example, his attack on grand theories takes this form:
liberal arguments for judicial review will only work if the regime can
draw on elements of republicanism, but if we have the republican elements, then we don't need judicial review. But it might be possible to
modify his argument in the following way. A "nostalgic originalist"
would follow the founders in saying that judicial review cannot be relied on *to the extent* that contemporary liberals would like to, but that
it is still a worthwhile "auxiliary aid" in a mixed liberal/republican regime. It can serve as a check to more extreme instances of "corruption"
of political power (a perennial republican concern), and it can also in
that way be a useful part of civic education (another republican theme).
At the same time, because not as much is expected from judicial review (the chief guarantees of liberty lying elsewhere in the regime, especially in the extended republic argument), perhaps the republican
elements necessary to make it workable in a more limited form need
not be so substantial (for example, a lesser degree of "civic virtue"
would be adequate).

On a deeper level, there are problems with the scholarship on which
Tushnet relies in his characterization of republicanism vis-a-vis liberalism.[13] The recent scholarship on the civic republican tradition puts
forward a version of republicanism that does not seem to take into account sufficiently the ambiguity of republicanism during the founding.
Most importantly, it fails to discuss this republicanism adequately in
the context of the most fundamental division of political thought, the

ancients versus the moderns. It was this ambiguity that was the Achilles' heel of the Anti-Federalists as well.

Classical and modern republicanism were substantially different, in ways that the Anti-Federalists, recent republican scholarship, and Tushnet do not account for. For a clearer vision of this problem, there is no better source of enlightenment than Montesquieu.

Montesquieu's *Spirit of the Laws* is a real puzzle. At the beginning of the book, Montesquieu provides a typology of regimes, breaking them down into monarchies, tyrannies, and republics. The republics described in this section of the book have generally "classical" features. They rely especially on the "virtue" of the citizenry, that is, their self-renouncing dedication to the fatherland (with which they identify their own good). This virtue is a product of an education of the whole people as a single family, with each of the citizens devoting close attention and care to one another's conduct. It requires frugality and equality, with a strict regulation of property to achieve both. Manners too are closely regulated to preserve purity of morals. The laws of such a regime are, as Martin Diamond aptly observed,[14] *harsh* and even sanguinary laws, far beyond what liberals and what early American "republicans" both would tolerate. "Civic republicans" quoted Montesquieu, but they did so somewhat selectively.

The puzzle in Montesquieu arises from the fact that later in *The Spirit of the Laws* Montesquieu has a long description and discussion of the English Constitution, which does not fit anywhere into the general typology of regimes at the beginning of the book. England, a modern commercial republic, is profoundly different from the classical republic, with an emphasis on political liberty rather than virtue. Citizens pursue not the good and glory of the fatherland, but primarily their economic self-interest. The society is characterized by a (relative, not complete) liberation of the private passions rather than the classical repression of them (shown, among other ways, by Montesquieu's efforts to mitigate the severity of different aspects of the criminal law). This form of government looks a good deal more like the liberal republicanism of Americans.

This is not the place to deal with the solution to the puzzle of why Montesquieu excludes the modern commercial republic from his original broad typology of regimes. I raise this issue here because it exemplifies some perennial problems of discussions of American "civic republicanism." The Anti-Federalists relied on Montesquieu's descriptions of both "virtuous republicanism" and "liberal republicanism" (the terms are Thomas Pangle's),[15] failing to see (as Montesquieu saw) that these republicanisms represented fundamentally different choices. As

Herbert Storing has argued, this was fatal to the Anti-Federalist position, since it amounted to an impossible desire to have their cake and eat it too: to be both ancient and modern. In the end, they had to choose, and they chose to go along with modernity, desiring the blessings of liberty and commerce that classical republicanism would have made impossible.

This is not to argue that the modern republican regime necessarily had to be "purely" liberal, absolutely without any admixture of the elements of "virtuous republicanism." To say that the regime could not be based on the citizens' self-renouncing dedication to the public good was not to say that the notion of civic virtue had to be dismissed entirely. But it did mean rejecting or at least minimizing the elements of classical republicanism most incompatible with modern liberal republicanism. Among other things, for example, it meant giving up the idea of legally enforced economic equality and a very broad censorial power to regulate manners, for example, in the form of sumptuary laws.

The question in my mind is exactly what form of republicanism Tushnet wants to use as the standpoint for his critique of liberalism. It is difficult for me to imagine that he would seriously consider the illiberal, virtuous republicanism of the classical world. At one point, for example, he rejects not only as "unrealistic" but also as "irresponsible" the idea of restricting the franchise to help make republicanism workable once more. Like the Anti-Federalists, Tushnet and other critics of liberalism are actually very attached to some aspects of liberalism (e.g., a very broad form of freedom of speech, occupational freedom, a very broad conception of political equality) that are incompatible with classical republicanism. But if the basis for Tushnet's critique is modern liberal republicanism, then there may not be a possibility of any robust contrast between it and liberalism.

One example of this problem in Tushnet, I think, is his frequent discussion of "community." Tushnet draws on the republican tradition and its greater emphasis on community in order to provide a contrast with and critique of liberal individualism. But the possibility of genuine community requires us to address the question of what a "community" has "in common." For classical republicanism, the sharing could be quite substantial, because classical regimes were founded on the notion of a shared way of life, in which citizens' habits of thought and opinions, their moral ideals and attitudes toward all the different facets of human life, and even their most fundamental religious beliefs—all were intimately bound up with community identity and life. There was no principled distinction between "public" and "private."

But I do not think that Tushnet and other contemporary students of civic republicanism want to go that far in resurrecting *classical* republicanism. While often showing effectively the illusory nature of the modern liberal attempt to separate public and private completely, and while yearning for a greatly reinvigorated sense of community, these critics usually produce only the hollow shell of community in their own theorizing. Deeply affected by modern (liberal) philosophy's skepticism about man's ability to know *the* human good, they have no substantive view of the human good on which to base their community. As a result, their community usually comes down to some kind of "joint self-determination," without substantive content, a kind of community for community's sake. But that is as illusory a goal as liberalism's purely private pursuit of happiness. Just as you cannot successfully pursue a "happiness" abstracted from a concrete substantive view of what truly brings happiness, so is it impossible to pursue a "community" abstracted from a concrete substantive view of what truly brings community. In both cases it is necessary to distinguish between the ersatz and the real. A theory of happiness that includes the "delight" a Klansman might take in burning blacks is not particularly useful. Nor is a theory of community that is open to foundation on a like evil. Tushnet doesn't engage in liberalism's pursuit of "neutral" law, but he seems to give no substantive criteria for evaluating different forms of community.

Religion receives a similar treatment. It becomes a community in which people share (invented) conceptions of reality. Much of Tushnet's critique of liberal constitutional law regarding religion is quite insightful. Liberalism has difficulty with intermediate associations such as churches, since they reflect human experiences at odds with liberalism (especially its individualism). But in general, Tushnet's own tendency is to relativize religions by regarding them as communities "narrower" than the political community.[16] That contrasts interestingly with both classical republicans and early Americans. Classical republicans (and modern imitators such as Rousseau, in his *Social Contract*) regard religion and politics as coextensive; religion is the "civil religion." Early Americans, it could be argued, regarded particular sects as narrower communities, but they also had a more universal conception of religion (particularly Christianity) that made it possible to regard religion as a *broader* community. All men, and even political communities, owed a certain recognition to God, as the Declaration of Independence's acknowledgment of "Divine Providence" showed. The basis for the distinctiveness of religion, for singling it out for protection, lay in its being that broader or more universal (though invisible) community. Tushnet's rejection of religion's distinctiveness (262, n.56) leads him not to take seriously Douglas's comment in *Zorach*, which reflects the views of early Americans: "We are a religious people whose institutions presuppose a Supreme Being." Tushnet downplays this statement as merely reflecting the diffuse religiosity of American civil religion. Its content is only that in "our public life we are allowed to, and may be encouraged to, bolster our positions by reference to a deity" (268–69). But what Douglas said was different: Our very political institutions *presuppose* a Supreme Being. Religion with content—"true" religion as opposed to an artificial human creation—seems as foreign to Tushnet's thought as to contemporary liberalism.

The ambivalent (postmodern?) character of Tushnet's republicanism also seems to appear in his comparative treatment of sex and money (the passions of lust and avarice). Tushnet emphasizes the strand of equality of wealth quite heavily. Private wealth leads to economic control over others, which in turn deprives them of the independence necessary for republican citizenship. The pursuit of wealth was also, according to the republican tradition, an absorption in one's private good that made public-spiritedness difficult. Thus, in the republican tradition, there was a place for sumptuary laws, which regulated consumption (especially conspicuous consumption) with a view to guaranteeing the requisites of republican citizenship.

But greed or avarice was not the only private passion that undermined the public good. Lust had similar effects, both in diverting the citizen from pursuit of the public good and in undermining the family, on which society was based. Yet this side of the republican tradition does not seem to play an important role in Tushnet's thinking. For example, his lengthy analysis of pornography turns on the feminist objections to violence and female subordination, without much concern for erotica or lust per se, or more broadly for the centrality of the family to political life. This is presumably because Tushnet shares the rejection of any normative conception of the family characteristic of most contemporary intellectuals. In this regard, Tushnet seems to depart from both classical and early modern republicanism. Does this suggest that Tushnet's thought is infected more deeply by liberal individualism than one might think at first glance?

Tushnet's republicanism emphasizes the importance of economic equality and government's duty to establish and maintain economic equality. This too is different from most modern republicanism, which saw the citizen's independence being compromised as much by dependence on public wealth as on private wealth (a theme emphasized strongly in Tocqueville). Perhaps, it may be said, changed circumstances in the modern world make government the only possible guarantor of this necessary economic equality. But as Tushnet suggests frequently, that may simply be an argument for the impossibility of republicanism in the modern world. It is curious, at least, that Tushnet does not seem to feel the need to deal with the problem of dependence on the state as another threat to the independence that republican citizenship demands.

One of the bigger unanswered questions of the book is what exactly Tushnet means by "socialism" when he advocates it. At the end of chapter 3 he refers to an earlier writing in which he responded to the "What would you do?" question by saying that he would make "an explicitly political decision: which result is, in the circumstances now existing, likely to advance the cause of socialism?" (146). And in his discussion of campaign financing in chapter 9, he comments that the capital market is likely to malfunction on at least one question, namely, the value of capitalism, because "the relatively less well-off face a more stringent budget constraint that reduces their ability to invest in political activity" (285). The most obvious remedy to this, he suggests, would be subsidies to socialist parties. That answer (especially as opposed to the available alternative of subsidies to "the relatively less well-off") suggests a simple assumption that socialist parties represent the interests of the less well-off, an assumption that perhaps may be taken for granted in some intellectual circles but might require discussion elsewhere.

But what does Tushnet mean by "socialism"? Sweden? Something more radical? A utopian future whose details are hidden in the mists of the future? It is hard to respond to an argument for a "republican socialism" without knowing what it is. Will republican socialism require a trade-off in economic efficiency and is that trade-off, with all its possible implications (e.g., less mobility, less occupational choice?), worth paying? Will republican socialism's control over the economy raise questions about political independence, especially the availability of resources for unpopular groups to criticize and oppose the government? In the absence of a more specific version of what this republican alternative would be, it is very difficult to compare the defects of what we have with the defects of what Tushnet would propose. Tushnet sometimes (less in *Red, White, and Blue* than in some of his other writings) seems to assume that the present order is so bad that whatever we would get in its place would have to be better. But with all of its defects, the present order seems better to me than most of the political communities that have employed the term "socialist" in their self-definition.

But Tushnet's decision not to spell out a more detailed alternative—rooted in his own belief, I think, that it would not be possible to do so, since it remains to be constructed—is less important in the final analysis because of his ultimate position that "[c]ritique is all there is" (318). The conclusion to *Red, White, and Blue* suggests that if a republican society were ever to be achieved, Tushnet would then feel compelled to switch hats and condemn it in the name of liberalism. Both liberalism and republicanism are rooted in genuine, though not fully compatible, human experiences. Just as Tushnet criticizes liberalism in the name of community, so would he be compelled to criticize republicanism in the name of autonomy.

He does not always seem to despair completely of every kind of synthesis. For example, in his discussion of religion, he argues that a revitalized republican tradition might be able to foster a "culture of mutual forbearance" that would seem to have some of the advantages of liberal toleration without marginalizing religion in the same way. This suggests to me that there may be some way of working out a common ground, respecting the "experiences" at the root of both republicanism and liberalism. One wonders whether Tushnet might find similar grounds in a "revitalized liberal tradition" for dealing with some of the problems of republicanism. Because we never see the (liberal) critique of the yet-to-be constructed republicanism, it's hard to know. But Tushnet in the end concludes that "[n]either the liberal tradition nor the republican one can accommodate the aspects of experience that the other takes as central" (318), and the whole book is predicated on the impossibility of any kind of effective synthesis of the two.

And so, for Tushnet, "critique is all there is." That is unfortunate, because the Constitution (especially if it is properly understood—that is, fairly interpreted) provides us with a political order that, whatever its deficiencies, makes possible a large measure of liberty, opportunity, prosperity, and human decency. In an imperfect world, that political order deserves not only appropriate criticism of its shortcomings, but considerable admiration and even loyalty.

8

Constitutional Interpretation
and Precedent

One final stone must be set in place to complete a discussion of judicial review in American politics. Even assuming that it were possible, over time, to secure the appointment of originalist justices to the Supreme Court, what would these justices do, confronted with a large body of constitutional law that is rooted tenuously if at all in the Constitution itself? This requires us to elaborate more fully what could be called an "originalist theory of adjudication."

If the justices merely applied precedents, their originalist convictions, as mere historical curiosities, would have little impact on constitutional law. If they maintained precedents, but avoided extending or even applying them (grasping at grounds to distinguish precedents, however unpersuasively), they would help to create an incoherent and unprincipled constitutional law. If they insisted on the Constitution as the standard (over precedent), and were willing to uproot precedent, then they would be the authors of a radical revolution in American law. If they at times did the former and at other times the latter, on what principled basis could they choose to draw the line between appropriate maintenance and appropriate overruling of precedents?

The Burger Court—in ways that I have discussed elsewhere[1]—fairly typically chose the route of incoherence. It was notably reluctant to overturn precedents explicitly, though it occasionally did so, as in *Garcia v. San Antonio Metropolitan Transportation Authority* (overturning its own earlier decision in *National League of Cities v. Usery*). But it was also notably reluctant to extend many liberal Warren Court precedents, as it refused in *San Antonio v. Rodriguez* (which turned down an equal protection challenge to local school financing, despite wide disparities in the wealth of school districts, holding that education was not a "fundamental right") to apply the reasoning of cases like *Shapiro v. Thompson* (which held that one-year residency requirements for welfare unconstitutionally burdened the "fundamental right" to travel). The result was a body of law in which many cases whose underlying principles seemed incompatible with each other were all "good" constitutional law, on the basis of unpersuasive "distinctions" between them.[2]

The Rehnquist Court seems, on the whole, to be similarly inclined. The Court is divided into "conservatives" generally oriented toward originalism (Scalia, Thomas, Rehnquist), "liberals" oriented toward some form of modern judicial review (Stevens, Ginsberg, and Breyer), and "moderates" (O'Connor, Souter, Kennedy). This last group typically provides the key votes on divided issues and, while they are moderately conservative on many issues, they are not consistently committed to originalism on principle. The "center of gravity" of the Court, then, lies in a moderate form of modern (essentially legislative) judicial review— a Court that is reluctant to extend past activist decisions or produce new ones, but is also opposed to uprooting activist precedents and is occasionally willing to engage in some judicial legislation. A particularly disconcerting result of this balance of forces is the lack of a truly principled jurisprudence—notwithstanding the many arguments elaborated by classic defenders of modern judicial activism such as Alexander Bickel and Ronald Dworkin that support an expanded modern judicial power because of a special judicial capacity to articulate principles.[3]

In this chapter I would like to examine the question of how an originalist Court would approach the task of judicial review today, when (arguably) most of the controlling precedents typically at issue are at best tenuously rooted in the Constitution and often lack constitutional foundations at all.

I will start by examining two contrasting recommendations from originalist scholars, and then move on to examine some materials from earlier American constitutional statesmen (James Madison and Abraham Lincoln), and finally try to provide some conclusions of my own.

One Extreme Alternative

Gary Lawson of Northwestern University Law School provides us with a striking and powerfully stated position in "The Constitutional Case Against Precedent."[4] He lays out the reasoning of *Marbury v. Madi-*

son: judges are called upon to decide cases according to law, the Constitution is the supreme law, and therefore in cases where the Constitution and a statute (or an executive act) are incompatible the Court should apply the Constitution, refusing to give effect to the law (or executive act). This reasoning, he says, provides a parallel argument to deny precedent *any* weight in constitutional adjudication.[5] If the precedent is correct (its reasoning is persuasive), then there is no need to rely on precedent. The weight of precedent is therefore an issue precisely in cases where the precedent was wrongly decided. If the previous judicial decision was wrongly decided, judges in a new case are in essence faced with the choice of giving effect either to the Constitution or to the incorrect prior judicial opinion. Just as the judges must place the Constitution above an unconstitutional law or executive act, so must they place it above a decision of a previous court that is contrary to the Constitution:

> If a statute, enacted with all of the majestic formalities for lawmaking prescribed by the Constitution, and stamped with the imprimatur of representative democracy, cannot legitimately be given effect in an adjudication when it conflicts with the Constitution, how can a mere judicial decision possibly have greater legal status?[6]

Reliance on incorrect precedent is not only *not* obligatory—it is affirmatively *unconstitutional*.

Several questions might be raised regarding this argument. First, Lawson's argument seems to be just as effective against the legitimacy of "vertical precedent," in which a lower court is compelled to follow the incorrect precedents from higher courts. An argument that effectively "saves" the practice of vertical precedent—and it is hard to imagine our legal system without such a practice—may very well provide grounds for a doctrine of horizontal precedent as well.[7]

Second, Lawson's argument appears to draw a simple either/or picture of constitutional decisions. They are either clearly right or clearly wrong. Does he give sufficient weight to the fact that some decisions are less clear?

He does take up the issue, to some extent, when he acknowledges that his "argument rests on the premise that the Constitution has, at least in principle, an objectively ascertainable meaning."[8] (This is a premise in which I strongly concur.) He rightly dismisses critics who assert the total indeterminacy of constitutional meaning, and points out that "the absence of right answers in some cases affects the practical

scope of my argument but not its formal soundness. The use of precedent will still be unconstitutional in any case in which a right answer
is ascertainable."[9]

Lawson goes on to argue that "the constitutional case against precedent is precisely coterminous with the constitutional case for judicial
review. To the extent that indeterminacy undermines the argument
against precedent, it also undermines the case for judicial review in the
first instance."[10] Again, I think that he is correct in assuming that the
indeterminacy of the Constitution in a given matter removes an essential condition for the exercise of judicial review, which is premised on
the existence of a clear conflict between the law or act and the Constitution. The question is whether there is anything in between an interpretation being clearly right or wrong and its being "indeterminate."

Another Extreme

Virtually no one says that precedent is completely sacrosanct. *Cooper
v. Aaron* does seem to argue that Supreme Court precedent is authoritative vis-a-vis all other political actors; that is, the decision identifies
the oath to uphold the Constitution with an oath to uphold the Supreme
Court's interpretation of the Constitution.[11] For reasons cited below (in
Lincoln's discussion of the authority of Court decisions), I think this
is clearly wrong, but for the moment I want to point out that even this
extreme claim does not make precedent absolute, for the Court did not
bind *itself* to follow its own precedents in every case.

Professor Henry Monaghan, in his "Stare Decisis and Constitutional Adjudication,"[12] goes quite far in attributing weight to constitutional precedent, even from an originalist perspective, and his thoughtful
article is worth considering. Monaghan contends that there have been
"significant and irreversible departures from original understanding" of
the Constitution (e.g., *Brown v. Board of Education*, the scope of the
national commerce power, the growth of the administrative state, and
the transformation of presidential power).[13] Stare decisis certainly helps
to explain why some of these decisions are and should be maintained.
Monaghan argues that there are sound grounds for this power of stare
decisis. "At its most general level, stare decisis operates to promote
systemwide stability and continuity by ensuring the survival of governmental norms that have achieved unsurpassed importance in American
society."[14] In addition, stare decisis helps to legitimate judicial review
(especially among elites) by contributing to the rule of law argument,
"the important notion that the law is impersonal in character."[15]

The *source* of stare decisis is either the "judicial power" of Article III or "constitutional common law," that is, it is "the natural result of judicial powers and duties established in the text and ultimately subject to the control of Congress."[16] The *content* of stare decisis is more complex. Briefly, it can be said that "[i]n the American common law, stare decisis states a conditional obligation: precedent binds absent a showing of substantial countervailing considerations."[17] But Monaghan uneasily concedes that "it may not be possible to go further and formulate relatively determinate implementing criteria, however general, that would guide, if not constrain, judgment."[18] The *meaning* of precedent includes the Court's rule or standard and also (because judicial opinion ought to be a reasoned elaboration of principle) the underlying reasoning.

What are the implications of this weighty but conditional authority of precedent for originalism? Monaghan argues that "we cannot know the framers' original understanding on the subject under discussion: deeply ingrained transformative change." Even conceding that they expected an adherence to original understanding, "our task is to make sense out of a nonoriginalist universe," in which the constitutional text plays "only a role, and an increasingly subordinate one at that."[19] He concludes that

> neither originalism nor the constitutional text has mystical qualities that compel a return to the fold in the face of transforming departures from the original understanding. At this point in our history, when adherence to stare decisis promotes the underlying values of stability and continuity better than does adherence to the original understanding, the latter cannot prevail.[20]

Monaghan carries the logic of his case to a consistent conclusion: it not only justifies maintaining transformative change, but also licenses (prospectively) "disregard of original understanding when the Court is satisfied that change is necessary to maintain systemic equilibrium," and disregard of precedents themselves for similar reasons.

Despite a final assertion that we cannot dismiss the Constitution of 1789, then, Monaghan's article ends by apparently abandoning originalism. If precedents have such great weight, constituting in at least some cases de facto constitutional amendments, the fixed standard of the Constitution, the "anchor" for interpretation, seems lost. Originalist justices are reduced to defending not the Constitution but previous, illegitimate constitutional decisions. Precedent seems like a one-way ratchet moving away from the Constitution.

Some Historical Materials

I would like to turn now from modern scholarship to earlier thinkers, in particular James Madison and Abraham Lincoln. Both of these constitutional statesmen can contribute in important ways to our understanding of the question.

On various occasions, Madison dealt explicitly with the question of the force of precedent in constitutional cases. Probably the most important of these was the attack on him for inconsistency at a time, later in his life, when he rejected the doctrine of nullification, though his critics alleged that he had embraced such a doctrine in the Virginia Resolutions of 1798. Critics said that Madison had manifested such inconsistency throughout his career, and they cited especially his prominent opposition to the national bank, on constitutional grounds, in the early 1790s and his later signing of a bill establishing a national bank when he was president.

In response, Madison strongly denied the charges of inconsistency. On the bank question, he said that he had signed the bank bill

> in conformity to an early & unchanged opinion, that in the case of a Constitution as of a law, a course of authoritative, deliberate, and continued decisions, such as the Bank could plead was an evidence of the Public Judgment, necessarily superseding individual opinions. There has been a fallacy in this case as indeed in others in confounding a question whether precedents could expound a Constitution, with a question whether they could alter a Const. This distinction is too obvious to need elucidation. None will deny that precedents of a certain description fix the interpretation of a law. Yet who will pretend that they can repeal or alter a law?[21]

And to another correspondent he wrote:

> the inconsistency is apparent only, not real; inasmuch as my abstract opinion of the text of the Constitution is not changed, and the assent was given in pursuance of my early and unchanged opinion, that, in the case of a Constitution as of a law, a course of authoritative expositions sufficiently deliberate, uniform, and settled, was an evidence of the public will necessarily overruling individual opinions. It cannot be less necessary that the meaning of the Constitution should be freed from uncertainty, than that the law should be so. That cases may occur which transcend all authority of precedents must be admitted, but they form exceptions which will speak for themselves and must justify themselves.[22]

Madison, then, clearly understood precedent to have force, even in cases where his "abstract opinion" remained that the meaning of the Constitution had been misstated by the precedent.

Lincoln's contribution to our topic is more indirect. It occurs in the context of a discussion of the authority of Supreme Court precedents, which was part of his response to the *Dred Scott* decision. Lincoln's position was quite nuanced. He distinguished between the *decision of the case* and the *interpretation of the Constitution* on which that decision was based. Republicans had no intent to disturb the decision in the particular case, he said. He went even further, conceding that normally the decisions of the Court should control not only the particular cases decided, but the general policy of the country, subject to be disturbed only by amendments. Nonetheless, as Lincoln argued in his First Inaugural:

> the candid citizen must confess that if the policy of the government, upon vital questions, affecting the whole people, is to be irrevocably fixed by decisions of the Supreme Court, the instant they are made, in ordinary litigation between parties, in personal actions, the people will have ceased, to be their own rulers, having, to that extent, practically resigned their government, into the hands of that eminent tribunal.[23]

Lincoln took a middle position on the question of the authority of Supreme Court precedents: "judicial decisions are of greater or less authority as precedents according to circumstances." Lincoln listed a variety of circumstances that undermined the authority of the *Dred Scott* decision, though there is no indication that he intended the list to be exhaustive. They include: the lack of unanimity of the decision; its apparent partisan bias; its discordance with educated public (especially legal) opinion and with the steady practice of the different branches of government throughout our history; its foundation upon false historical opinions (e.g., that the Declaration's "all men are created equal" meant "all white men are created equal"), and (given the presence of these factors) the lack of authority that comes from being affirmed and reaffirmed over time.

Although Lincoln was addressing the question of the authority of Supreme Court precedents for other actors in the political system (e.g., legislators), the factors that affect that authority of Supreme Court precedents for them would presumably also be at least some of the factors in the Court's own judgment about its precedents.

Some Basic Principles

With these materials to help us examine the question of the legitimate
force of precedent for an originalist, I would like to try to sift through
the various arguments and provide what I think are some reasonable
guidelines.

The first factor to note in evaluating the weight of precedent is that
settled precedents, especially, carry weight in constitutional adjudication. Lincoln's list of factors that undermine the authority of Supreme
Court precedents provides us with a good starting point. The more divided the Court, the less weight its opinion carries;[24] the greater the appearance of partisanship, the less weight; the more the opinion
"surprises" or goes against the grain of educated (especially legal) expectations and the less it is supported by the practice of other branches of the government, the less weight; the more dubious the historical
arguments on which it is based, the less weight; the more recent the
contested decision, the less weight. Settled decisions, then, will be especially those that are agreed to by large or unanimous Court majorities, that conform to the expectations of the educated public, that are
supported by the practice of government generally, and that have been
reaffirmed over time.

These considerations seem to overlap with Madison's reasons for the
force of precedent. His reasoning gives weight to the need for "deliberate, uniform and settled" constitutional meaning. But he connects these
factors to a deeper *political* argument derived from the nature of our
republican form of government: "a course of authoritative expositions
sufficiently deliberate, uniform, and settled" is "evidence of the public
will necessarily overruling individual opinions," "evidence of the Public Judgment, necessarily superseding individual opinions." The ultimate
rulers in republican government are the people, and it is their opinion
that is finally authoritative. When by various signs it becomes clear that
a decision has become "settled," that is a kind of tacit consent argument that the people have determined the matter. (At the same time,
recall—as I will discuss further below—that Madison indicates that
there may be cases that "transcend all authority of precedents.")

It is important to note here that settled precedent reflects not only
the reaffirmation by the Court of its earlier decisions, but also the
acceptance of those decisions by the other branches of government.
Justice Scalia made a form of this argument in *Pennsylvania v. Union
Gas Co.*:

> Moreover, unlike the vast majority of judicial decisions, Hans has had
> a pervasive effect upon statutory law, automatically ensuring that pri-

vate damages actions created by federal law do not extend against the States. Forty-nine Congresses since Hans have legislated under that assurance. It is impossible to say how many extant statutes would have included an explicit preclusion of suits against States if it had not been thought that such suits were automatically barred. Indeed, it is not even possible to say that, without Hans, all constitutional amendments would have taken the form they did [citing the Seventeenth Amendment].[25]

Precedents may have become part of the fiber of the law, the assumptions on which other branches of government have based the performance of their duties.

A second factor in considering the weight of precedent must be its "distance" from the Constitution. The further the precedent is from the Constitution, the less its weight. A decision that is *clearly* wrong will have less weight than one that is at least a plausible interpretation or application of the document.

Lawson argues that indeterminacy of the Constitution adds nothing to the weight of precedent, since the case for judicial review is precisely coterminous with the case for precedent. If the meaning or application of the Constitution is indeterminate, then an essential ground for judicial review is absent, and the resultant precedent carries no weight.

While I strongly agree that indeterminacy makes judicial review inappropriate in the first instance, that indeterminacy may cut the other way when it is a question of overruling precedent. It seems to me that precedent should carry greater weight especially when judges are confronted with a precedent that is not so much "affirmatively unconstitutional" (i.e., clearly wrong in its substantive interpretation of the Constitution) as it is "unjustifiable," that is, not clear enough to justify judicial review although its substantive interpretation of the Constitution may be quite plausible (but not compelling).

For example, I would argue that the constitutional question in *Champion v. Ames* could have gone either way. The minority opinion, which would have struck down the prohibition of the interstate shipment of lottery tickets, could rightly appeal to Marshall's admonition in *McCulloch v. Maryland* that the Court would be compelled to strike down laws when enumerated powers were used as a "pretext" for regulating matters intended to be left to the states. (What about a Congressional law that prohibited the interstate transportation of people not married or divorced in accord with Congressional specifications?) On the other hand, the majority rightly pointed to Marshall's statement in *Gibbons v. Ogden* that the abuse of an enumerated power—given that those powers were "plenary"—could only be rectified by electing new representatives. Both positions are reasonable.

Because the law was not *clearly* unconstitutional, the Court was correct in upholding it. Why should the Court's preference between two concededly reasonable constitutional interpretations take precedence over the legislature's? Suppose, however, that the Court had wrongly struck down the law, and that this decision had become a settled precedent. What should a later Court then do in a case where the precedent was invoked? It seems to me that there are reasonable grounds to say that precedent, if settled, should have stronger weight in such a case, even though the original act of judicial review would have been unjustified.

Lawson might possibly agree with this, since the "unjustifiable" decision (as opposed to the *substantively* mistaken one) can be viewed as not positively violating the Constitution, and hence as not unconstitutional. Perhaps this is simply another limit on the scope of his argument.

However, it seems more likely that he would disagree, arguing that what I am calling an "unjustifiable" decision is substantively wrong in a broader sense in that it constitutes a judicial usurpation of the legislative power granted by the Constitution. From that perspective, he might argue that today's Court cannot, on the basis of the previous unjustifiable decision, continue to restrict legitimate legislative power.

But Madison notes that it is "necessary that the meaning of a Constitution should be freed from uncertainty" just as it is true that ordinary statutes ought not to be left uncertain in meaning. This necessity inheres in the nature of law, for an unsettled and changing law is harder to know and to apply consistently and impartially. Combined with the argument that constitutional law properly regarded as "settled" can be viewed as having received public acquiescence, this provides a reasonable ground for recognizing the force of precedent in constitutional decisions.

But what is the source of this recognition of the "nature of the law" that justifies giving precedent weight? The most plausible contender would appear to be "the judicial power" of Article III. Lawson contends that invoking this provision begs the question. Since the judicial power turns on what the sources of law are in deciding cases, and since the Constitution is hierarchically superior to any other source of law, Article III contains no basis for a judicial power to prefer incorrect precedent to the Constitution. Lawson does concede, however, that Article III grounds a case-deciding power that is final, so that the executive must enforce a judicial decision even when he believes it to be unconstitutional. But if the executive can be required to enforce a wrong judicial decision on grounds relating to an Article III case-deciding power, why cannot courts be required to give weight to precedents (even when incorrect) as part of an Article III judicial power understood to include the respect for precedent indisputably at the core of Anglo-American judging?

Another level of this problem of indeterminacy emerges when we ask "exactly how 'indeterminate' is the Constitution on the point at issue?" This is a variation of the question "*how* plausible or reasonable are competing interpretations of a constitutional provision?"

The very important qualification that Madison adds to his position— that some cases will transcend all authority of precedent—seems to suggest that it is too simple to distinguish only between "clearly wrong decisions" and "decisions where the Constitution is indeterminate." Madison's abstract opinion on the constitutionality of a national bank never changed—in that sense, his decision to uphold the constitutionality of the bank was "clearly wrong." And yet, the fact that Madison found that wrong decision about the bank in some sense tolerable—it did not fit in the category of cases that transcend all authority of precedent—suggests, perhaps, that the opinion was "reasonable" in at least some weak sense of that term.

Perhaps we can say that Madison believed in a certain kind of constitutional humility. He was willing to defer to what he saw as long-term popular agreement to a constitutional position, even one he considered wrong in the abstract. He acknowledged that his opinion was subject to a form of popular overruling. This suggests that those popularly supported opinions are "reasonable" in some sense, especially since they can be contrasted with some decisions that—even with the support of precedent—are not authoritative, that are in some sense so "unreasonable" as to lack authority.

What are these limits that apply to even the popular authority manifested to settled precedent? The most plausible interpretation of this Madisonian position is that some constitutional principles are so "fundamental" that even precedent cannot displace them; precedent would not authorize maintaining decisions based on principles incompatible with the essential nature of our form of government.

We do know that this category does not include the important question of a national bank—though Madison's language on the bank issue was very strong. He argued in House debate that accepting the bank meant permitting Congress to choose any means to achieve its constitutionally specified ends, and thus "the essential characteristic of the Government, as composed of limited and enumerated powers, would be destroyed."[26] Would cases that transcended all authority of precedent have to go beyond that somehow?

I take Madison's deference to settled precedent on the bank as a tacit admission that his earlier case is overstated. The power of Congress to have plenary power to choose means to the ends entrusted to it by the Constitution—rather than have those means limited in some implied way—was, after all, compatible with a government of limited, enumerated powers. Of course, the power to choose means might be pushed so far as to change the nature of the Constitution, and if it did so, judges ought to strike down such laws.[27] But the constitutional interpretation on which the bank was based did not make that inevitable.

Madison's acceptance of the bank precedent reflects in part, I think, the fact that the constitutional differences among the founders, however great, were generally contained within boundaries set by their common agreement on rules for interpreting the Constitution.

The more difficult question—given that the founders did not have to confront the question of what Monaghan calls "deeply ingrained transformative change"—is what Madison would say about precedent in our "nonoriginalist universe," that is, a later America in which most constitutional law has been systematically detached from the anchor of the written document. Would these cases (or some of them) be cases that transcend all authority of precedent?

Precedents and the Originalist Today

It was established early in American history that "the judicial power" of Article III referred to the decision of "cases" and "controversies." Judges, for example, were not to issue "advisory opinions."[28] The "judicial power" to which the framers referred was not a newly devised power, but one that had been exercised for centuries in the country from which America took root. In particular, the judicial power reflected the influence of the common-law system, in which judges acknowledged the great weight of precedent.[29] Alexander Hamilton gives testimony to this in *Federalist* No. 78:

> There is yet a further and weighty reason for the permanency of the judicial offices; which is deducible from the nature of the qualifications they require. It has been frequently remarked with great propriety, that a voluminous code of laws is one of the inconveniences necessarily connected with the advantages of free government. To avoid an arbitrary discretion in the courts, it is indispensable that they should be bound down by strict rules and precedents, which serve to define and point out their duty in every particular case that comes before them; and it will readily be conceived from the variety of controversies which grow out of the folly and wickedness of mankind, that the records of

those precedents must unavoidably swell to a very considerable bulk, and must demand long and laborious study to acquire a competent knowledge of them.[30]

The necessity of the authority of precedents, to limit the discretion of judges, is assumed by Hamilton to be an ordinary and essential part of the judicial power.[31]

Should constitutional cases be somehow exempted from the ordinary attributes of the judicial power? A more plausible case for this might be made if the power of judicial review were a distinct and independent power of American judges. But the fact is that judicial review is nowhere mentioned in the Constitution, and is actually a *derivative* power, something that flows from the ordinary power of judges to decide cases. This suggest that it ought to be exercised according to the usual forms of judicial power. That is, the nature of judicial review differs from ordinary common-law adjudication; but since judicial review is exercised in the context of such adjudication, it ought to be exercised in the common-law mode—always remembering that the ground for judicial review is judicial judgment, not will, and the principle of legislative deference thereby entailed.

Precedent, however, was not an *absolute* principle in the common-law system. In addition to the countervailing considerations in common law, there are special considerations related to the nature of constitutional adjudication. Justice Louis Brandeis's qualification of precedent is one of the best known:

Stare decisis is usually the wise policy, because in most matters it is more important that the applicable rule of law be settled than that it be settled right . . . This is commonly true even where the error is a matter of serious concern, provided correction can be had by legislation. But in cases involving the Federal Constitution, where correction through legislative action is practically impossible, this Court has often overruled its earlier decisions. The Court bows to the lessons of experience and the force of better reasoning, recognizing that the process of trial and error, so fruitful in the physical sciences, is appropriate also in the judicial function.[32]

An originalist can be concerned about part of the argument—the reference to experience suggests the kind of adaptability that is characteristic of modern, nonoriginalist judicial review[33]—but the references to the difficulty of correcting errors in constitutional cases and to the force of better reasoning seem to be sensible admonitions that qualify the force of precedent somewhat.

The conclusion that I would draw from these observations is that there ought to be, as Monaghan says, a presumption in favor of precedent. The burden of proof is on the one who seeks to overturn precedent.

How heavy that burden will be, however, very much depends on how settled a precedent is. Once a precedent is very settled in the terms we noted above—large Court majorities have affirmed and reaffirmed the decision over a long period of time in accord with educated public opinion and with the apparent acquiescence of the other branches—the burden of proof will be a heavy one. But if a precedent is young, controversial, and subject to substantial and ongoing debate, it does not seem to qualify for the kind of respect and deference that Madison ascribed to settled precedent.

Likewise, the greater the distance between the precedent and the "true law" of the Constitution, the less deference it deserves. A "clearly wrong" precedent needn't automatically be overturned, but other things being equal, it ought to be more vulnerable to overturning than a constitutional precedent that is a close call.

What cases seem most fairly to fall into Madison's category of cases that transcend all authority of precedent? *Roe v. Wade* would clearly be a major instance, since, besides the federalism issue, it implicates the question of the right to life, one of the most fundamental principles of our form of government. *Roe*, moreover, is already extremely vulnerable because it has clearly never been "settled" (and that can still be said after *Planned Parenthood v. Casey,* I believe) and because its basic principle is a substantial distance from the command of the Constitution (being a dubious interpretation of a privacy right that is already on its own terms a dubious interpretation).

Another example might be the extreme form of the incorporation of the Bill of Rights into the Fourteenth Amendment that applies virtually all of its rights (now dramatically expanded) to the states and does so "jot-for-jot and tittle-for-tittle." Such a dramatic transformation of federalism, it might be reasonably argued, cannot be closed off to reconsideration.

Hypothetically, were the Supreme Court to adopt the extravagant claims of recent presidents about the warmaking power of the president (e.g., that a United Nations resolution is a sufficient basis for the president to commit troops to war, apart from any Congressional authorization), those claims would involve such a transformation of separation of powers that they would have to be considered open to revision.

Perhaps most fundamentally, judicial decisions that commit the Court itself to the ongoing exercise of nonjudicial power would seem open to question. On this ground it was sensible for the Court to reconsider its free exercise doctrine, which under *Sherbert v. Verner* and *Wisconsin v. Yoder* had required constant judicial balancing or policy-making, and to return to the more traditional doctrine reinstituted in *Employment Division v. Smith*, which relieved it of the task of constant legislating in this area.

The Pragmatic Case for Precedent

There is another, more minimalist form of the case for precedent today. There seem to be no sound reasons for committing originalist judges to what might be called "Don Quixotism." It is a form of tilting at windmills to try to fight battles that are decisively and irreversibly lost. Of course, it may not always be easy to say when defeat is indeed final. But sometimes it will be clear, and there are at least strong practical grounds for the originalist judge not to contend against well-settled precedents. For example, *Brown v. Board of Education*, at least as to the fundamental principle of prohibiting genuine legal segregation (that is, understanding *Brown* on its on terms rather than the way subsequent Courts have interpreted it since 1969) does seem to be a literally irreversible decision. There is virtually no support for its overruling and no sound reason, as a matter of broad public policy principles, to want it overruled. Even originalists who regard it as a judicial modification and extension of the Fourteenth Amendment, therefore, are right not to press for its overruling.

Likewise, one could mount a powerful case against the existence of substantially independent federal agencies exercising quasi-legislative, quasi-executive, and quasi-judicial power. (Are the "quasi-"s just a way of trying to downplay the reality that separation of powers is being violated?) Yet the administrative state, as Monaghan points out, is clearly with us to stay—it is so deeply embedded that it cannot be uprooted—and so it would be a foolish exercise to try to declare these agencies unconstitutional. Nor, to give a third example, is there any likelihood that the incorporation of the Bill of Rights into the Fourteenth Amendment due process clause, despite its dubious textual and historical basis, can be completely uprooted. And, finally, even if there is strong evidence that the original First Amendment freedom of speech was a prohibition against prior restraint, the extension of that protection of speech to most forms of subsequent punishment seems irreversible.

This position does, however, leave some room for judges to *limit* (as opposed to simply rejecting outright and fully) such settled precedents. In fact, that is one of the strongest arguments for permitting judges to accept the weight of precedent to some degree: if they are not bound in principle to dissent from all decisions based on incorrect precedents ("wasting" their votes on positions that have no practical chance of being adopted), judges generally committed to originalism will be free to provide (perhaps necessary) votes for positions that are at least *closer* to the proper interpretation of the Constitution.

It is possible, for example, to accept that a given precedent is settled in part, but in other respects not fully settled. *Brown* may be settled, but later school desegregation cases are not. It may be simply settled that the First Amendment (as to both its speech and religion positions) applies to the states. Is it clear that there must be a completely uniform standard applied to both? I do not think so. It is not at all unthinkable that, for example, given the traditional state police power regarding regulation of morals (and the absence of a general federal police power), different obscenity standards apply to the states (and localities) and to the federal government.[34] It seems settled that the most basic search-and-seizure requirements apply to both federal and state governments, but the rather indeterminate language of the clause (no "unreasonable" searches and seizures) and the different demands of criminal law enforcement and the constitutional principle of federalism make different minimum standards for them plausible.

Some hard questions remain here as to what exactly has been "settled" by precedent and what remains subject to revision. And since this ground for giving weight to precedent is a practical one (the futility of opposing what seems to be beyond dispute), it is subject to change if the empirical judgment on which it is based ("x is a lost cause") turns out to be wrong. Causes that seemed hopelessly lost have on occasion, surprisingly, been resuscitated.

Conclusion

This kind of discussion is necessarily a very dissatisfying one for an originalist. Originalism is a theory whose roots generally reside in the recognition that republican principles are incompatible with unchecked (or insufficiently checked[35]) judicial power.[36] While traditional constitutional jurisprudence was never a "mechanical jurisprudence" that claimed to eliminate completely the need for a certain measure of political prudence in judges, it certainly tried to confine judges to the interpretation (rather than the making) of law. The general guidelines for originalist judges discussed above recognize that there is no absolute rule on precedent: it is neither always illegitimate to uphold incorrect constitutional precedents nor always illegitimate to overturn them. They tell originalist judges to give considerable weight to precedent that is settled and less sharply opposed to (or less dramatically an extension of) the Constitution. They also say that practical necessity will require conceding great precedential weight to cases that seem so deeply rooted that opposition to them would accomplish nothing. On the other hand, they also recognize that many decisions are not fully settled and that some principles are so fundamental that contrary decisions can never be exempted from reconsideration. In the final analysis, then, originalist judges will have to make prudent determinations about which precedents to consider beyond debate and which to regard as open to challenge. If this is an uncomfortable position for originalist judges— and it is—that may simply be an inevitable feature of living in what Monaghan calls a "nonoriginalist universe."

Notes

Chapter 1

1. On the question of how much agreement there was, see my discussion of H. Jefferson Powell's critique of my argument in the "Afterword: A Response to Critics" in the revised edition of *The Rise of Modern Judicial Review* (Lanham, Md.: Rowman & Littlefield, 1994), pp. 384–88.

2. The following discussion of Blackstone draws heavily on my discussion of the same topic in *The Rise of Modern Judicial Review* (New York: Basic Books, 1986).

3. *Federalist*, ed. Wills (New York: Bantam, 1982), No. 83.

4. For a discussion of this issue, see the afterword of the revised edition of *The Rise of Modern Judicial Review*, where I respond to H. Jefferson Powell's review of the book in the *Texas Law Review*.

5. My own examination of these materials is contained in "Constitutional Interpretation in the American Founding" (Ph.D. diss., Boston College, 1978).

6. 12 Wheaton 213, 332 (1827).

7. *McCulloch v. Maryland* 4 Wheaton 316, 415 (1819).

8. See, for example, Marshall's arguments in *Cohens v. Virginia* 6 Wheaton 264, 385 (1821).

9. The classic discussion of this point occurs in Marshall's opinion in *McCulloch v. Maryland* 4 Wheaton 316, 418.

10. 4 Wheaton 316, 415, and 419.

11. *The Works of Alexander Hamilton*, ed. Henry Cabot Lodge (New York: Putnam and Sons, 1904), III, 463.

12. For a more extensive discussion of this issue, see "Constitutional Interpretation in the American Founding," pp. 76–87.

13. Madison discusses this in a letter to Lee 25 June 1824, *The Writings of James Madison*, Hunt, ed. (New York: G. P. Putnam's Sons 1900–1910) IX, 191.

14. On this dialectic, see my "Afterword" in the revised edition of *The Rise of Modern Judicial Review*, in particular the section dealing with Michael Zuckert's description of constitutional interpretation, pp. 381–84.

15. John Henry Newman, *An Essay in Aid of a Grammar of Assent* (Garden City, N.Y.: Doubleday, 1955), p. 254.

16. Aristotle, *Nichomachean Ethics*, Book I, chapter 3.

17. 7 Peters 243 (1833).

18. The fact that they are clear and noncontroversial is a reasonable guarantee of their objectivity in this context. For the record, I don't mean to assert that noncontroversiality is an essential requirement for objectivity (a contention I would deny).

19. On Jefferson, see "Constitutional Interpretation in the American Founding," pp. 90–101; on Marshall, see my "John Marshall and Constitutional Law," *Polity* 15, no. 1 (Fall, 1982), 5–25; and on modern constitutional law, see *The Rise of Modern Judicial Review*, Parts II and III.

20. See the seminal article by Thomas Grey, "Do We Have an Unwritten Constitution?" 27 *Stanford Law Review* 703 (1976).

21. Thus, for example, the need in Ronald Dworkin's theory of judicial interpretation—which allows judges to rework precedents and put them into a new theoretical framework—for considering some of the earlier decisions "mistakes." *Taking Rights Seriously* (Cambridge: Harvard University Press, 1977), chapter 4.

22. "Is evolved" in this sentence parallels the phrase "was suicided," in sentences such as "Jan Masaryk was suicided by Communists in 1949"—i.e., he was thrown out a window and then reported as a suicide.

A fine example of this is described in Raoul Berger's *Government By Judiciary: The Transformation of the Fourteenth Amendment* (Cambridge: Harvard University Press, 1977), where Berger shows (pp. 340–46) the contradictions within Leonard Levy's work between statements that argue that constitutional interpretation is inevitably result-oriented and other statements that condemn the Burger Court for being result-oriented.

23. See my *Judicial Activism* (Pacific Grove, Calif.: Brooks/Cole, 1991), especially chapter 1.

24. *Works* V, 458–63.

25. Hunt, ed., *The Writings of James Madison*, IX 74 (Letters to Ritchie 15 September 1821 and Jackson 27 December 1821).

26. *Federalist* No. 40, pp. 200–01.

27. Higby of California, *Congressional Globe*, 39th Congress, 1st session, 27 February 1886, p. 1056.

28. So, for example, the First Amendment cannot be limited to protecting the religious liberty of Christians on the grounds of what Justice Story said was the "real object of the First Amendment": namely, "not to countenance, much less to advance, Mahometanism, or Judaism, or infidelity, by prostrating Christianity; but to exclude all rivalry among Christian sects, and to prevent any national ecclesiastical establishment which should give to a hierarchy the exclusive patronage of the national government." Quoted from Robert L. Cord's *Separation of Church and State* (New York: Lambeth Press, 1982), p. 13. Note

that I am not contending that Justice Story himself would have so limited it; but I do believe that some of the founding generation might have.

29. For a more extensive discussion of this topic, see "Constitutional Interpretation in the American Founding," chapters 6 and 7.

30. A more extensive discussion of modern constitutional interpretation and judicial review can be found in *The Rise of Modern Judicial Review*, Part III.

31. As it turns out, once the principles of loose modern interpretation are established with phrases such as "due process" and "equal protection," other apparently more determinate (though still general) phrases, such as the contract clause and the First Amendment, can be interpreted in a similarly loose manner.

32. The clause forbidding laws respecting an establishment of religion is treated a bit differently, because it is more often regarded as an "absolute." The differences in such cases shift to questions about the definition of establishment. The difference of treatment suggests that there is an underlying agenda here, i.e., the complete marginalization of religion from public life.

33. The best example of such an approach is Benjamin Cardozo's *The Nature of the Judicial Process* (New Haven: Yale University Press, 1921), e.g., pp. 69–71.

34. Alexander Bickel, *The Least Dangerous Branch* (Indianapolis: Bobbs-Merrill, 1962), p. 26.

35. *Scott v. Sandford* 19 Howard 393 (1857).

36. A longer response can be found in "John Marshall and Constitutional Law," pp. 14–17.

37. *Sturges v. Crowninshield* 4 Wheaton 122, 202–203 (1819).

38. 6 Wheaton 264, 387 (1821).

39. As might be expected, a number of these factors were cited by Lincoln in his response to Southern secession, e.g., in his message to Congress in special session 4 July 1861.

40. On the original meaning of the due process clause, see chapter 2.

41. For reasons discussed in chapter 5 of *The Rise of Modern Judicial Review*, it *is* plausible that the framers of the post-Civil War Reconstruction Amendments were content to leave those amendments somewhat unclear, with a view to *Congressional* specification of their content.

42. "Judicial legislation" is a term that has its limits. It may be thought to imply that judges have a wider range of choice than in fact they have. But it highlights the discretionary power of the judge, which tells an essential and all-too-often obfuscated part of the truth about this form of judicial review.

Chapter 2

1. The only other possible reading of "process" would seem to be that the law according to which one is deprived of life, liberty, or property must have been established by the appropriate law-making process. But to say that the law must really be a law, at least in this sense, seems trivial. Nor would this interpretation fit what seems to be the order of the Bill of Rights—see below.

2. The narrower interpretation would limit the legislative only in the sense that the legislature could not itself move to deprive a particular person of life, liberty, or property without the legal procedure guaranteed by the standing law. It would leave the legislative free to modify the general law regarding legal procedure.

3. See *Hurtado v. California,* 110 U.S. 516 (1884), following *Murray's Lessee v. Hoboken Land & Improvement Co.,* 18 Howard 272 (1856).

4. See *Hurtado,* 110 U.S. 516 (1884).

5. Parts of the above outline are from *Sources of Our Liberties,* ed. Richard L. Perry (Chicago: American Bar Foundation, 1959) pp. 427–429. Leaving out the other two proposed amendments, passed by Congress but rejected by the states, does not disturb the order. The two rejected amendments (at the head of the list approved by Congress) differed from the others considerably; one regulated the size of the House, and the other regulated Congressional increases in compensation. The latter, of course, was finally ratified in 1992 as the 27th Amendment.

6. Whether there are *any* limitations on legislative modifications of common-law legal procedure—e.g., whether it can abolish "procedure" altogether—may be a more difficult question. This narrower interpretation seems to leave the legislature free to do so, but perhaps it might be possible to formulate a principle that guaranteed that there be "some" procedure, but no *particular* form. (I'm doubtful about that, largely on "slippery slope" grounds. Moreover, the abolition of all procedure is unlikely—and if the political process ever gets to the point of passing a law like that, amendments are not likely to be very helpful.)

7. The argument that due process includes all of the guarantees of the Bill of Rights *and more* would also give the due process clause a *raison d'etre,* but it is even more incompatible with the placement and unsupported by historical evidence. An alternative argument that it contains the more fundamental parts of Bill of Rights guarantees, or some of them, as well as other rights, also creates problems explaining the placement, and has no historical evidence to support it.

8. *Murray's Lessee v. Hoboken Land & Improvement Co.* 18 Howard 272 (1856), described below.

9. *American Journal of Legal History* 19 (1975): 265.

10. Letters of Phocion, *Works of Hamilton,* IV, 232.

11. James Kent, *Commentaries on American Law* (New York: Kent, 1864), Part IV, Lecture 24 (citing Story as well).

12. Joseph Story, *Commentaries on the Constitution* (Boston: Hilliard, Gray, and Company, 1833) III, 38 sect. 1789.

13. *Works* IV, 232.

14. 18 Howard 272, 280.

15. As W. W. Crosskey pointed out in *Politics and the Constitution in the History of the United States* (Chicago: University of Chicago Press, 1953) II, 1109. The quality of Crosskey's treatment of the Constitution is erratic, but

his discussion of the original intent of the due process clause is very profitable reading, though I think he rejects narrower interpretations of it too easily (at II, 1104).

16. Nor is this evolutionary view of the common law merely a twentieth-century reading, although the philosophical foundation for legal change may have been different in earlier writers. A traditional discussion of the adaptability of the common law appears, for example, in James Wilson's *Lectures on Law*, in 1792. See also *The Works of James Wilson*, ed. Robert McCloskey (Chicago: University of Chicago Press, 1967), e.g., pp. 335, 353–54.

17. Crosskey II, 1108.

18. 110 U.S. 516 (1884).

19. 96 U.S. 97, 104 (1878).

20. 2 Hayward (N.C.) 310 (1804).

21. 4 Wheaton 518, 581.

22. 4 Hill (N.Y.) 140 (1843).

23. These cases and many others are discussed in Edward Corwin's *Liberty Against Government* (Baton Rouge: Louisiana State University Press, 1948), chapter 3.

24. 6 Cranch 87 (1810).

25. 6 Cranch 87, 135–36.

26. 4 Wheaton 235, 244 (1819).

27. See 2 Peters 380, 414, and note.

28. 13 N.Y. 378 (1856); Corwin, *Liberty Against Government*, pp. 101–110; it should be noted, however, that most other state courts rejected this reasoning.

29. 19 Howard 393, 450 (1857).

30. Other evidence that might be cited for a broader view would draw on English constitutional history, giving weight especially to various historical meanings and uses of the Magna Carta. See also Frank R. Strong's *Substantive Due Process of Law: A Dichotomy of Sense and Nonsense* (Durham, N.C.: Carolina Academic Press, 1986). This argument is subject to many of the same objections (e.g., from the placement of the clause in the Bill of Rights) and also seems to lack support from the time of the framing of the Bill of Rights itself. Professor Strong's book, for instance, leaps from English history to nineteenth-century American history with hardly any discussion of the founding or the text of the Constitution itself.

For a contrary view of historical evidence, see the excellent chapter on due process in George Carey's *In Defense of the Constitution* (Cumberland, Va.: James River Press, 1989).

31. On the approach to judicial review characteristic of the early or "traditional" era of American constitutional history, see *The Rise of Modern Judicial Review*, Part I.

32. When asked about the meaning of due process, Congressman John Bingham of Ohio responded, "the courts have settled that long ago, and the gentleman can go and read their decisions." Quoted in Berger's *Government*

by Judiciary, pp. 203–204. *Murray* being the most authoritative Supreme Court decision on due process prior to the Civil War, it seems reasonable to presume that he had that case in mind as representing the settled meaning of the clause.

33. The state provisions for indictment by information are evidence emphasized by Justice Frankfurter in his discussion of the Fourteenth Amendment in *Adamson v. California* (1947) and by Charles Fairman in his famous article "Does the Fourteenth Amendment Incorporate the Bill of Rights?" *Stanford Law Review* 2 (1949): 5.

Chapter 3

1. *Harvard Law Review* 98 (1985): 885.

2. For example, Harry Wellington in his *Interpreting the Constitution* (New Haven: Yale University Press, 1990) treats Powell's article as the irrefutable final word on the subject: "H. Jefferson Powell, of Duke University, has done the seminal work on the subject. . . . Powell's conclusion seriously diminishes a basic attraction that originalism (or, as he calls it, intentionalism) would otherwise have. Since the founders did not themselves intend 'that the Constitution would be construed in accordance with what future interpreters could gather of the framers' own purposes, expectations, and intentions,' the founders' will, or desire, cannot be claimed today as authority for the use of their recorded intentions. . . . Contemporary interpreters moved by that past may also employ original intent, but if they do it is only because they respect a tradition of interpretation. No longer can they see themselves as being under an obligation to obey the commands of the founding fathers. They must come to terms with the realization that no such commands were issued" (50–51).

3. *George Washington Law Review* 54 (1986): 296.

4. Charles A. Lofgren has also analyzed Powell's piece, in *Constitutional Commentary* 5 (1988): 77. While some of our conclusions are similar, we tend to reach them by different paths.

Professor Lofgren properly places primary emphasis on ratifier intent, as early Americans did, but seems to discount framer intent too much on that basis (going so far as to say, for example, that Madison "condemned resort to framer intent" (111). Given the paucity of sources of ratifier intent (the limited records of debates and the resolutions of the state ratifying conventions), however, framer intent (if sufficiently clear) may often be the best indication of ratifier intent (after the text itself). Evidence that Powell and Lofgren themselves employ suggests that it would be better to say that ratifier intent had precedence over framer intent, in cases of conflict (to the extent—at most, very limited—that there was such conflict), but that framer intent was a legitimate, subordinate factor in interpretation. Berger has this right (at 327).

5. These summaries will generally paraphrase the authors, employing their own words as possible, but with quotation marks reserved only for longer quotations, not for short phrases.

6. Jefferson said: "On every question of construction, carry ourselves back to the time when the Constitution was adopted, recollect the spirit manifested in the debates, and instead of trying what meaning may be squeezed out of the text, or invented against it, conform to the probable one in which it was passed" (Berger, p. 329). For Jefferson, this seems to come close, at times, to: "don't haggle with the words, just put yourself back in the place of those who wrote and ratified it—whose spirit is most accurately represented by the Republican party—and follow what they intended."

7. An early American example of this kind of unwritten legislative history is Marshall's description in *Barron v. Baltimore* of the forces that led to the passage of the Bill of Rights, sources that everyone recognizes to have been fearful of national, rather than state, abuses.

8. Powell, p. 899.

9. Blackstone, *Commentaries on the Laws of England,* ed. George Sharswood (Philadelphia: George W. Childs, 1866), p. 59.

10. Blackstone, *Commentaries,* I, 381, n. 16.

11. *Federalist,* No. 37, p. 179.

12. *Records of the Federal Convention of 1787,* ed. Max Farrand (New Haven: Yale University Press, 1937), II, 648.

13. On the import of the decision not to destroy the records, see Lofgren, *Constitutional Commentary* 5 (1988): 81–82.

14. I want to make it clear that I do not myself think that these arguments justify a free judicial hand in constitutional interpretation. Constitutional ambiguities due to multiple authorship need not be resolved by judges: why should judicial interpretations take precedence to legislative-executive ones, if the Constitution really is ambiguous? And the need to apply constitutions to a broader range of activities over a much longer period of time could support legislative-executive discretion as much or more than judicial discretion in interpretation. Here, I am arguing only that the simple analogy between will and constitution is not, by itself, a convincing argument.

15. There is really no substitute for going back to the major constitutional debates of the 1790s and reading them carefully. I believe that such a reading would confirm my assertion here that in early constitutional debates, resort to extrinsic sources of the intention of the lawgiver (in the case of the Constitution, the framers and ratifiers) was exceptional and secondary (i.e., to confirm a reading of the text, the main source for the lawgiver's intent) rather than common and primary. I tried to describe three of these debates in "Constitutional Interpretation in the Founding" (Ph.D. diss., Boston College, 1978), chapter 3.

16. Other evidence cited by Powell in this section is not convincing. The arguments of the Anti-Federalist Brutus have relatively little authority, coming as they do from the "losing" side, and they have few implications for the central point of the debate between Powell and Berger. Likewise, Powell's evidence that statutory (and constitutional) meaning were to be liquidated by particular discussions and adjudications is not very helpful, since the whole

point at issue is what standards were to be used in these discussions and adjudications. Like Berger's argument about common law intent, therefore, it is circular.

17. For a more detailed treatment of Powell's article on the Jay Treaty debate, see Lofgren, *Constitutional Commentary* 5 (1988): 94–102.

18. See also Clyde Jacobs's *The Eleventh Amendment and Sovereign Immunity* (Westport, Ct.: Greenwood Press, 1972), chapter 2.

19. Joseph Story, *Commentaries on the Constitution of the United States* (Boston: Hilliard, Gray, and Co., 1833), p. 392 (Book III, chapter 5, s. 407, note 1) (emphasis added).

20. This is obscured if one adopts a modern and distorted reading of Story—more typically seen in assertions about Hamilton—that makes his opposition to state attacks on national sovereignty into a hostility to those prerogatives the Constitution *did* reserve to the states).

21. *Annals of Congress* 2 February 1791, p. 1952.

22. For another discussion of Powell on Madison, see Lofgren, *Constitutional Commentary* 5 (1988): 102–111.

23. Madison, letter to C. E. Haynes 25 February 1831, in *The Writings of James Madison*.

24. Lincoln makes a similar point in his speech on the *Dred Scott* case, arguing that Court decisions ordinarily not only decide cases but also settle the meaning of the Constitution. But, of course, he goes on to argue that there are limits to the authority of the Court, giving various grounds for considering Court decisions as not settling an issue. See his speech on the *Dred Scott* decision in *The Political Thought of Abraham Lincoln,* ed. Richard N. Current (Indianapolis: Bobbs-Merrill, 1967), pp. 84–93.

25. It raises the very important question of what a justice oriented toward original intent in its proper sense would do today, given that large parts of American constitutional law no longer bear any arguable relation to the Constitution as it was written. On this topic, see chapter 8.

26. *The Writings of James Madison,* IX, 74.

27. See, for example, Madison's letter to Spencer Roane of 2 September 1819, commenting on Roane's attack on *McCulloch v. Maryland*. Madison joins in many of Roane's criticisms of Marshall's construction, without doubting the authority of the Court to interpret the Constitution. (Indeed, he suggests that the Court may be disqualifying itself excessively from striking down usurpations of power by the federal government.)

28. 12 Wheaton 353–54 (1827).

29. An issue that is to some extent distinct from the authority of original intent itself, though it is inextricably entwined with it, is the role of the judiciary when even a careful interpretation of the text, as outlined above, yields the conclusion that the Constitution is ambiguous. It is on this point, I think, that Powell and I are farthest apart. I would argue that the power of judicial review, properly understood as a power granted the judges by implication from the Constitution's text, does not include the power to give ambiguous phrases

of the Constitution a definitive content. There is no reason why the judiciary's preferred reading of an admittedly ambiguous text ought to take precedence to that of the political branches in such cases. The only ground in our constitutional system for judges to strike down acts of the other branches is a clear incompatibility between those acts and the Constitution. (For a more extensive discussion of this point, see *The Rise of Modern Judicial Review*, chapters 3 and 4, and pp. 141–43.)

While Powell's position on this point is not clear from this article, other writings by him indicate that he would give the judges power to interpret the document authoritatively and to strike down acts of the political branches even in cases where it is ambiguous or unclear. See his reviews of Laurence Tribe's "Constitutional Choices" in *Northwestern Law Review* 80 (1986): 1128 and of Murphy, Fleming, and Harris's *American Constitutional Interpretation* (Mineola, N.Y.: The Foundation Press, Inc., 1986) in *Duke Law Journal* (1986): 915.

30. Lofgren makes a similar point: "As a modern student of Madison asks, 'Why should we assume that those who *merely* ratified the Constitution grasped its meaning better than those who wrote it—or those who have since seen how it works in practice?' The answer from an 'intentionalist' perspective is that whether the ratifiers better grasped the instrument's meaning is beside the point; rather, how the ratifiers understood the Constitution, and what they expected from it, *defines* its meaning. The act of ratifying cannot be dismissed with the adverb 'merely'" (112).

My only caveat is that I would not use the term "expectations" to describe the authority of the ratifiers' *intent*. What is binding is the ratifiers' understanding of the *principles* they were consenting to. It is at least conceivable that ratifiers (or framers) had *expectations* that were not fully compatible with the *principles*. For example, there is evidence that some of the founding generation thought that the First Amendment protections of religious liberty extended only to Christians. (This view is sometimes mistakenly attributed to Justice Joseph Story, by those who neglect to read his entire treatment of the First Amendment in his *Commentaries on the Constitution of the United States*.) But the principle adopted in the First Amendment cannot be interpreted fairly to be limited only to protection of Christianity. In general, however, I think these instances were limited, especially among the most thoughtful proponents of the Constitution, on whose understanding the document was generally adopted.

Chapter 4

1. See, for example, Grey, "Do We Have an Unwritten Constitution?" *Stanford Law Review* 27 (1975): 703; J. Ely, *Democracy and Distrust: A Theory of Judicial Review* (Cambridge, Massachusets: Harvard University Press, 1980).

2. *Federalist* No. 78, pp. 392–99.

3. 1 Cranch 137 (1803).

4. See, for example, Tushnet, "Following the Rule Laid Down: A Critique of Interpretivism and Neutral Principles," *Harvard Law Review* 96 (1983): 781; Brest, "The Misconceived Quest for the Original Understanding," *Boston University Law Review* 60 (1980): 204.

5. It also helps to explain a senatorial preference for arguments that focus on "legal ethics" or sexual harassment or the like, since these arguments are "nonpolitical" on their face—they do not involve a frank admission that opposition is due to the political implications of the constitutional philosophy of the nominee.

6. This subject will develop earlier discussions in *The Rise of Modern Judicial Review* but with less attention to the historical dimension.

7. This discussion is based on a lengthier analysis contained in Wolfe, "Woodrow Wilson: Interpreting the Constitution," *Review of Politics* 14 (1979): 121.

8. W. Wilson, *Congressional Government* (Baltimore: Johns Hopkins University Press, 1885, 1981).

9. W. Wilson, *Constitutional Government in the United States* (New York: Columbia University Press, 1908).

10. W. Wilson, *Constitutional Government*, p. 206.

11. W. Wilson, *Constitutional Government*, p. 8.

12. W. Wilson, *Constitutional Government*, pp. 54–55.

13. W. Wilson, *Constitutional Government*, p. 55.

14. W. Wilson, *Constitutional Government*, p. 57.

15. W. Wilson, *Constitutional Government*, p. 70.

16. W. Wilson, *Constitutional Government*, p. 60.

17. W. Wilson, *Constitutional Government*, p. 60.

18. W. Wilson, *Constitutional Government*, p. 60.

19. W. Wilson, *Constitutional Government*, p. 70. Whether Wilson's view really is consistent with actual provisions of the Constitution is hard to say, because he is not too clear on what the president can do. One suspects that his view may be close to Theodore Roosevelt's "stewardship theory" of the presidency, which *is* inconsistent with the Constitution, as William Howard Taft persuasively argued in *Our Chief Magistrate and His Powers* (New York: Columbia University Press, 1916), pp. 136, 143-146.

20. 290 U.S. 398 (1933).

21. Ch. 339, 1933 Minn. Laws 514.

22. It differed only in providing some kind of rental value during the moratorium. See also Charles Miller, *The Supreme Court and the Uses of History* (Cambridge, Massachusetts: Belknap Press of Harvard University Press, 1969), chapter 3, pp. 39–51.

23. *Home Building and Loan v. Blaisdell*, 290 U.S. at 442–43.

24. *Home Building and Loan v. Blaisdell*, at 449–53 (Sutherland, J., dissenting).

25. A much clearer indication of what the Court was doing in *Blaisdell* can be found in an unpublished concurring opinion by Justice Cardozo. Citing previ-

ous Court decisions, Justice Cardozo notes that, "From the beginning it was seen that something must be subtracted from the words of the Constitution in all their literal and stark significance." A. Mason & W. Beaney, *American Constitutional Law* (Englewood Cliffs, N.J.: Prentice-Hall, 1978), pp. 393–94.

For an attempt to defend *Home Building and Loan v. Blaisdell* from a more traditional interpretive standpoint, see Gary Jacobson, *Pragmatism, Statesmanship and the Supreme Court* (Ithaca, N.Y.: Cornell University Press, 1977), pp. 181–93.

26. 304 U.S. 458 (1938).

27. *McCulloch v. Maryland*, 17 U.S. (4 Wheat.) 316, 415 (1818), quoted in *Home Building & Loan Assoc. v. Blaisdell*, 290 U.S. 398, 443 (1933). Raoul Berger has noted the extraordinarily frequent misuse of Chief Justice Marshall's statement. See R. Berger, *Government by Judiciary*, pp. 375–79.

28. *Lochner v. New York*, 198 U.S. 45, 75–76 (1905) (Holmes, J., dissenting).

29. B. Cardozo, *The Nature of the Judicial Process* (New Haven: Yale University Press, 1921).

30. B. Cardozo, *The Nature of the Judicial Process*, p. 77.

31. B. Cardozo, *The Nature of the Judicial Process*, p. 83.

32. B. Cardozo, *The Nature of the Judicial Process*, p. 88.

33. For a discussion of the privileges and immunities clause, see J. Ely, *Democracy and Distrust*, pp. 22–30; C. Wolfe, *Rise of Modern Judicial Review*, pp. 127–31.

34. *Craig v. Boren*, 429 U.S. 190, 197 (1976).

35. See *Trimble v. Gordon*, 430 U.S. 762 (1977) (Rehnquist, J., dissenting).

36. *McCulloch v. Maryland*, 17 U.S. (4 Wheat.) 316, 415 (1818). See also Wolfe, "John Marshall and Constitutional Law," *Polity* 15 (1982): 5.

37. See Blackstone, *Commentaries on the Laws of England* at *134. See also R. Berger, *Government By Judiciary*, pp. 20–21.

38. John D. Frank & Robert F. Munro, *The Original Understanding of "Equal Protection Of the Laws,"* *Washington University Law Quarterly* (1972): 466–72.

39. *The Federalist* No. 81, pp. 408–417; C. Wolfe, *Rise of Modern Judicial Review*, pp. 77, 104–05.

40. 83 U.S. 394 (1873).

41. 83 U.S. 394 (1873) at 409.

42. Nor do I mean to concede that one can bring whatever he wants: The above discussion indicates that there is a restrained and limited *constitutional* understanding of judicial power that should be brought to bear on other parts of the Constitution as well.

43. See, for example, J. Ely, *Democracy and Distrust*, p. 340; Kelly, "Clio and the Court: An Illicit Love Affair," *Supreme Court Review* I (1965): 19. The most prolific writer on the subject has been Randy Barnett, with his two-volume *The Rights Reserved to the People* (Fairfax, Va.: George Mason University Press, 1989–1993).

44. Nor does the simple inclusion of the words "others [rights] retained by the people" justify judicial specification of enumerated rights, any more than the words "necessary and proper" in Article I, section 8, justify a judicial evaluation of the necessity and propriety of congressional legislation.

45. *The Federalist* No. 84, p. 437.

46. 1 *Annals of Congress*, 8 June 1789, p. 456 (J. Gales ed. 1789).

47. J. Ely, *Democracy and Distrust*, pp. 34–35.

48. See Letter from James Madison to Thomas Jefferson (17 Oct. 1788), *The Writings of James Madison*, 271.

49. See Letter from James Madison to Thomas Jefferson (17 Oct. 1788), *The Writings of James Madison*, 271–72.

50. For Madison's position and the First Amendment's meaning as adopted, see M. Malbin, *Religion and Politics: The Intention of the Authors of the First Amendment* (Washington, D.C.: American Enterprise Institute, 1979).

The "confusion" attributed to Madison by Professor Ely, (*Democracy and Distrust*, 34–36) is, in fact, his own: Madison knew what he wanted to say and said it quite well. What confusion existed in 1789 was in the minds of those who thought that this amendment was necessary—adding something significant and novel to the original Constitution. As noted above, Madison did not regard the Bill of Rights itself as necessary, let alone the Ninth Amendment standing by itself.

51. To attribute to Madison the view that the Ninth Amendment was an open-ended judicially enforceable guarantee of rights shows a serious misunderstanding of Madison's attitude toward judicial review as well.

Madison argued that the judiciary was not intended by the Convention to make the final determination on constitutional questions at the expense of the other two branches.

> In the State Constitutions and indeed in the Federal one also, no provision is made for the case of a disagreement in expounding them; and as the Courts are generally the last in making ye decisions, it results to them by refusing or not refusing to execute a law, to stamp it with its final character. This makes the Judiciary Department paramount in fact to the Legislature, which was never intended and can never be proper.

J. Madison, "Observations on the 'Draft of a Constitution for Virginia,'" in *Writings of James Madison*, p. 294.

In the classic formulation of the separation of powers doctrine in *Federalist* No. 51 (J. Madison), there is a striking absence of any reference to the power of judicial review, an obvious "check" that should have been included for one who accepts judicial review of Congressional enactments.

On the whole, it seems that Madison shared Jefferson's theory of "coordinate review" at the federal level, with a broader judicial review of state acts (primarily with a view to protecting the uniformity of national law, and a small number of specified constitutional rights). The point of recounting this material is that Madison did not have an unqualified confidence in judicial review. Given *that* context, it is even easier to see that a judicially enforceable, open-ended Ninth Amendment would never have come from his pen.

52. *Marbury v. Madison*, 5 U.S. (1 Cranch) 137, 176–79 (1803).

53. For Justice Black's view, see *Smith v. California*, 361 U.S. 147 (1959). Let me hasten to add that I do not accept Justice Black's interpretation.

54. For a more adequate interpretation of First Amendment freedom of speech, see what are widely assumed to be Chief Justice John Marshall's views, in J. Marshall, "Address of the Minority in the Virginia Legislature" in *John Marshall: Major Opinions and Other Writings,* ed. J. Roche (Indianapolis: Bobbs-Merrill, 1967), pp. 34, 45–48.

55. Justices Black and Douglas are correct in formulating the Court's position in roughly this way. See also H. Black, *A Constitutional Faith* (New York: Knopf, 1968), p. 52.

56. See also *Southern Pacific Co. v. Arizona*, 325 U.S. 761 (1945).

57. *United States Trust Co. v. New Jersey*, 431 U.S. 1 (1977).

58. It should be clear that I am using the term "balancing" here not in the sense of Felix Frankfurter's deferential approach to legislative actions, but in a generic sense that includes both Justice Frankfurter's approach and those of more activist judges (which include heavy presumptions against legislation, as in the "compelling state interest" test).

It could be argued that this balancing was implicit in the economic substantive due process cases that began in the late nineteenth century—see, for example, *Lochner v. New York*, 198 U.S. 45 (1905)—and later in the clear and present danger test formulated in opinions in the 1920s by Justices Holmes and Brandeis. See *Schenck v. United States*, 249 U.S. 47, 52 (1919); *Abrams v. United States*, 250 U.S. 616, 624 (1919) (Holmes, J. dissenting); *Gitlow v. New York*, 268 U.S. 652, 668–70 (1925); id. at 672–73 (Holmes, J. dissenting). It first became explicit in state regulation of interstate commerce cases—see *South Carolina State Highway Dept. v. Barnwell Bros.*, 303 U.S. 177 (1938); *Southern Pacific Co. v. Arizona*, 325 U.S. 761 (1945)—and soon appeared in civil liberties decisions thereafter, either in Justice Frankfurter's more deferential form or in more restrictive forms that flowed from the "preferred position" of the First Amendment (and eventually other "fundamental") rights. See, for example, *Schneider v. State*, 308 U.S. 147 (1939); *Dennis v. United States*, 341 U.S. 494, 517 (1951) (Frankfurter, J., concurring); *Wisconsin v. Yoder*, 406 U.S. 205, 213–15 (1972); *Roe v. Wade*, 410 U.S. 113 (1973).

59. See, for example, *Southern Pacific Co. v. Jensen*, 244 U.S. 205, 221 (1916) (Holmes, J. dissenting).

60. 17 U.S. (4 Wheat.) 316 (1819).

61. 17 U.S. (4 Wheat.) 428 (1819)

62. 17 U.S. (4 Wheat.) 429-30 (1819).

63. *Panhandle Oil Co. v. Mississippi*, 277 U.S. 218, 223 (1928) (Holmes, J., dissenting). Note that it was not necesary for Holmes to rely on this argument in order to allow for some use of the taxing power. Marshall himself in

McCulloch v. Maryland allowed for the use of the taxing power in cases where an "intelligibile standard" that did not endanger federal supremacy was available, by distinguishing the case of a nondiscriminatory property tax applied to bank property.

64. My argument here is not that traditional judges never decided any question of degree. Perhaps there were cases where no "intelligible" standard was available. The argument is that judges would have been reluctant to make such decisions and would not have done so where it was not necessary. Certainly they would not have unhesitatingly made them the "normal" way of making constitutional law distinctions.

65. See Bradford Wilson, "The Origin and Development of the Federal Rule of Exclusion," *Wake Forest Law Review* 18 (1982): 1073.

66. 232 U.S. 383 (1914). Note that I cite here the case that is conventionally given as the origin of the federal exclusionary rule. I think that Bradford Wilson has shown that this understanding is inaccurate, in *Enforcing the Fourth Amendment* (New York: Garland Publishing Co., 1986).

67. 232 U.S. 393 (1914) On *Weeks* and the exclusionary rule, however, see Bradford Wilson's *Enforcing the Fourth Amendment* (New York: Garland Publishing Co., 1986).

68. 381 U.S. 479 (1965).

69. 381 U.S. 483–84 (1965)

70. 381 U.S. 483–84 (1965)

71. 381 U.S. 483–84 (1965)

72. 381 U.S. 479.

73. 410 U.S. 113 (1973).

74. 378 U.S. 478 (1964).

75. 378 U.S. 484–85 (1964).

76. *Griswold*, 381 U.S. at 509 (Black, J. dissenting). For the record, I do not generally subscribe to Justice Black's approach to constitutional interpretation and judicial review.

77. 316 U.S. 535 (1942).

78. 316 U.S. 541 (1942).

79. 316 U.S. 541 (1942).

80. 394 U.S. 618 (1969).

81. 394 U.S. 634 (1969).

82. 197 U.S. 11 (1905).

83. 361 U.S. 516 (1960).

84. Most of the examples given in the first part of this article concern judicial activism of a liberal bent. I should at least note that much of what I have said would apply equally to a conservative judicial activism based, for example, on the takings clause. See especially R. Epstein, *Takings: Private Property and the Power of Eminent Domain* (Cambridge, Mass.: Harvard University Press, 1985).

85. Andrew Lipscomb and Albert Bergh, *The Writings of Thomas Jefferson* (Washington D.C.: Thomas Jefferson Memorial Association, 1939), 14, 449.

86. See G. Wood, *The Creation of the American Republic, 1776–1787* (New York: Norton, 1969), pp. 463–75.

87. See G. Wood, *The Creation of the American Republic, 1776–1787*, pp. 471–564.

88. This brief discussion is condensed from C. Wolfe, "Constitutional Interpretation in the American Founding" (Ph.D. diss., Boston College, 1978).

89. R. Berger, *Government By Judiciary.*

90. R. Berger, *Government By Judiciary*, pp. 52–98.

91. See, for example, *Yick Wo v. Hopkins*, 118 U.S. 356 (1886). See also Frank and Munro, "The Original Understanding of Equal Protection of the Laws."

92. R. Berger, *Government By Judiciary*, pp. 117–33.

93. R. Berger, *Government By Judiciary*, pp. 140–51.

94. R. Berger, *Government By Judiciary.*

95. R. Berger, *Government By Judiciary*, p. 49. "Little weight has been attached by the Supreme Court to postenactment remarks, even of the Congress itself." Id. But Chief Justice Marshall's willingness to take postratification factors into account is suggested by his reliance on the practice of government in many cases. See, for example, *Marbury v. Madison*, 5 U.S. (1 Cranch) 137 (1803); *Gibbons v. Ogden*, 22 U.S. (9 Wheat.) 1 (1824). It seems to me that post-ratification remarks should, like other aspects of historical evidence, be evaluated with care and carry the weight that the evidence justifies.

96. R. Berger, *Government By Judiciary*, p. 120.

97. R. Berger, *Government By Judiciary*, pp. 99–116.

98. Although I have deep reservations about the positivism of Part Two. See Jacobsohn, "Hamilton, Positivism and the Constitution: Judicial Discretion Reconsidered," *Polity* 14 (1980): 70.

99. See also Grey, "Do We Have an Unwritten Constitution?" *Stanford Law Review* 27 (1975): 703; J. Ely, *Democracy and Distrust: A Theory of Judicial Review* (Cambridge, Massachusetts: Harvard University Press, 1980).

Chapter 5

1. For my discussion of Ely, Choper, and Dworkin, see the conclusion of *The Rise of Modern Judicial Review.*

2. See, for example, books such as Gerald Rosenberg's *The Hollow Hope* (Chicago: University of Chicago Press, 1991).

3. Gerard V. Bradley, *Church-State Relationships in America* (New York: Greenwood Press, 1987).

4. See Wolfe's "The Contemporary Supreme Court and Federalism" in *Federalism and the Constitution* (Washington, D.C.: Advisory Commission on Intergovernmental Relations, 1987).

5. 367 U.S. 552–553.

6. 431 U.S. 717.

7. *Annals of Congress* 1, 8 June 1789, p. 456 (J. Gales ed. 1789)

8. For a more extended discussion, see chapter 4.

Chapter 6

1. As I argued in chapter 3, the reliance on Powell by nonoriginalists as a critique of originalism is misplaced. Powell's article, which is billed (indeed bills itself) as a critique of originalism, is actually a fairly good statement—on the level of general principle—of originalism properly understood. The description of the founders' approach to interpretation described in the body of the article--as opposed to the more provocative introduction--describes a method of interpretation that can be described as textualism, supplemented by careful and limited recourse to history. Where Powell ultimately departs from originalism (and this is clearer in other articles) is not so much in his understanding of constitutional interpretation, but in his nonoriginalist conception of judicial review that would permit judges to make their preferred readings of concededly unclear provisions authoritative.

2. See chapter 2.

3. On religion, see Gerard V. Bradley's *Church-State Relationships in America*, and on voting see Raoul Berger's *Government by Judiciary*.

4. *Wesberry v. Sanders* 376 U.S. 1, 8 (1964).

5. He rejects the argument of some critical legal scholars "that there is no difference between law and partisan politics . . . Surely we can accept this limited retreat from orthodoxy [i.e., the vision of an apolitical court] without abandoning ourselves to the long night of nihilism" (157). But brave assertions like that are just whistling in the dark—unless he starts giving reasons why we needn't abandon ourselves to nihilism, at which point he must jettison legal realism and construct an argument for the possibility of a law apart from politics.

6. Ad hoc constitutional law was one of the distinguishing features of the Burger Court, in particular—a Court that was reluctant to overturn precedent and also too politically conservative to push the principles of Warren Court decisions to the limits of their logic. The "political indigestibility" of the implications of Warren Court decisions thus led to a more politically conservative court that was (excessively) respectful of precedents but unwilling to extend them. The result—an altogether foreseeable one, given the dominance of modern views exalting judicial discretion—makes the ideal of courts rigorously adhering to principle seem like a bad joke. See Wolfe, *The Rise of Modern Judicial Review*, chapter 13.

7. *Texas v. Johnson* 491 U.S. 397 (1989) and *U.S. v. Eichman* 496 U.S. 310 (1990).

8. Thomas Grey argued that the Burger Court decisions in this area were part of a policy to increase social stability. See his "Eros, Civilization, and the Burger Court" *Law and Contemporary Problems* 43 (1980): 84–85, 90.

9. See William Galston, "A Liberal-Democratic Case for the Two-Parent Family," *The Responsive Community* 1 (1990): 14.

10. This is another revealing instance of a decision by a court that "many students of law would say finds its authority in the ideal of a rigorous adherence to principle" (79). The court's job is made easier, apparently, by the fact that it need not articulate the principle very well itself—that can be left for commentators to figure out subsequently.

Chapter 7

1. I confine my observations about concern for citizen character here to the importance of religion and morality for the founders and for many contemporary originalists. One could also argue, however, that the founders' liberalism contained other important character-shaping elements. As examples, I would cite Tocqueville's discussion of free institutions and individualism in Book II of Volume II of *Democracy in America*, and Martin Diamond's essay "Ethics and Politics: The American Way" in Horwitz, ed., *The Moral Foundations of the American Republic* (Charlottesville: University Press of Virginia, 1986).

2. Consent takes two forms here. First, it refers to the requirement of consent in altering the decision-making process or substantive guarantees specified in the Constitution. Second, it refers to the requirement of consent in the ordinary operations of government, especially the accountability of government officials, directly or indirectly, to majorities through elections.

3. For the latest convincing statement of original intention (building on earlier work by Robert Cord and Michael Malbin), see Gerard V. Bradley's *Church-State Relationships in America*.

4. Bradley, Gerard V., *Church-State Relationships in America*, ch. 5, (New York: Greenwood Press, 1987).

5. I must concede that the religion clauses of the First Amendment are not completely theoretically coherent, for reasons I suggest in chapter 3 of *Essays on Faith and Liberal Democracy* (Lanham, Md.: University Press of America, 1987). For example, I do not believe that they succeed as well as the framers thought in achieving neutrality on questions relative to the differences between different religions. But I do not believe that the meaning of the clauses as they understood them could legitimately be set aside on the grounds that their goals could be achieved better if the clauses were read differently (even if such a reading existed, which I doubt).

6. This minority report is found in *John Marshall: Major Opinions and Other Writings* (ed. J. Roche).

7. For a discussion of this as a typical ploy of modern constitutional interpretation, see chapter 4.

8. I am making two points here. The second one is that even if the amendment is ambiguous, the conservative originalist such as myself does not consider this a justification for judicial review, since our position is that only clear-cut constitutional violations justify judicial review. Tushnet's functional equivalence argument cannot be plausibly held to represent the clear-cut meaning of the Fourteenth Amendment.

The first point concerns the original intention of the equal protection clause. The wording does not explicitly say what matters call for "equal" treatment. But we know from the Constitution that it cannot mean equal in everything. Most importantly, both section two of the amendment and the Fifteenth Amendment indicate clearly that equality of *voting* rights was not guaranteed. One presumes, therefore, that equal protection is not guaranteed with respect to the category of "political rights" in general. The best candidates for what *is* protected are a) "security of person and property"—on the basis of the connotations of the word "protection"—and b) "civil rights"—on the basis of extrinsic sources of the framers' intent, especially the Congressional debates, which emphasized the rights described in *Corfield v. Coryell* and in the Civil Rights Act of 1866. Neither of those categories would include public education.

9. If this most radical view is accepted, then all supposed knowledge and speech is meaningless. If that is so, then the most accurate reflection of reality is to be found in existentialist authors—not the inconsistent ones like Sartre or Camus, who find some "meaning" in bravely facing the meaninglessness of reality, but ones like Kafka, who write stories where people are put on trial without knowing the charge and in the end die like dogs. In such a world, trying to talk to anyone else is, like everything else, a waste of time.

10. Tocqueville makes this argument in *Democracy in America*, Vol. 1, chapter 7 (in the section on "tyranny of the majority"). In fact, I think that his book is one long argument for a "balanced republic" (i.e., one that contains elements that moderate the democratic principle). In this he follows Aristotle, who (in his *Politics*, Book IV, chapter 4 and Book VI, chapter 6) describes a range of democracies, and then argues that the best one is one of the less democratic forms of democracy.

11. A good example of the former is David A. J. Richards—see especially his "Rights and Autonomy" in *Ethics* 92 (October 1981): 3–20. Tushnet and other critical legal-studies thinkers are good examples of the latter.

12. George Orwell has some interesting remarks on this tendency in an essay on James Burnham. He sees it rooted in intellectuals' worship of power.

13. When I say that Tushnet "relies" on republicanism scholarship, I am not saying that he simply accepts it. As I note below, Tushnet does finally distance himself from it as well as from liberalism.

14. "Ethics and Politics: The American Way" in Robert H. Horwitz, ed., *The Moral Foundations of the American Republic*.

15. See Thomas Pangle's *Montesquieu's Philosophy of Liberalism* (Chicago: University of Chicago Press, 1973).

16. "Worship differs from speech, then, by manifesting a commitment to a community less encompassing than the whole society" (261). "This principle is attractive precisely because it allows the law of religion to gloss over the fact that religious communities stand apart from, and in many ways stand in opposition to, the wider community of which they are simultaneously a part" (262).

Chapter 8

1. See *The Rise of Modern Judicial Review*, chapter 13, and "Burger Court Disappointments" in *This World* (1987).

2. One of the most salient instances of this process occurred in the area of church-state law. After years of tug-of-war on the Court between "stricter separationists" and "accommodationists," attempts to make sense out of the Court's precedents regarding what was "a primary effect that advanced or inhibited religion" seemed impossible. Perhaps the ultimate expression of this occurred in *Lynch v. Donnelly*, 465 U.S. 668 (1984), in which the Court upheld the constitutionality of a nativity scene contained in a larger municipal Christmas display. Chief Justice Burger, writing for the Court, said that the benefits for religion of a municipal creche scene were not greater than the benefits of many other programs that had been upheld (e.g., textbooks and transportation for parochial schools, grants for buildings at religiously affiliated colleges, tax exemptions for church property, Sunday closing laws, released time programs for religious education). "We are unable," said Burger, "to discern a greater aid to religion deriving from inclusion of the creche than from these benefits and endorsements previously held not violative of the establishment clause." His assertion was quite right, but beside the point. It would also have been easy enough to say that the effect of the creche advanced religion no *less* than a string of *other* cases the Court had decided (e.g., overturning state provision of maps and field-trip transportation and other "secular" services to private, nonprofit—including parochial—schools and tax credits for parents of students in those schools, public school "nondenominational" prayer—none of which could be said to single out and support *particular* religious views, as the creche scene clearly did.

3. See Bickel, *The Least Dangerous Branch* (Indianapolis: Bobbs-Merrill, 1962), chapter one, and Ronald Dworkin, *Taking Rights Seriously*, chapters four and five.

4. *Harvard Journal of Law and Public Policy* 17 (1994): 23.

5. Lawson explicitly confines his analysis to *federal* cases involving *horizontal precedent* (i.e., precedent made by an equal or inferior, not a superior, court) and dealing with *constitutional* issues (not common-law adjudication).

6. Lawson, "The Constitutional Case Against Precedent" *Harvard Journal of Law and Public Policy* 17 (1994): 27.

7. Akhil Reed Amar makes this point in his response, "On Lawson on Precedent," *Harvard Journal of Law and Public Policy* 17 (1994): 41. He makes a similar point respecting Lawson's acceptance of *res adjudicata*—that the final judicial decision in a case is binding as to the parties to that case. But if the decision is binding on the parties even if it is based on an incorrect reading of the Constitution, then it is not *always* inadmissible to give effect to a decision contrary to the Constitution, as Lawson's argument suggests it is.

8. Lawson, "The Constitutional Case Against Precedent," p. 31.

9. Id.

10. Lawson, "The Constitutional Case Against Precedent," pp. 31–32 (emphasis omitted).

11. 358 U.S. 1, 18 (1958).

12. *Columbia Law Review*, 88 (1988): 723.

13. *Columbia Law Review*, 88 (1988): 727–39; the quote is at p. 724.

14. *Columbia Law Review*, 88 (1988): 749.

15. *Columbia Law Review*, 88 (1988): 752

16. *Columbia Law Review*, 88 (1988): 754. The notion of constitutional common law was developed more fully by Monaghan in an earlier article, "The Supreme Court 1974 Term—Foreword: Constitutional Common Law," *Harvard Law Review*, 89 (1975): 1.

17. *Columbia Law Review*, 88 (1988): 757.

18. *Columbia Law Review*, 88 (1988): 761.

19. *Columbia Law Review*, 88 (1988): 770, 771.

20. *Columbia Law Review*, 88 (1988): 772.

21. Letter to N. P. Trist, December 1831 in *The Writings of James Madison*, IX, 476–77.

22. Letter to C. E. Haynes, 25 February 1831, in *The Writings of James Madison*, p. 442–43.

23. *The Political Thought of Abraham Lincoln*, pp. 175–76. This is a restatement of a position taken earlier in his speech on the *Dred Scott* decision in Springfield, Illinois, 26 June 1857.

24. Madison agreed with this point. See his letter to Spencer Roane, 2 September 1819 in his *Writings*, pp. 447–48, wishing that the Court had given seriatim opinions in *McCulloch v. Maryland,* since "[t]his might either by the harmony of their reasoning have produced a greater conviction in the Public mind; or by its discordance have impaired the force of the precedent now ostensibly supported by a unanimous & perfect concurrence in every argument & dictum in the judgement pronounced."

25. 105 L.Ed.2d 1, 37 (1989).

26. Gales and Seaton's *History of Debates in Congress*, p. 1948 (debate of 2 February 1791).

27. 4 Wheaton 423 (1819).

28. See *The Rise of Modern Judicial Review*, pp. 102–03.

29. It might be argued that the Constitution does not explicitly adopt common-law judicial procedure, and that my reliance on the importance of precedent in the common law is therefore inadmissible. I believe that this reads the Constitution too narrowly. At some points, the Constitution's text itself seems to presume a common-law background, e.g., the Seventh Amendment: "In Suits at common law . . ."; Article III, section 2: "The judicial Power shall extend to all Cases, in Law and Equity . . ." (the reference to "Law and Equity" being more plausibly a reference in the context of the Anglo-American legal system than to more generic uses of the term, e.g., in Aristotle's *Politics*). This, and similar language, only confirms a noncontroversial historical fact

that our legal system "flowed out of" the English legal system, and initially bore its general features, except where the colonists and founders took steps to change it. (One of those areas was, of course, judicial review itself. But even here, it is important to recognize that the power of judicial review is not a distinct and independent prerogative of the judiciary, but a power derivative from, and limited to the context of, their more fundamental task of deciding cases.

30. Hamilton, Madison, Jay, *The Federalist Papers* (ed. Wills), pp. 398–99.

31. While there is no specific mention of precedent in it, I believe that another passage makes similar assumptions. Hamilton says in Federalist No. 81 (p. 411) that the danger of judicial usurpation on legislative authority "can never be so extensive as to amount to an inconvenience, or in any sensible degree to affect the order of the political system. This may be inferred with certainty *from the general nature of the judicial power*; from the objects to which it relates; *from the manner in which it is exercised*; from its comparative weakness, and from its total incapacity to support its usurpations by force" (emphasis added). The italicized passages, especially the second one, seem very likely to include an implicit reference to a system of case law in which great weight is given to precedent.

32. *Burnet v. Coronado Oil & Gas Company* 285 U.S. 393, 406–08 (1931) (internal citations omitted).

33. See *The Rise of Modern Judicial Review*, chapters nine and ten.

34. See, for example, Justice Harlan's dissent and concurrence in *Roth v. U.S. and Alberts v. California* 354 U.S. 476, 496 (1957).

35. One does not have to consider judicial power completely unchecked to regard it as excessive and dangerous. It is sufficient that it not be *adequately* checked.

36. Originalism, that is, while initially a theory of interpretation of the Constitution, naturally extends into a theory of adjudication as well. A large part of the reason for this is that an originalist examination of the consitutional foundations of judicial review in the Constitution will recognize the very limited form judicial review should take in order to make it compatible with the overall republican design. I discuss this in chapters 3 and 4 of *The Rise of Modern Judicial Review*.

Index

abortion, 125, 132–34, 136, 143–46
absurdity, 5
adjudication, constitutional. *See* constitutional adjudication
ambiguity: in Constitution. *See* Constitution; historical, 155; inevitability of, 56–57; of intent, 45, 48; in law, 50; from multiple authorship, 60, 199n14; originalism and, 158; as reason for extratextual investigation, 104; republicanism and, 168; in word meaning, 4; in wording of statutes, 46
amendment power, 14, 15, 22–23
appointment process, 135
Arcara v. Cloud Books, 110
Aristotle, 10
assistance of counsel, 89
autonomy, xiii

Backus, Isaac, 118
Bacon, Matthew, 52
balancing process, 20; competing interests, 98–99, 205n58; state interests, 115–16
Baldwin, Abraham, 58, 61
Bank of Columbia v. Okely, 38
Barron v. Baltimore, 6, 10, 79, 80, 199n7
Bates v. Little Rock, 103
Berger, Raoul, xii, 107, 108; critique

of Powell, 44–80; on judicial activism, 125; on Justice Story, 66–69; on Madison's view of interpretation, 71–78; on meaning of "intention," 53; on primacy of intent, 46–55; on school segregation, 104–5, 106; on use of historical materials, 63, 64–66, 81, 104
Berns, Walter, 153
Bickel, Alexander, 107, 119, 127, 130; on judicial review, 137, 176
Bill of Rights: application to states, 10, 11; connection of rights in, 112; due process clause and, 195n1; Fourteenth Amendment incorporation of, 188, 189; organization of, 28–29; procedural guarantees in, 30, 37; purpose of, 31; rejected amendments, 196n5
bills of attainder, 36, 110
Bingham, John A., 105
Black, Hugo, 89, 102, 129, 139, 157
Blackstone, William, 56; on due process, 32–33; on factors in interpretation, 66, 68; on intent, 45, 48, 53; on liberty, 93; on primacy of text, 49; on rules of interpretation, 4–5, 9, 52–54; use of extratextual sources by, 53
Bork, Robert, 85, 108, 111, 112, 123; on constitutional

209n8; constitutional interpretation and, 86; contemporary, 85, 107, 108; finality of, 127; justification for, 85, 127, 178; legislative deference principle, 35, 42, 61, 91, 106, 139; legitimacy of, 86; limitations on, 130; modes of, 85; natural justice and, 37–38; precedent in. *See* precedent; Rehnquist Court and, 176; role of interpretation in, 97; theories of, 24, 35, 40, 149, 151; time of, 130, 140; undemocratic aspects of, 127, 137; Wellington on, 127, 130, 134, 140, 143. *See also* judicial power

judiciary: adaptation of constitution by, 14; adherence to principle, 140, 209n10; authority of, 58, 128; control of, 128, 135–36, 187; definition of values by, 125, 127, 129, 140–47; discretion of, 140; function of, 100; independence of, 57; objectivity in, 163–64; political nature of, 163–64; role of, 93; self-restraint of, 140; value judgments by, 129–30. *See also* judges; judicial power; judicial review

Jurow, Keith, 32

just compensation clause, 30, 37

Kennedy, Anthony, 176

Kent, James, 33

Kentucky Resolution, 70

King, Rufus, 58, 61

knowledge, certainty of, 162–63

Lakatos, 113

language: broad, 14; capabilities of, 49; changes in, 154–55, 159, 164, 166; fluidity of, 71, 72; meaning of, 154, 210n9; subjectivity of, 10, 128; weight in adjudication, 141

law, 92; age of, 140; ambiguity in, 50, 75, 184; changing, 126, 135–

38; characteristics of, 36, 50; enforcement of, 142; gaps in, 20, 99; generality of, 36; making versus applying, 128; meaning of, 49; natural. *See* natural law; neutral, 171; objects of, 6; political character of, 140; public support for, 142; sources of, 127, 131, 135; spirit and reason of, 4, 5, 52, 80

law of the land. *See* due process; law

Lawson, Gary, 176–78, 183, 184

Least Dangerous Branch, The, 107

legal interpretation, 4

legal profession, 126, 137

legislative history: founders' use of, 80; interpretation using, 46, 51, 54, 60; lack of, 49, 51, 54–55, 60, 66, 68, 79, 80, 81, 141; public morality and, 133; unwritten, 51, 199n7

legislature: due process limitations on, 28, 33, 34, 196n6; judicial deference to, 35, 42, 61, 91, 106, 139; modification of common law by, 30, 33, 34, 41; prerogatives of, 45; procedural modifications by, 196n6; prohibition of actions by, 39; protection of rights by, 123; response to change, 136–37; response to public values, 131, 141; Wellington on, 140

Levy, Leonard, 155, 156, 161

liberal legal theory, 150

liberalism, Tushnet's critique of, 167–68, 170–72, 174

liberty, xiii, 93; means of protection of, 151; nontraditional, 115; political, 169; relation to property, 128

Lincoln, Abraham, 135, 147, 162, 176, 181

Lochner, 132, 143, 147

Lofgren, Charles A., 198n4

loose construction, 13, 195n31

Madison, James, 8, 23, 60, 63, 176; on ambiguity, 56–57; on authority

About the Author

Christopher Wolfe is professor of political science at Marquette University. He graduated summa cum laude from Notre Dame in 1971 and went on to study political philosophy at Boston College, receiving his Ph.D. in 1978. During his graduate studies he "migrated" from political philosophy to American political thought and constitutional law.

He is the author of *Judicial Activism: Bulwark of Liberty or Precarious Security?* (Brooks/Cole, 1991; second revised edition Rowman & Littlefield, forthcoming 1997), *The Rise of Modern Judicial Review: From Constitutional Interpretation to Judge-Made Law* (second edition Rowman & Littlefield, 1994), and *Essays on Faith and Liberal Democracy* (University Press of America, 1987), and the editor (with John Hittinger) of *Liberalism at the Crossroads* (Rowman & Littlefield, 1994). He is currently working on a project on liberalism, American public philosophy, and natural law.

He is a founder and president of the American Public Philosophy Institute (1989).

Professor Wolfe is married to Anne McGowan Wolfe, and they have been blessed with ten children.